Hands-On Cybersecurity for Finance

Identify vulnerabilities and secure your financial services from security breaches

Dr. Erdal Ozkaya
Milad Aslaner

BIRMINGHAM - MUMBAI

Hands-On Cybersecurity for Finance

Commissioning Editor: Vijin Boricha
Acquisition Editor: Heramb Bhavsar
Content Development Editor: Nithin George Varghese
Technical Editor: Komal Karne
Copy Editor: Safis Editing
Language Support Editor: Storm Mann
Project Coordinator: Drashti Panchal
Proofreader: Safis Editing
Indexer: Pratik Shirodkar
Graphics: Tom Scaria
Production Coordinator: Arvindkumar Gupta

First published: January 2019

Production reference: 1310119

Published by Packt Publishing Ltd.
Livery Place
35 Livery Street
Birmingham
B3 2PB, UK.

ISBN 978-1-78883-629-6

www.packtpub.com

This book is dedicated to: my wonderful wife, Arzu, my better half, who helps me to be me. I am who I am today because of her, my son Jemre, my best friend and supporter and My daughter Azra, my best friend and my source of energy.

– Dr. Erdal Ozkaya

This book is dedicated to the three most important women in my life: my mother, Hasine, who has always looked after me; my sister, Aylin, who helped me to become a better person; and my better half, Salpie, who made me realize what is truly important in life.

– Milad Aslaner

`mapt.io`

Mapt is an online digital library that gives you full access to over 5,000 books and videos, as well as industry leading tools to help you plan your personal development and advance your career. For more information, please visit our website.

Why subscribe?

- Spend less time learning and more time coding with practical eBooks and Videos from over 4,000 industry professionals

- Improve your learning with Skill Plans built especially for you

- Get a free eBook or video every month

- Mapt is fully searchable

- Copy and paste, print, and bookmark content

Packt.com

Did you know that Packt offers eBook versions of every book published, with PDF and ePub files available? You can upgrade to the eBook version at `www.packt.com` and as a print book customer, you are entitled to a discount on the eBook copy. Get in touch with us at `customercare@packtpub.com` for more details.

At `www.packt.com`, you can also read a collection of free technical articles, sign up for a range of free newsletters, and receive exclusive discounts and offers on Packt books and eBooks.

Foreword

As cybercrime continues to be a growing threat to critical-business infrastructure, global economies, and financial stability, there is a need for vigilance across all sectors, geographies, and industries. There are many techniques, tools, and technologies that financial services organizations can employ to protect their infrastructure, data, and people from a compromise. On occasion, it appears as if there is a surfeit of such techniques, tools, and technologies—and the number of available solutions is overwhelming to even the largest global organizations, and even more so to those who do not have mature, well-funded, and well-staffed security organizations. In this book, Dr. Erdal Ozkaya and Milad Aslaner explore the many different aspects of building a comprehensive and segment-specific offense and defense against current and emerging threats to global financial services organizations. Their objective is to reduce the complexity and focus on the fundamentals of cyber resilience and good cyber hygiene by means of practical advice. As global threats continue to increase in volume and complexity, it is often important to make certain we are doing the basics well. The advanced tools will be valuable, but our ability to construct and operate a scalable and sustainable security program with relevant processes, people, and tools is what will allow us to be successful over the long term. Both of the authors have relevant, boots-on-the-ground experience to share, and I encourage you, the reader, to read this book with a pragmatic view of what is possible today, while regarding it as a building block for the future success of your security program.

Ann S. Johnson

Corporate Vice President, Microsoft

Contributors

About the authors

Dr. Erdal Ozkaya is a leading cybersecurity professional skilled in business development, management, and academics. He spends his time securing the cyberspace and sharing his knowledge as a security adviser, speaker, lecturer, and author. Erdal is passionate about reaching communities and creating cyber-aware campaigns. He leverages new and innovative approaches and technologies to holistically address information security and privacy needs for people and organizations worldwide. He has co-authored many cybersecurity books as well as security certification courseware and exams for different vendors. Erdal is also a part time lecturer at Australian Charles Sturt University.

> *My special thanks to all my family and friends for sharing their feedback and helping me be better. When I look back at my life so far, you are always a part of my best memories. You have always been there when I needed you, and I promise that I will be there when you need me. I will not mention any names specifically as I do not want to risk forgetting any of you. You know who you are.*

Milad Aslaner is a security professional with over 10 years' experience in product engineering and management. He has published white papers and books on social engineering, the practical application of cybersecurity, and cybersecurity in the financial services industry, with a technical focus on EDR, TVM, incident response, and real-world exploitation techniques. During his time at Microsoft since 2012, he has led the commercial software engineering team for the Surface Book and Laptop, and built security features such as SEMM. As a senior security program manager, he aims to transform strategic enterprise customer requirements to realize new scenarios, thereby safeguarding Microsoft customers against the evolving threat landscape.

> *Albert Einstein once said, once you stop learning, you start dying. This has always resonated well with me and was one of the motivating factors for me to start writing. I still remember writing the very first chapter, and how I felt a feeling of pride and joy as I was imagining how readers would digest this knowledge and adapt it to be more successful in their roles. This would not have been possible without the support of my family, friends, and colleagues.*

About the reviewers

Dr. Aditya Mukherjee is a cybersecurity veteran, with more than 11 years of experience in security consulting for various Fortune 500's and government entities, managing large teams focusing on customer relationships, and building service lines. He started his career as an entrepreneur, where he specialization in implementation of cybersecurity solutions/cyber-transformation projects, and solving challenges associated with security architecture, framework and policies. Over the tenure of his career he has been bestowed with various industry recognition and awards, of which most recently are the—Most Innovative/Dynamic CISO of the Year 2018, Cyber Sentinel of the Year and an Honorary Doctorate—for excellence in the field of management.

> *I would like to thank the people who supported me throughout especially my mother, without whose support anything I do wouldn't be possible. The writers of this book, Erdal and Milad for their hard work and dedication in bringing out a quality literature. A big thanks to the Packt team for creating a wonderful, enabling and fostering learning environment and Drashti for her co-ordination in bringing out the final product that is in your hands.*

Kunal Sehgal has been heading critical cybersecurity roles for financial organizations, for over 15 years now. He is an avid blogger and a regular speaker on cyber related topics across Asia. He also holds a bachelor's degree in computer applications from Punjab University, and a post graduate diploma from Georgian College in cyberspace security. He has numerous cyber certifications including: Certified Information Systems Auditor (CISA), Certified Information Systems Security Professional (CISSP), Certified Information Security Manager (CISM), Tenable Certified Nessus Auditor (TCNA), Certificate of Cloud Security Knowledge (CCSK), ISO 27001 Lead Auditor, Offensive Security Certified Professional (OSCP), CompTIA Security+, and many more.

> *Dedicated to my darling daughter.*

Packt is searching for authors like you

If you're interested in becoming an author for Packt, please visit `authors.packtpub.com` and apply today. We have worked with thousands of developers and tech professionals, just like you, to help them share their insight with the global tech community. You can make a general application, apply for a specific hot topic that we are recruiting an author for, or submit your own idea.

Table of Contents

Preface   1

Chapter 1: Introduction to Cybersecurity and the Economy   5
  What is cybersecurity – a brief technical description?   5
    People   6
    Processes   6
    Technology   7
  The scope of cybersecurity   7
    Critical infrastructure security   7
    Network security   8
    Cloud security   8
    Application/system security   9
    User security   9
    Internet of Things security   10
    Terminologies   10
  General description of hacking groups and cyber espionage   11
    Hacking groups   12
    Cyber espionage   13
  Cybersecurity objectives   14
    Importance of cybersecurity and its impacts on the global economy   14
      The number of cyber attacks is growing   14
      Cyber attacks are getting worse   15
    Impacts on the global economy   15
      Estimation of financial losses related to cybercrime   16
      Finance and cybersecurity   18
        Critical dependency of business, processes, and IT infrastructure   18
      Economic loss   20
    Banking and financial systems – changes from a risk and security
    perspective   21
    Data breach means money   22
  **Financial repercussion of reputational damage caused by cyber
  attacks**   23
  Digital economy and related threats   24
    Smart threats   24
    Ransomware   25
    Critical infrastructure attacks   26
  Summary   26
  Further reading   26

Chapter 2: Cyber Crime - Who the Attackers Are   27
  Introduction to cyber crime   27

Threat actors 29
  Hacktivism 30
    Case study – Dakota Access Pipeline 31
    Case study – Panama Papers 32
  Cyber terrorists 33
    Case study – Operation Ababil 33
  Cyber criminals 34
    Case study – FIN7 34
    Case study – Carbanak APT Attack 35
    Case study – OurMine operation 36
Summary 37
Chapter 3: Counting the Costs 39
The cost of a cybersecurity attack 39
  The cost of different cyber attacks 41
Breakdown of the costs of a cyber attack 43
  Production loss 44
  Economic losses 45
  Damaged brand and reputation 46
  Loss of data 47
  Fines, penalties, and litigations 47
  Losses due to recovery techniques 48
Breakdown of the cost of securing an organization 49
  Every financial institute should know Carbanak 49
  Antivirus systems 50
  Endpoint Detection and Response solutions 51
  Firewall systems 52
  Intrusion-prevention systems 52
  Encryption 53
Bonus 54
  What is Microsoft offering? 54
  Windows 10 Defender Security Center 55
  Windows Defender 56
  Windows Defender Exploit Guard 57
  Controlled folder access 58
  Network protection 59
  Attack surface reduction 61
  Windows Defender Credential Guard 61
  Windows Defender Application Guard 62
  Windows Event Forwarding 63
  Windows Defender Advanced Threat Protection 64
  Protecting privileged identities 66
    How do privileged identities get compromised? 66
    How to prevent attackers from gaining access to privileged identities 67
Summary 67
Further reading 68

Chapter 4: The Threat Landscape   69
  Threats against end customers   69
    Credit card fraud   70
    Application fraud   70
    Card-not-present fraud   71
    Compromised account fraud   72
    Credit card testing   72
    Financial Trojans   73
      Case study – BackSwap Trojan   73
      Case study – Ramnit   74
      Case study – Bebloh   74
    Phishing   75
      Case study – immediate action required   76
    Pretexting   77
    Dumpster diving   77
    Mobile fraud   77
  Threats against financial institutes   78
    ATM attacks   78
    POS attacks   78
    Denial of service   79
    Ransomware   79
    Blackmailing   79
  Summary   79
Chapter 5: Phishing, Spamming, and Scamming to Steal Data and Money   81
  Phishing scams   82
    Evolution of phishing   83
      Social engineering emails   85
    Spear phishing   90
    Business email compromise or whaling   94
      Credential theft using malicious software   95
        Ardamax   95
        LokiBot   96
    Characteristics of phishing emails   98
  Spamming   98
    How spammers get email addresses   99
    How spammers make money   100
      Advertising   100
      Malware   100
        Storm   101
        Triout   102
        Botnets   103
    Characteristics of spam emails   103
  Summary   105
  Further reading   105

Chapter 6: The Malware Plague   107
  Malware categories   108
    Computer virus   110
    Computer worm   110
      SQL Slammer worm   111
      Crypto worm   111
        WannaCry   112
    Trojan   113
      Bebloh   113
      Zeus   114
    Rootkit   116
      Torpig   116
    Spyware   116
    Adware   117
  Malware trends   117
  Malware infection vectors   118
    Injected by remote attacker   118
    Email   119
    Auto-executed web infection   119
    User-executed web infection   119
    Installed by other malware   119
    Network propagation   119
    Portable media   120
    Coded into existing software   120
  Summary   120

Chapter 7: Vulnerabilities and Exploits   121
  Detecting vulnerabilities   122
  Exploitation techniques   124
    Buffer overflow   125
    Integer overflow   126
    Memory corruption   126
    Format string attacks   127
    Race condition   127
    Cross-site scripting   128
    One-click attack   128
    SQL injections   129
  Exploitation delivery   130
  Summary   130
  Further reading   130

Chapter 8: Attacking Online Banking Systems   131
  Online banking benefits for financial services   133
  The online banking process   133
  Attack techniques   134
  Summary   135

Further reading   136

Chapter 9: Vulnerable Networks and Services - a Gateway for Intrusion   137
  Vulnerable network protocols and network intrusions   138
    Simple Mail Transfer Protocol   138
    Secure Sockets Layer   138
    Domain Name System   139
      Packet sniffing   139
      Distributed denial of service   140
  Attacking web servers and web-based systems   140
    SQL injection   140
    Buffer overflow   141
    Advanced Google search operators   141
    Brute-force attacks   142
      Medusa   143
      Brutus   144
    Bypassing web protection   144
      Bypassing captcha   145
      Bypassing two-factor authentication   146
      Bypassing firewalls   146
  Hacking wireless networks   147
    Hacking wireless networks   147
      Aircrack-ng   148
      Kismet   149
      Wireshark   150
    Hacking Bluetooth   150
  Vulnerable network devices   151
  Summary   151
  Further reading   152

Chapter 10: Responding to Service Disruption   153
  Cybersecurity incidents   154
  Fundamentals   154
    Data knowledge   154
    Monitoring   155
    Attack surface analysis   155
    Vendor management   156
  Incident response and management   156
    Phase 1 – preparation   157
    Phase 2 – detection and analysis   157
    Phase 3 – containment   158
    Phase 4 – eradication and recovery   158
    Phase 5 – post-incident activity   158
  Summary   159
  Further reading   159

Chapter 11: The Human Problem - Governance Fail   161

Business versus security 162
Failing security management 163
    Lack of adoption of cybersecurity initiatives 163
    Lack of organization and planning 163
    Poor leadership 164
Careless online behavior 164
Insider threats 166
Technological transformation of financial services 168
Failure in implementing security policies 171
Summary 173
Further reading 174

Chapter 12: Securing the Perimeter and Protecting the Assets 175
Network models 176
    Single trust network model 176
    Dual trust network model 177
    Zero trust network model 178
        Microsoft 365 zero trust network models 179
Endpoint security 180
    Endpoint security threats 180
        Physical access 181
        Malicious code execution 181
        Device-based attack 182
        Communication interception 182
        Insider threats 183
        Decreased productivity 184
    Modern endpoint security 184
        Device protection 185
        Threat resistance 185
        Identity protection 186
        Information protection 186
        Breach detection investigation and response 186
Summary 187
Further reading 187

Chapter 13: Threat and Vulnerability Management 189
Vulnerability management strategy 190
    Asset inventory 190
    Information management 190
    Risk assessment 191
    Vulnerability analysis 191
    Threat analysis 191
    Risk acceptance 192
    Vulnerability assessment 192
    Reporting and remediation 192
Defining vulnerabilities in a few steps 193

From vulnerability to threat 193
Multiplying threats 194
Multiplying risk 195
The root cause of security issues 196
Vulnerability management tools 196
Implementation of vulnerability management 205
Best practices for vulnerability management 207
Assess yourself 209
Tying vulnerability assessments into business impact 209
Take an active role 210
Identify and understand the business processes 211
Pinpoint the applications and data 211
Try to find hidden data sources 211
Determine the hardware structure 211
Map the network infrastructure to hardware 212
Identify the controls 212
Run the vulnerability scans 212
Read the results of the scans 212
Conduct penetration testing by third parties as well 213
Understanding risk management 214
Defense in depth approach 216
Best practices for protecting your environment 217
Summary 218
Further reading 218
Chapter 14: Audit, Risk Management, and Incident Handling 219
IT auditing 220
Evaluating the systems, policies, and processes that secure the
organization 221
Determining the risks to the company's assets 221
Ensuring that the organization is compliant with the relevant regulations 222
Determining inefficiencies in the IT infrastructure and management 222
Risk management 223
Identification 224
Risk analysis 224
Risk assessment 225
Risk mitigation 225
Risk monitoring 225
Incident handling 226
Preparation 226
Identification 226
Containment 227
Recovery and analysis 227
Summary 227
Further reading 228

Chapter 15: Encryption and Cryptography for Protecting Data and Services 229
Encryption 230
Early encryption methods 230
Encryption today 232
Symmetric encryption 232
Asymmetric encryption 233
Protecting data and services with cryptography 235
Data at rest 235
Full disk encryption 236
File encryption 236
Data in transit 237
End-to-end encryption 237
Encrypted web connection (SSL and TLS) 238
Encrypted email servers 238
Examples of encryption algorithms 238
Advanced Encryption Standard (AES) 238
Triple DES 239
RSA 239
Blowfish 239
Encryption challenges 240
Summary 241
Further reading 241

Chapter 16: The Rise of the Blockchain 243
Introduction to Blockchain technology 244
Consensus mechanisms in a Blockchain 244
Proof of work 245
Proof of stake 246
Applications of Blockchain technology 246
Recording purposes 246
Digital identity 247
Government purposes 247
Financial applications 248
Cryptocurrencies 249
Cryptocurrency wallets 251
Desktop wallets 251
Web wallets 251
Mobile wallets 251
Hardware wallets 252
Paper wallets 252
Challenges to cryptocurrencies 252
Unstable value 252
Theft 252
Exchange risks 253
Blockchain challenges and future 253
Summary 254

Further reading — 254

Chapter 17: Artificial Intelligence and Cybersecurity — 255
  Threat landscape evolution — 257
  Artificial Intelligence — 257
    Narrow Artificial Intelligence — 258
    True Artificial Intelligence — 258
    Technologies powering Artificial Intelligence — 260
  Artificial Intelligence-powered cybersecurity — 260
    Use cases — 262
  Summary — 263
  Further reading — 264

Chapter 18: The Quantum Future — 265
  Evolution of the quantum technology — 266
    1965 — 266
    1980 — 266
    1985 — 266
    1994 — 266
    1995 — 267
    1996–present — 267
  The quantum technology race — 267
    Quantum communication — 268
    Quantum computation — 269
    Quantum simulation — 269
    Quantum sensing — 270
    Quantum software — 270
  Quantum technology breakthroughs — 270
  Impacts of the quantum technology — 272
    Communication — 272
    Mining — 273
    Finance — 273
    Defense — 273
    Health — 273
    Energy — 274
    Big data — 274
    Artificial Intelligence — 274
  Summary — 274
  Further reading — 275

Other Books You May Enjoy — 277

Index — 281

Preface

Welcome to *Hands-On Cyber Security for Finance*. This book will present a step-by-step guide on understanding threats to the financial cyberspace and help you learn how to secure your organization against such threats.

This book aims to overcome financial cyber threats by taking you through some of the most well-known case studies and real-life scenarios and elucidate ways to tackle them. As you make progress with the book, you will discover different vulnerabilities and bugs (including the human risk factor), and thus gain an expert-level view on identifying attackers. By the end of the book, rest assured you will have excellent insight into the future of cybersecurity and gained hands-on experience in protecting financial services and their related infrastructures.

Who this book is for

Hands-On Cybersecurity for Finance is for you if you are a security architect, cyber risk manager, or pentester looking to secure your organization.

What this book covers

Chapter 1, *Introduction to Cybersecurity and the Economy*, provides a general overview of the current technologies, the infrastructures, and the general economy related to the financial world, which happens to be the primary target of cybercrime.

Chapter 2, *Cyber Crime - Who the Attackers Are*, gives an in-depth explanation particularly on cybercrime and cybercriminals, covering several associated case studies.

Chapter 3, *Counting the Costs*, covers the costs associated with cyber attacks and cybersecurity by analyzing different reports from cybersecurity experts.

Chapter 4, *The Threat Landscape*, briefly discusses threats against end users and financial institutes.

Chapter 5, *Phishing, Spamming, and Scamming to Steal Data and Money*, will provide the reader with an in-depth study on the malicious techniques frequently used by an attacker to obtain sensitive information.

Chapter 6, *The Malware Plague,* introduces different malware families and explains how they spread; this will eventually help you plan your defense strategy in a better way.

Chapter 7, *Vulnerabilities and Exploits,* will deep dive into the different exploitation techniques such as buffer overflow, race condition, and memory corruption, and explain how these exploits are delivered by threat actors.

Chapter 8, *Attacking Online Banking Systems,* will focus on the online economy and related security systems. We will describe how protections are implemented and how hackers are able to penetrate and acquire their target.

Chapter 9, *Vulnerable Networks and Services - a Gateway for Intrusion,* will introduce the important aspects of cybersecurity that are related to communication and network protocols.

Chapter 10, *Responding to Service Disruption,* will cover in depth what a cybersecurity incident is and how to establish an incident response plan.

Chapter 11, *The Human Problem - Governance Fail,* will briefly consider the human factor impacting the entire cybersecurity implementation, including standards, policies, configurations, architecture and so on.

Chapter 12, *Securing the Perimeter and Protecting the Assets,* will go deep into the most commonly adapted IT perimeter security model, which is single trust, then share insights into dual trust and finish up with the zero trust network model.

Chapter 13, *Threat and Vulnerability Management,* will cover three important processes in any organization and the different steps associated with it.

Chapter 14, *Audit, Risk Management, and Incident Handling,* will take us through the detailed version of encryption from its early methods and give us a brief idea of how far it has evolved. This chapter will cover various techniques along with the associated challenges.

Chapter 15, *Encryption and Cryptography for Protecting Data and Services,* will touch upon one of the most important changes facing the global economy currently: Blockchain and cryptocurrency.

Chapter 16, *The Rise of the Blockchain,* will talk about quantum computing at length, particularly the different ways in which it will shape the future.

Chapter 17, *Artificial Intelligence and Cybersecurity,* will focus in detail how to defend an asset using threat model, analysis, bug testing, software life cycle, accomplishing monitoring of software engineering processes used to ensure quality.

`Chapter 18`, *The Quantum Future,* will evaluate the impact of the increasing use of AI (Artificial Intelligence), which could soon be the next game changer.

To get the most out of this book

Basic understanding of cybersecurity tools and practices will help you get the most out of this book.

Download the color images

We also provide a PDF file that has color images of the screenshots/diagrams used in this book. You can download it here: `https://www.packtpub.com/sites/default/files/downloads/9781788836296_ColorImages.pdf`.

Conventions used

There are a number of text conventions used throughout this book.

Any command-line input or output is written as follows:

```
Set-MpPreference -EnableNetworkProtection Enabled
```

 Warnings or important notes appear like this.

 Tips and tricks appear like this.

Get in touch

Feedback from our readers is always welcome.

General feedback: If you have questions about any aspect of this book, mention the book title in the subject of your message and email us at `customercare@packtpub.com`.

Errata: Although we have taken every care to ensure the accuracy of our content, mistakes do happen. If you have found a mistake in this book, we would be grateful if you would report this to us. Please visit www.packt.com/submit-errata, selecting your book, clicking on the Errata Submission Form link, and entering the details.

If you are interested in becoming an author: If there is a topic that you have expertise in and you are interested in either writing or contributing to a book, please visit authors.packtpub.com.

Reviews

Please leave a review. Once you have read and used this book, why not leave a review on the site that you purchased it from? Potential readers can then see and use your unbiased opinion to make purchase decisions, we at Packt can understand what you think about our products, and our authors can see your feedback on their book. Thank you!

For more information about Packt, please visit packt.com.

Disclaimer

The information within this book is intended to be used only in an ethical manner. Do not use any information from the book if you do not have written permission from the owner of the equipment. If you perform illegal actions, you are likely to be arrested and prosecuted to the full extent of the law. Packt Publishing does not take any responsibility if you misuse any of the information contained within the book. The information herein must only be used while testing environments with proper written authorizations from appropriate persons responsible.

Introduction to Cybersecurity and the Economy

The relationship between cybersecurity and the economy has only been growing stronger, with cyber attacks on the rise. Cyber attacks have brought a new recognition of the importance of cybersecurity efforts. Attacks have now become widespread, common, and expected in some firms. New attacks are emerging within weeks due to an underground economy that has seen specialists create built-to-sell malware to a waiting list of cyber criminals. The impacts of cyber attacks have been felt and there are reports that these attacks are only going to get worse. The current and forecasted impacts are a devastation to the global economy. Here, we will introduce cybersecurity and link it to cyber attacks and the global economy. In this chapter, we will cover the following topics:

- What is cybersecurity?
- The scope of cybersecurity
- Terminology related to the cybersecurity world
- General description of hacking groups, cyber criminals, and cyber espionage
- Importance of cybersecurity and its impacts on the global economy
- Financial repercussion of reputational damage caused by cyber attacks
- Digital economy and related threats

What is cybersecurity – a brief technical description?

Cybersecurity can be summarized as efforts aimed at preserving the confidentiality, integrity, and availability of computing systems. It's the practice of affording security to networks and systems to protect them from cyber attacks.

According the definition of cybersecurity by Cisco, (`https://www.cisco.com/c/en/us/products/security/what-is-cybersecurity.html`), cybersecurity is the practice of protecting systems, networks, and programs from digital attacks. These attacks are usually aimed at accessing, changing, or destroying sensitive information; extorting money from users; or interrupting normal business processes.

Implementing effective cybersecurity measures is particularly challenging today because there are more devices than people, and attackers are becoming more innovative.

Cyber attacks have been on the rise and are targeted at accessing, modifying, or deleting data, money extortion, and the interruption of normal services. Cybersecurity is of great concern to today's businesses since there has been a high adoption of information technology to achieve efficiency and effectiveness in business operations. The current business environment is such that there are many devices, systems, networks, and users. All these are targeted by cyber criminals, and multiple techniques have been devised and used against them. Cyber attacks are only becoming more effective and sophisticated. Therefore, cybersecurity is becoming a survival mechanism rather than a luxury for many businesses. Cybersecurity has multiple layers, which cover devices, networks, systems, and users. These layers are intended to ensure that these targets are not compromised by attackers. In organizations, these layers can be compressed into three categories: people, processes, and technology.

People

This is the category that includes users. Users are known to be particularly weak in the cybersecurity chain. Unfortunately, cyber criminals are aware of this and often target them rather than systems during attacks. Users are the culprits in creating weak passwords, downloading attachments in strange emails, and easily falling for scams.

Processes

This category encompasses all the processes used by the organization. These can include business processes, such as the supply chain, that could be exploited by attackers to get malware inside companies. Supply chains are, at times, targeted in organizations that are well secured against other methods of being attacked.

Technology

Technology relates to both the devices and software used by an organization. Technology has been a prime target for cyber criminals and they have developed many techniques to compromise it. While security companies try to keep abreast of the threats facing technology today, it seems that cyber criminals have always had the upper hand. Cyber criminals can source new types of malware from underground markets and use them in multiple attacks against different technologies.

The scope of cybersecurity

The importance of cybersecurity can't be overstated. The world is in a state of interconnection, and therefore an attack on one host or user can easily become an attack against many people. Cyber attacks can range from the theft of personal information to extortion attempts for individual targets. For companies, many things are always at stake. There is, therefore, a broad scope of what cybersecurity covers for both individuals and corporate organizations—let's look at this in more detail.

Critical infrastructure security

Critical infrastructure is systems that are relied on by many. These include electricity grids, traffic lights, water supply systems, and even hospitals. Inevitably, these infrastructures are being digitized to meet current demands. This inadvertently makes them a target for cyber criminals. It is, therefore, necessary for critical systems to have periodic vulnerability assessments so that attacks that can be used against them can be mitigated beforehand. There have been several attacks on critical infrastructures in different countries. Commonly-targeted sectors include transport, telecom, energy, and the industrial sector. The most significant one was on Iran's nuclear facility. The facility was targeted using a speculated state-sponsored malware called **Stuxnet**. Stuxnet caused the total destruction of the nuclear facility. This just highlights the effect of cyber attacks against critical infrastructure.

The following is an excerpt from an article that describes the malware attack on Iranian nuclear facility computers (`https://www.engadget.com/2014/11/13/stuxnet-worm-targeted-companies-first/`):

> *Once the malware hit their systems, it was just a matter of time before someone brought compromised data into the Natanz plant (where there's no direct internet access) and sparked chaos. As you might suspect, there's also evidence that these first breaches didn't originate from USB drives. Researchers saw that Stuxnet's creators compiled the first known worm mere hours before it reached one of the affected companies; unless there was someone on the ground waiting to sneak a drive inside one of these firms, that code reached the internet before it hit Natanz.*

Network security

There is no way businesses can be conducted without networks today. Countries that have isolated themselves from internet connectivity have been left behind financially, since a big part of the global economy is currently powered by the internet. North Korea is an example of one country where the internet is highly restricted and only accessed by a few people. However, having connectivity to networks comes with its own cons. Individual and corporate networks have been subjected to unauthorized access, malware, and denial of service from cyber criminals. There are some techniques that can be used to perform actions on networks that can hardly be detected by network admins without the use of tools such as intrusion-detection systems. Other cyber attacks include sniffing packets, theft, and manipulating data during transit. The tools that are being used to protect against network security threats have become overwhelmed with the amounts of traffic that they have to filter. They have also been facing challenges due to the number of false positives that are getting reported. Because of this, security companies are turning to new technologies, such as machine learning, to enable them to detect malicious and abnormal traffic in a more efficient and effective manner.

Cloud security

Among the new technologies that are receiving massive adoption is the cloud. The cloud allows organizations to access resources that they could previously not access due to the financial constraints of acquiring and maintaining the resources. It's also a preferred option for backing up due to its reliability and availability compared to other backup options. However, the cloud has its own set of challenges where security is concerned. Organizations and individuals are concerned about the theft of their cloud-stored data. There have already been incidences of data theft in the cloud. Cloud security ensures that cloud users can secure their data and limit the people that can access it.

According to McAfee security, as many as one in every four organizations has been a victim of cloud data theft (`https://venturebeat.com/2018/04/15/mcafee-26-of-companies-have-suffered-cloud-data-theft/`):

> *Enterprises are moving their data to the cloud, but not everybody is certain that the cloud is as secure as it could be, according to the third annual report on cloud security from cybersecurity firm McAfee. This is due in part to the fact that one in four companies has been hit with cloud data theft.*

Application/system security

Many business processes are run with the aid of applications or systems. However, these systems have introduced a weak point in organizations. If these systems are hacked, they can lead to the halting of services or production activities, theft of business secrets, and loss of money. A study by Trustwave SpiderLabs in 2017 revealed that 100% of randomly-selected and -tested web apps had at least one vulnerability. App security is, therefore, receiving attention in many organizations that have set up cybersecurity strategies.

A 2017 study showed that 100% of sampled web apps had at least one vulnerability (`https://www.trustwave.com/en-us/resources/blogs/trustwave-blog/don-t-sleep-on-web-applications-the-5-most-common-attack-types-and-how-to-better-defend-them/`):

> *In fact, a stunning 100 percent of web apps that the Trustwave SpiderLabs team tested in 2017 contained at least one vulnerability.*

User security

As said before, these are the weakest weak points, and they are particularly hard to protect since they are targeted using social-engineering techniques. These techniques cannot be prevented by using security tools. Attackers get to users through normal interactions, using media such as phones, emails, or face-to-face encounters. Organizations have lost a lot of money due to their employees being attacked using social-engineering attack methods. Therefore, user-awareness programs have been incorporated into most cybersecurity strategies.

Internet of Things security

Internet of Things (IoT) is an emerging technology that has been plagued with security threats. However, its practicality has seen it being adopted in many organizations despite the security challenges. IoT devices have been shipping in an insecure state, which poses threats to organizations and individuals. Cybersecurity has therefore been extended to cover this threat landscape.

Terminologies

Here are some terms related to the cybersecurity world:

- **Cybercrime**: Any crime that involves the use of a computer as the object of a crime or as an accessory used to commit a crime. The perpetrators of such a crime are known as cyber criminals. They mostly use computer technology to illegally access sensitive information, scam, or carry out malicious actions.
- **Ransomware**: Malware built to extort money from victims by blocking access to their computers and files until they pay a ransom amount. However, the payment of the ransom is never a guarantee of file recovery.
- **Malware**: Malicious software. There are three categories of malware: viruses, worms, and Trojans. These are used to either allow unauthorized access or to damage computers.
- **Social engineering**: An attack technique that is increasingly being used by cyber criminals to manipulate people into revealing some information or carrying out some actions. The end goal is either monetary gain or access to sensitive information, such as business secrets.
- **Phishing**: A common exploitation attack that involves sending fraudulent emails, that claim to be from reputable sources, to users. Phishers aim to get sensitive data or money from their targets. With advancements in technology, phishing attacks are becoming more sophisticated and advanced, and thus more successful.

- **Botnet**: A network of zombie devices that have been infected with malware to make them perform certain tasks, such as denial of service attacks. Personal computers were once key targets for recruitment in botnets, but since the introduction of IoT devices, hackers have been shifting focus to this largely insecure technology. A particularly dreadful botnet is the Mirai botnet, which is made up of IoT devices and has been used in several attacks.

- **Data breach**: A corporate network is attacked by cyber criminals and some valuable data is stolen. In many cases, customer authentication details, addresses, and their financial information is stolen. Stolen data is valuable and can be sold in black markets or ransomed. Even when the stolen data is encrypted, hackers can find ways to decrypt it, especially if the encryption algorithm was weak.

- **DDoS attack**: Attackers target a machine with an overwhelming number of requests, thus clogging its bandwidth and ability to respond to legitimate requests. DDoS attacks are carried out by botnets, which have been discussed previously. DDoS attacks can be used as a diversion technique where hackers cause security personnel to focus their efforts on recovering from the DDoS attack while another attack is taking place.

- **Spyware**: Malware used to spy on people for the purposes of obtaining their personal information, login credentials, or other sensitive information. They mostly infect browsers or come hidden in apps and programs. For mobile devices, malware can use GPS sensors to communicate back the whereabouts of a user's device, and they can also access the call history and SMS.

General description of hacking groups and cyber espionage

Hacking groups and cyber espionage have frequently featured in cybersecurity reports; here, we will discuss both of them.

Hacking groups

Hacking groups have been active with their engagements in both legal and illegal activities. Legal activities are those that don't violate any government regulations, such as the spreading of user awareness, while illegal activities violate government regulations, such as electronic fraud. Hacking groups are an association of hackers that act in unison during cyber attacks. Due to their unity during attacks, they are often more successful than solo attackers. There has been significant activity from hacking groups that has led to both good outcomes, such as user awareness, and bad outcomes, such as the theft and destruction of data. Here are some famous hacking groups:

- **Shadow Brokers**: A notorious hacking group known for taking the fight directly to law-enforcement agencies. This group has taken credit for attacks against the US **National Security Agency** (**NSA**) many times. In their hacks, the Shadow Brokers have released to the public some of the alleged NSA hacking arsenal, which comprises exploits, bugs, and malware. This hacking group is associated with one of the most dreadful ransomware attacks. The group hacked the NSA and released an exploit called EternalBlue, which could be used against Windows computers. The exploit was released in March 2016 in black markets, and in May, hackers had already used it as part of the WannaCry ransomware attack. This is the exploit that made the encryption mechanism to execute by the Windows OS security mechanisms. The NSA was partially blamed by Microsoft for harboring these exploits instead of notifying the company so that they could be fixed. Shadow Brokers have not been associated with any illegal activity that targets corporate organizations or individuals. It seems that their main target is the NSA, due to speculations that this agency continually stocks exploits that it can use for espionage purposes inside and outside the US.

- **Bureau 121**: This hacking group is said to be from North Korea, which contradicts the common assumption that North Korea is lagging behind technologically. Defectors from North Korea have said that there are military hackers that are well-paid in the country to keep up with hacking operations. The group is said to be massive, with over 1,500 people who work outside North Korea. The group has attacked South Koreans through apps and websites, and has even destroyed banking records. They said to be behind the 2015 Sony hack, which cost the company $15,000,000. The hack came just after Sony released a movie that had depicted Kim Jong-un in a bad light.

- **Anonymous**: The most recognized hacking group in the world. It's said to be from 4chan and has, over the years since 2003, grown in number and capabilities. The group operates in a decentralized manner, and even if one of their members is arrested, there are more than sufficient personnel to keep the group running. The group is associated with a hacktivist movement that takes the form of vigilante actions. The group has played a role in anti-child-pornography movements, where its members have brought down numerous websites that offer such content. What makes Anonymous so special is that it has been adopted as an idea rather than a hacking group. Therefore, it has received adoption around the world and has a higher chance of staying relevant. This group has been branded with the iconic Guy Fawkes mask.

Apart from these hacking groups, there are many others. Some emerge and then cease to exist once their top leaders are arrested. Hacking groups are not necessarily evil since some of them hack with good intentions. However, they are still a threat to cybersecurity since they use tools and techniques that can be ultimately harmful to users and computers.

Cyber espionage

This is a growing cybersecurity problem where cyber criminals target an organization in an attempt to steal information that could be used by competitors or to undermine the company. Companies worldwide have fallen victim to these types of hack, where their business secrets are stolen by foreign countries. Manufacturing companies that have fallen victim to cyber espionage have seen counterfeits of their products being released at cheaper prices in overseas markets. Cyber espionage is becoming an economy menace since it affects the revenues of many organizations. It's estimated that a large number of organizations that have fallen victim to cyber espionage still don't know that they're victims.

In some incidents, cyber espionage has been directly attributed to hacking groups. There are fears, however, that some espionage attacks are state-sponsored. Some countries have been accused of having special units that conduct cyber-espionage attacks.

Cybersecurity objectives

The aim of cybersecurity is to ensure that the confidentiality, integrity, and availability of data and systems is preserved. This section discusses the different objectives of cybersecurity.

Importance of cybersecurity and its impacts on the global economy

Cybersecurity has of vital importance today ever since the world was networked. Many processes in organizations are enabled by interlinked technologies. However, the penetration of technology into normal lives and organizational processes has introduced people to cyber threats. With every improvement in technology, the threat of cyber attacks increases. New technology, such as IoT, have met the harsh reality of cybercrime. However, current cybersecurity efforts ensure that the use of technology is not hindered by cyber criminals. There are several reasons why organizations and individuals are emphasizing cybersecurity; they are outlined here.

The number of cyber attacks is growing

With the rapid development of technology, the number of cyber attacks has been growing exponentially. Cybersecurity reports show that, each year, there is a rise in the number of threats that have been detected for the first time. There are specialists in underground markets that have focused on creating new types of malware that they sell to hackers. Cyber criminals are spending long hours doing background research on individuals and organizations to find weaknesses that they can target. Social engineers are perfecting their manipulation tactics to help them net more victims. At the same time, users have not significantly improved or taken individual responsibility for their own security or that of the companies they work for. The only hope in securing individuals' data, money, and systems lies in enhancing cybersecurity. With all the developments on the part of cyber criminals, cybersecurity is fast becoming a necessity.

Cyber attacks are getting worse

Cybercrime has evolved from what it used to be. The aftermath of a cyber attack today is often devastating, as can be seen from the companies that have fallen prey to cyber criminals. Yahoo lost its value after it was confirmed that cyber criminals had penetrated its systems and stolen the data of 3,000,000,000 users. Ubiquiti Networks lost over $40,000,000 to cyber criminals that executed a social-engineering attack on its employees. Many other top companies have lost sensitive data to hackers. Individuals are not spared either. The WannaCry ransomware indiscriminately encrypted individuals' and organization' computers in over 150 countries. In general, cybercrime is getting worse. More money is involved, and huge chunks of sensitive data are being stolen. The targets are not limited to small organizations, since big companies, such as Uber and Yahoo, have already fallen victim. Cybersecurity is therefore essential for organizations and individuals.

Impacts on the global economy

The economic implications of cyber attacks are being felt on a global scale. Organizations are losing billions of dollars to attacks every year. Forbes has estimated that with the current pattern, cybercrime will cost the globe $2,000,000,000,000,000,000 in 2019. In 2015, this number was only at $400,000,000. Prior to the estimate from 2015, early estimates done in 2013 reported that cybercrime only costs $100,000,000 globally. As can be seen, the pattern has been such that the cost keeps growing. The World Economic Forum has taken note of this, and with concern. It has warned that the figures could be higher since a large percentage of cybercrime goes undetected. It has identified industrial espionage as one crime where many victims don't even know that they're victims.

As per the estimation of the cost of cybercrime by Steve Morgan (`https://www.forbes.com/sites/stevemorgan/2016/01/17/cyber-crime-costs-projected-to-reach-2-trillion-by-2019/#466996b73a91`), from 2013 to 2015, the cost of cybercrime has quadrupled, and it looks like there will be another quadrupling from 2015 to 2019. Juniper research recently predicted that the rapid digitization of consumers' lives and enterprise records will increase the cost of data breaches to $2,100,000,000,000,000,000 globally by 2019 (`https://www.juniperresearch.com/press/press-releases/cybercrime-cost-businesses-over-2trillion`).

Estimation of financial losses related to cybercrime

The financial losses related to cybercrime are incomparable to the cost of cybersecurity. While cybersecurity costs remain almost constant, cybercrime costs increase every year. In 2017, it was estimated that annual breaches had increased by 27.4%.

Accenture has estimated the cost of cybersecurity for the year 2017, as follows:

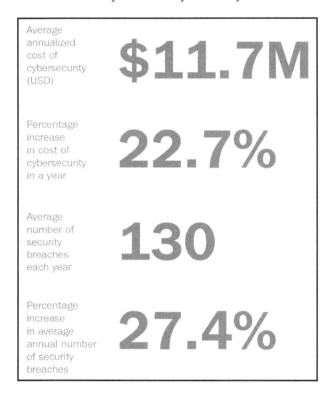

Average annualized cost of cybersecurity (USD)	**$11.7M**
Percentage increase in cost of cybersecurity in a year	**22.7%**
Average number of security breaches each year	**130**
Percentage increase in average annual number of security breaches	**27.4%**

These numbers are more than just a statistic. It shows that more organizations will fall victim to cybercrime in 2018 than in 2017. The average cost of a breach or malware attack on an organization is currently at $2,400,000. However, this number is just an average. There are organizations that lose much more than that. Take, for instance, the Sony attack that happened in 2015: the organization lost a whopping $15,000,000 due to the attack; the Ubiquiti Networks case led to a $40,000,000 loss. Therefore, the average cost of a cyber crime should not be used to depict the reality, since some companies lose several times the average.

The time it takes to resolve a cyber attack is becoming longer than ever. It now takes an average of 23 days to recover from a ransomware attack. Insider threat attacks take up to 50 days to recover from. DDoS attacks take only a few days to recover from, but by then a lot of damage will have been done. In general, the attack duration has increased and that adds to the effects on the victims. The financial consequences can only go higher with more exposure time to an attacker.

Globally, the US has witnessed the highest average cost of cyber attacks. The country's average has been higher than the global average since 2017, when it was estimated at $21,000,000. This estimate has grown from $17,000,000 in 2016. The second country in the ranking of those with the highest cost of cybercrime is Germany; it jumped from $7,800,000 in 2016 to $11,500,000 in 2017. Japan is third, with an estimated cybercrime cost of $10,000,000. The UK, France, and Italy follow with estimates of $8,000,000, $7,900,000, and $6,300,000, respectively.

The following screenshot estimates cybersecurity costs by Accenture:

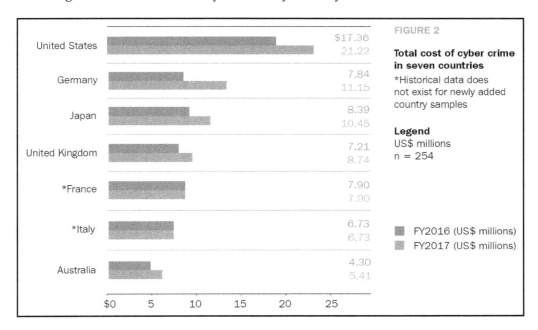

FIGURE 2

Total cost of cyber crime in seven countries
*Historical data does not exist for newly added country samples

Legend
US$ millions
n = 254

■ FY2016 (US$ millions)
■ FY2017 (US$ millions)

Country	FY2016	FY2017
United States	$17.36	21.22
Germany	7.84	11.15
Japan	8.39	10.45
United Kingdom	7.21	8.74
*France	7.90	7.90
*Italy	6.73	6.73
Australia	4.30	5.41

Reference: `https://www.accenture.com/t20170926T072837Z__w__/us-en/_acnmedia/PDF-61/Accenture-2017-CostCyberCrimeStudy.pdf`.

There are also other financial losses that arise from cybercrime that cannot be directly estimated. The loss of customer loyalty is a hidden impact that can have financial consequences. Fewer customers directly translates to lower revenue. Lost reputation is another impact that leads to financial loss. Without a good reputation, very few clients will choose to do business with a company that's perceived to be unsecured. Legal fees from cases relating to loss of user data also add to the financial consequences of hacks that a company has to meet. These fees, therefore, make cybercrime very costly to organizations.

Finance and cybersecurity

There is a strong relationship between finance and cybersecurity. Finance can be viewed in two perspectives in line with cybersecurity. Finance is used to procure cybersecurity products that can be used to prevent cybercrime. Finance is also a direct victim of cyber attacks. Therefore, it continues to be linked to cybersecurity. There have been attacks targeted specifically at the finance departments in organizations. Other than this, **Chief Finance Officers** (**CFOs**) are having to work closely with **Chief Information Security Officers** (**CISOs**) in organizations to ensure that they adequately fund their cybersecurity endeavors. Today, the links between finance and IT are closer than ever.

Critical dependency of business, processes, and IT infrastructure

Today, business is run through computer systems that coordinate processes from different business lines, while making the individual processes more efficient and effective. For instance, in a production company, the supplies department has to be linked with the production department, which then has to be linked with the sales department. This type of chain will ensure that the supply department has already procured input before the production department depletes the ones it has. The production department will control its output depending on the sales such that there is no over-production. To ensure that these three departments continue to operate smoothly, the organization might acquire **enterprise resource planning (ERP)** systems that will be integrated. The ERPs will ensure that the supplies department automatically gets notified when the production department needs more input. The production department will get actual and forecasted sales to ensure that it doesn't overproduce products that may go to waste. The ERP solution will be the backbone of all this coordination between departments.

This hypothetical example is just a snapshot of what takes place in actual organizations. Different departments are linked using IT systems. When these systems are down, business processes in different business lines will be affected. Therefore, it's in the best interest of all organizations to ensure that IT systems are running as expected at all times. Another critical linkage between departments is the internal network. Organizations that have branches in different places normally want to ensure that data stored in different physical locations can easily be accessed. Therefore, a WAN is established to keep all branches connected. If this network goes down, many operations can't take place. There are other components of the IT infrastructure in an organization that are equally important for the functioning of day-to-day operations. If these components go offline, operations can't go on as usual. This is the current state in most organizations. To survive in the current business environment, it has become necessary to make IT a resource. There are some industries where competitiveness is only judged by the systems that an organization has.

With a good view of the current dependence of businesses on IT infrastructures, one can appreciate the consequences of having components of the infrastructure failing or being attacked. Without some critical components, such as ERP systems, networks, and computers, business operations can come to a halt. One of the main reasons IT systems go down is cyber attacks. There are other causes, such as natural disasters, human error, and normal failures. However, of major concern today is attackers targeting the IT infrastructure. Not only can they stop operations, attackers can purposefully destroy the infrastructure. This will in turn cripple the organization. Therefore, organizations resort to protecting their IT infrastructures, since they cannot afford to lose some of the functionalities that are supported by the different components of the infrastructure.

Economic loss

As a consequence of the increasing cost of cybercrime, there has been a resultant loss in global and local economies. Based on estimates from McAfee, it is expected that 2018 will see 0.8% of the global economy gross domestic product being lost to cybercrime. This is estimated at $600,000,000,000. Estimates for 2019 show that the economic loss will hit the trillion-dollar mark. This shows that the economic impact of cybercrime is only getting worse. In 2014, the estimated loss was at 0.7% of the global economy. The US has seen a relatively constant increase in the number of cybercrimes reported. Europe, however, has seen the highest rise in cybercrime. It might appear that cyber criminals were once not particularly focused outside the US market. With time, there has been an influx of hacking activity, and the hacks have sporadically grown in the previously-unexplored Europe region. Also, since the US has seen consistent cybercrime, organizations have been preparing themselves for the attacks. Europe is now facing the highest economic loss to cybercrime. An estimated 0.84% of its regional gross domestic product has been lost to cybercrime. In the US, the percentage is at 0.78%.

There are several reasons why the economic loss due to cybercrime seems to be going up. To begin with, there are more cybercrime tools being released. The new cybercrime tools are more effective. As was explained in the *Hacking groups* section, the most damaging ransomware attack thus far was successful due to the use of a three-month-old exploit that had been stolen from the NSA by a hacking group. Another reason for the increase of economic losses is because of the adoption of new technologies by threat actors. These technologies enable them to decrypt encrypted files, gain access to systems without causing alarms to be raised, and overwhelm security tools, among other things. Another driver for the increased economic loss is the growing sophistication of hacks. A good example is phishing. Phishing has evolved over time. Years ago, it was done through plaintext email, which narrated an unfortunate occurrence and asked the recipient to offer some assistance to the person in peril. Early phishing emails were characterized by grammatical errors and an outright feeling of vagueness. However, phishing has recently developed a new face. It's done through professionally-formatted HTML emails that resemble those of legitimate companies. Phishing emails contain links to cloned websites that have a similar look, feel, and interactive quality to legitimate websites. The targets don't know when they're handing over their information to hackers or sending money to them. This type of revolutionary development in attack techniques has also been witnessed in other types of attacks. This has led to a high number of successful attack. For example, the number of victims of the IRS scam of 2017 was around 170,000. This is a number that didn't exist five years ago since these types of phishing attacks hadn't been used.

Banking and financial systems – changes from a risk and security perspective

Banking and financial systems have been the targets of cyber criminals. There are listings on some underground economies of malware that can be used against automated teller machines to cause them to spit out cash. There are malware that can be used to intercept the communication between bank servers and customers to steal sessions or login information. There are malware that have been developed to spy on users once they visit certain banking websites. There are phishing scams that have been specifically targeted at customers of certain online banks and payment systems. These are just a few of the threats that are facing banks and have caused them to innovate their risk and security perspectives. The following is a screenshot of a PayPal phishing email:

Please Update Your Account

Dear valued **PayPal** member:

It has come to out attention that your **PayPal** account information needs to be updated as part of our continuing commitment to protect your account and to reduce the instance of fraud on our website. If you could please take 5-10 minutes out of your online experience and update your personal records you will not run into any future problems with the online services.

However, failure to update your records will result in account suspension. Please update your records on or before 10 Dec. 2011.

Once you have updated your account records, your **PayPal** session will not be interrupted and will continue as normal.

To update your **PayPal** records click on the following link:
https://www.paypal.com/cgi-bin/webscr?cmd=_login-run

PayPal, Inc.
P.O. Box 45950
Omaha, NE 68145

Sincerely,

PayPal

 WARNING - This is a phishing email. If you receive an email like this, do not click on any links.

Banks have had to upgrade their machines and operating systems used to control their ATMs to prevent malware attacks that can cause money to be stolen. They recognize that there are hackers conversant with the systems used by ATMs, who can easily break into these systems and steal money directly from the machines. Banks have also come to recognize that there are threats with the transmission of data on the internet in plaintext form. Therefore, they have switched to secured HTTP to ensure that data is encrypted from the source to the destination. Therefore, a user's input for logging in cannot be stolen while in transit. This is a risk that they didn't have to contend with in the past, but now are forced to. Antivirus companies are creating browser add-ons that can be integrated with common browsers to detect and remove spyware, or to prevent any spying activities from taking place during data entry into websites. Previously, spyware was not a risk but today security companies have to respond to it. As for the phishing scams, banks have been spreading user awareness to prevent users from falling for scams. There has been a PayPal scam doing the rounds, with emails and websites that are similar to the legitimate PayPal sites and they have caused many users to lose money. Years ago, these scams didn't exist, but today banks have to pay attention to them so as to keep their users secure. In short, there are many changes taking place in banking and financial systems to account for new risks and security threats that didn't exist or weren't as serious in the past.

Data breach means money

When an organization is breached, data is stolen, and then it is leaked, the end result is the exchange of money. Therefore, data leakage almost always translates to money. The beneficiary of a data leak is the hacker. The hacker has everything to gain from the leaked data. The hacker could hold the stolen data ransom and ask the victim to pay so that the data isn't released or sold in underground markets. This has happened several times. A Dubai bank was once threatened by a hacker that they would release bank records that had been hacked from the bank's website. The bank defied the orders to send a ransom amount to the hacker, and the end result was that sensitive information was released on Twitter by the hacker. Another way that a hacker can make money out of a data breach is by selling it to third parties. When Yahoo was hacked and data belonging to 3,000,000,000 users stolen, it was listed for sale in dark markets. Black markets on the darknet are almost always the place where stolen data is sold. There are willing buyers for stolen data even if it's encrypted. The buyers tend to either be advertisers or other cyber criminals. Advertisers will use the stolen data to create profiles of people that they can advertise to some products. Cyber criminals will, on the other hand, try to user details, such as login credentials, to hack the user whose data has been stolen.

The other cashflow in a data breach relates to the loss of money from the victim organization. When a data breach occurs, and either user data or personally identifiable information is lost, the victim organization can be sued by the users. It is the responsibility of the organization that collects user data to ensure that this data is secured at all times from theft. There have been cases where users have dragged some companies to court after a data breach. Courts often side with users as they are the most aggrieved parties when personal data has been stolen. Financial loss also occurs to the victim organization due to the loss of credibility, reliability, and trust that customers had in it.

Financial repercussion of reputational damage caused by cyber attacks

A good example of how a cyber attack can damage a company's reputation can be drawn from Yahoo. Since Yahoo's cyber attack resulting in the theft of a whopping 3,000,000,000 accounts' data, the company significantly lost reputation and value. Verizon, the company that wanted to buy Yahoo, slashed $350 million from the amount that it had offered to acquire the company. There was also a mass exodus of users from Yahoo to rival companies such as Gmail. Today, fewer people want to create a Yahoo account, due to the thought of hacking and data theft. Yahoo serves as a lesson to many organizations of just how badly cyber attacks can damage the reputation of an organization.

Therefore, the financial repercussions of the loss of a good reputation as a result of a hack are real and more pronounced than other types of attack, such as physical theft. The first repercussion of loss of reputation is the loss of customers. Today, Yahoo barely controls the market share that it used to control prior to the hack. Users are scared of their data being stolen by hackers. Yahoo has repeatedly been hacked, such that the security controls put in place to secure its systems and data are doubted. The way that the organization handled the hacks is another contributor to the loss of customers. The organization didn't immediately warn users that a large number of account data had been stolen. Instead, it was seemingly playing games with its users, informing them that the hack had only affected a fraction of accounts. When the initial figures were released, it was said that only 500 accounts had been hacked. However, it turned out that there were more than 3,000,000,000 affected accounts. Users felt cheated and that the attack was not dealt with as it should have been . At the same time, competitors of Yahoo, such as Google, didn't have any security scares since their security records had remained spotless for so long. It's not known how long it will take Yahoo to recover from its damaged reputation.

Digital economy and related threats

The digital economy refers to the wide range of economic activities and commercial transactions that take place through IT. The digital economy has been growing partly due to the evolution of some part of the traditional economy to this type of economy. This makes it quite hard to draw a distinct line between what remains as the traditional economy and what is to be referred to as the digital economy. Many organizations have adopted information technology to enable them to run their processes faster, more efficiently, and with competitiveness. Individuals are also part of this economy, since they are engaging in tasks and transactions that they couldn't participate in previously. New technology is causing more people and organizations to join this economy. The addition of IoT, big data analytics, the cloud, wireless networks, and social media networks has continued to pull more people into this economy.

However, cyber threats exist in this economy. Without physical intrusion and theft, this economy can be sabotaged using technology similar to what powers it. Particularly, it has been said that this economy might cease to grow if the security to protect it isn't adequate. This economy is fragile and cyber threats have been marked as its greatest challenges. A single cyber threat can bring it to stagnation. Over the last few years, there has been a growth on the cyber threats that face this economy. Some attacks have shown the capability to bring the digital economy to its knees. It seems that the threats facing this economy are only getting more advanced. The following are some of threat trends facing the digital economy.

Smart threats

With the proliferation of IoT and cloud-connected devices, a new breed of cyber threat is emerging. There are now smart threats developed to target devices which are interconnected using the IoT technology and also the cloud. Since IoT devices are still fresh in the economy, they are being targeted more because they haven't yet been hardened to the threats that exist on the internet. IoT devices connect to the internet just like many other devices, but their security features are lacking, thus they are sitting ducks for hackers. The cloud is also seeing massive adoption from companies. This is a new frontier where hackers have moved their expertise to. The cloud is not the same as local servers, where organizations can closely monitor the security of their applications and sensitive information. If a wave of successful attacks sweeps through major cloud vendors, massive losses will be witnessed.

Ransomware

Hackers have already demonstrated that they can topple the digital economy using a single ransomware. The WannaCry ransomware attack serves as a basis for this statement. The attack was waged globally as it affected over 150 countries. Experts have said that if it hadn't been for the sloppiness of the coder of the ransomware, an end to the attack wouldn't have been found in time to prevent a global-scale panic. Within just 24 hours, this single ransomware caused huge loses to companies, deaths in hospitals, loss of individuals files, and other types of losses. Ransomware still remains a severe threat to the digital economy after that demonstration. It's estimated that ransomware threats have been growing and this should be of concern to the economy.

The following is the screen presented by WannaCry after encrypting a computer:

Critical infrastructure attacks

A perilous attack landscape for the digital economy is critical infrastructures. Countries are increasingly automating critical infrastructures that provide services to the masses. These infrastructures can be attacked, putting a stop to the critical services that they offer. For instance, the WannaCry ransomware attack of 2017 crippled the **National Health Service** (**NHS**) in the UK. Hospital systems were affected to a point where medical appointments and surgeries had to be postponed until the attack was resolved.

Summary

The chapter has given you an introduction to cybersecurity and the economy. It explained the scope of cybersecurity, the terms used in cybersecurity, and a general description of some relevant actors in cyber attacks. The chapter also looked at the objectives of cybersecurity. It outlined the importance of cybersecurity and its impact on the global economy. The financial repercussions of cyber threats have been highlighted, showing the devastation that can be caused by threat actors. Finally, this chapter focused on the digital economy and the threats it currently faces. These threats include smart threats, ransomware, and critical infrastructure attacks; all of these can be performed on a large scale, thus toppling the digital economy. In the next chapter, you will learn about different threat actor groups and their motivation.

Further reading

The following are resources that can be used to gain more knowledge on the topics covered in this chapter:

- *Glossary of cybersecurity terms*: https://www.bsigroup.com/en-GB/Cyber-Security/Cyber-security-for-SMEs/Glossary-of-cyber-security-terms/
- *COST OF CYBER CRIME STUDY*: https://www.accenture.com/t20170926T072837Z__w__/us-en/_acnmedia/PDF-61/Accenture-2017-CostCyberCrimeStudy.pdf

Cyber Crime - Who the Attackers Are

2

This chapter gives an in-depth understanding specifically of cyber crime and Cyber criminals, analyzing from different perspectives, the motivations and the evolution of individuals and group, that are part of the invisible world of black-hat hackers. Cyber criminals are consistently improving their techniques and malicious activities. The chapter will cover hacktivism, Cyber terrorists, and Cyber criminals in detail along with some real world examples.

Introduction to cyber crime

According to an independently conducted research by the Ponemon Institute LLC on the cost of cyber crime in 2017 (`https://www.accenture.com/t20171006T095146Z__w__/us-en/_acnmedia/PDF-62/Accenture-2017CostCybercrime-US-FINAL.pdf#zoom=50`), successful breaches per company continue to increase by 27% per year. The economic impact of these cyber attacks is one of the highest costs to the financial services industry. This means that companies within this sector need to drive for a change in how they approach cyber security.

The following diagram shows the average annual cost according to each industry sector:

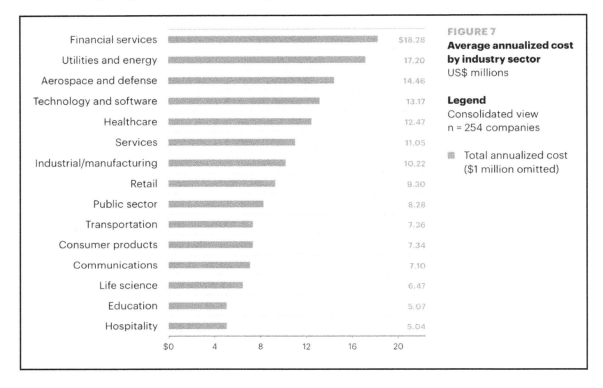

Financial services	$18.28
Utilities and energy	17.20
Aerospace and defense	14.46
Technology and software	13.17
Healthcare	12.47
Services	11.05
Industrial/manufacturing	10.22
Retail	9.30
Public sector	8.28
Transportation	7.36
Consumer products	7.34
Communications	7.10
Life science	6.47
Education	5.07
Hospitality	5.04

FIGURE 7

Average annualized cost by industry sector
US$ millions

Legend
Consolidated view
n = 254 companies

Total annualized cost
($1 million omitted)

The financial services industry is very appealing to threat actors, hacktivists, and nation states because of the data that companies within the financial services industry store. They have records of money transactions, details of the net wealth of individuals and companies, and much more.

Regardless of what industry sector they operate in, no company is safe against cyber attacks. In particular, companies in the financial services industry remain a very lucrative target. The following diagram shows the average client organization monitored by IBM security services in 2016 a cross industry versus financial services:

Threat actors

The attackers behind cyber attacks can be classified into the following categories:

- Cyber criminals
- Cyber terrorists
- Hacktivists

"What really concerns me is the sophistication of the capability, which is becoming good enough to really threaten parts of our critical infrastructure, certainly in the financial, banking sector."

– Director of Europol Robert Wainwright

Hacktivism

Hacktivism (`https://ics-cert.us-cert.gov/content/cyber-threat-source-descriptions#hack`), as defined by the **Industrial Control Systems Cyber Emergency Response Team (ICS-CERT)**, refers to threat actors that depend on propaganda rather than damage to critical infrastructures. Their goal is to support their own political agenda, which varies between anti-corruption, religion, environmental, or anti-establishment concerns. Their sub-goals are propaganda and causing damage to achieve notoriety for their cause. One of the most prominent hacktivist threat actor groups is Anonymous. Anonymous is known primarily for their **distributed denial of service (DDoS)** attacks on governments and the Church of Scientology. The following screenshot shows "the man without a head," which is commonly used by Anonymous as their emblem:

Hacktivists target companies and governments based on the organization's mission statement or ethics. Given that the financial services industry is responsible for economic wealth, they tend to be a popular target for hacktivists.

The ideologies held by hacktivists can vary, but at their core, they focus on bringing attention to social issues such as warfare or what they consider to be illegal activities. To spread their beliefs, they choose targets that allow them to spread their message as quickly as possible. The primary reason why hacktivists are choosing organizations in the financial services industry sector is that these organizations typically have a large user base, allowing them to raise the profile of their beliefs very quickly once they have successfully breached the organization's security controls.

Case study – Dakota Access Pipeline

The **Dakota Access Pipeline** (DAPL) was a 2016 construction of a 1.172-mile-long pipeline that spanned three states in the US. Native American tribes were protesting against the DAPL because of the fear that it would damage sacred grounds and drinking water. Shortly after the protests began, the hacktivist group Anonymous publicly announced their support under the name *OpNoDAPL*. During the construction, Anonymous launched numerous DDoS attacks against the organizations involved in the DAPL. Anonymous leaked the personal information of employees that were responsible for the DAPL and threatened that this would continue if they did not quit. The following screenshot shows how this attack spread on Twitter:

Case study – Panama Papers

In 2015, an offshore law firm called Mossack Fonseca had 11.5 million of their documents leaked. These documents contained confidential financial information for more than 214,488 offshore entities under what was later known as the Panama Papers. In the leaked documents, several national leaders, politicians, and industry leaders were identified, including a trail to Vladimir Putin. The following diagram shows how much was exposed as part of this attack:

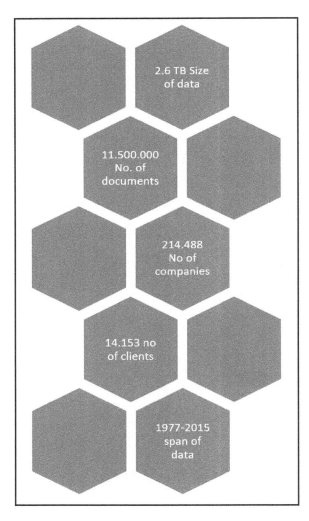

While there is not much information available on how the cyber attack occurred, various security researchers have analyzed the operation.

 You can find a screenshot that shows the tweet send by WikiLeaks on Twitter at this link: `https://www.pronews.gr/amyna-asfaleia/spy-news/420495_sta-adyta-ton-panama-papers-pos-katafere-mia-kryfi-pigina`.

According to the WikiLeaks post, which claims to show a client communication from Mossack Fonseca, they confirm that there was a breach of their *"email server"*. Considering the size of the data leak, it is believed that a direct attack occurred on the email servers.

Cyber terrorists

Extremist and terrorist organizations such as Al Qaeda and **Islamic State of Iraq and Syria** (**ISIS**) are using the internet to distribute their propaganda, recruiting new terrorists and communicating via this medium. An example of this is the 2008 attack in Mumbai, in which one of the gunmen confirmed that they used Google Earth to familiarize themselves with the locations of buildings. Cyber terrorism is an extension of traditional terrorism in cyber space.

Case study – Operation Ababil

In 2012, the Islamic group Izz ad-Din al-Qassam Cyber Fighters—which is a military wing of Hamas—attacked a series of American financial institutions. On September 18th 2012, this threat actor group confirmed that they were behind the cyber attack and justified it due to the relationship of the United States government with Israel. They also claimed that this was a response to the *Innocence of Muslims* video released by the American pastor Terry Jones. As part of a DDoS attack, they targeted the New York Stock Exchange as well as banks such as J.P. Morgan Chase.

Cyber criminals

Cyber criminals are either individuals or groups of hackers who use technology to commit crimes in the digital world. The primary driver of cyber criminals is financial gain and/or service disruption. Cyber criminals use computers in three broad ways:

- Select computers as their target: These criminals attack other people's computers to perform malicious activities, such as spreading viruses, data theft, identity theft, and more.
- Use computers as their weapon: They use computers to carry out "conventional crime", such as spam, fraud, illegal gambling, and more.
- Use computers as an accessory: They use computers to save stolen or illegal data.

The following provides the larger picture so we can understand how Cyber Criminals has penetrated into the finance sector and wreaked havoc:

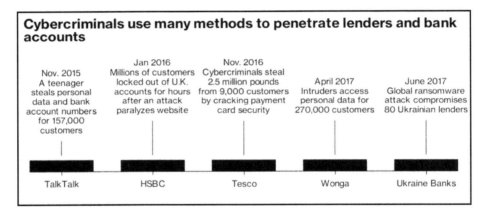

Cybercriminals use many methods to penetrate lenders and bank accounts

Nov. 2015 A teenager steals personal data and bank account numbers for 157,000 customers	Jan 2016 Millions of customers locked out of U.K. accounts for hours after an attack paralyzes website	Nov. 2016 Cybercriminals steal 2.5 million pounds from 9,000 customers by cracking payment card security	April 2017 Intruders access personal data for 270,000 customers	June 2017 Global ransomware attack compromises 80 Ukrainian lenders
TalkTalk	HSBC	Tesco	Wonga	Ukraine Banks

Becky Pinkard, vice president of service delivery and intelligence at Digital Shadows Ltd, states that *"Attackers can harm the bank by adding or subtracting a zero with every balance, or even by deleting entire accounts"*.

Case study – FIN7

On August 1st 2018, the United States District Attorney's Office for the Western District of Washington announced the arrest of several members of the cyber criminal organization FIN7, which had been tracked since 2015. To this date, security researchers believe that FIN7 is one of the largest threat actor groups in the financial services industry. Combi Security is a FIN7 shelf company.

The screenshot presented here: `https://www.theverge.com/2018/8/1/17639914/carbanak-indictment-hacking-credit-card-records-ukraine-campaign-chipotle-chilis-arbys` shows a phishing email sent by FIN7 to victims claiming it was sent by the US **Food and Drug Administration (FDA)**

Case study – Carbanak APT Attack

Carbanak is an **advanced persistent threat (APT)** attack that is believed to have been executed by the threat actor group Cobalt Strike Group in 2014. In this operation, the threat actor group was able to generate a total financial loss for victims of more than 1 billion US dollars. The following depicts how the Carbanak cyber-gang stole $1bn by targeting a bank:

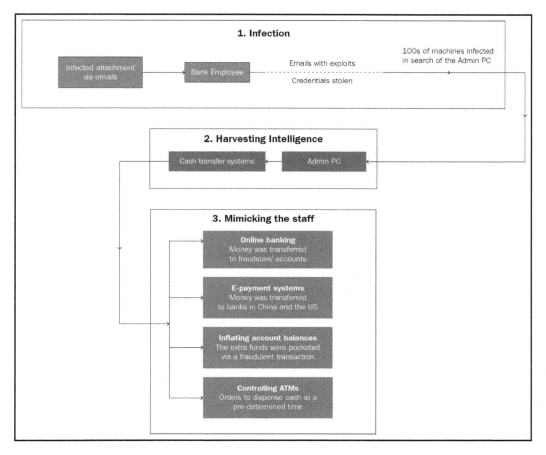

Case study – OurMine operation

In 2016, the threat actor group OurMine, who are suspected to operate in Saudi Arabia, conducted a DDoS attack against HSBC's websites, hosted in the USA and UK. The following screenshot shows the communication by the threat actor:

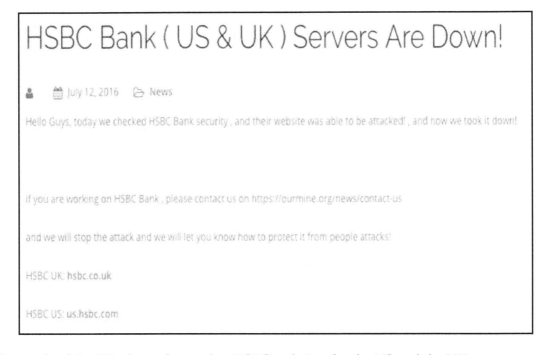

The result of the DDoS attack was that HSBC websites for the US and the UK were unavailable. The following screenshot shows the HSBC USA website after the DDoS attack:

Summary

The financial services industry is one of the most popular victim industries for cyber crime. In this chapter, you learned about different threat actor groups and their motivations. It is important to understand these in order to build and execute a successful cyber security strategy. In the next chapter, we will talk about the costs associated with cyber attacks and cyber security.

3
Counting the Costs

Reports from cybersecurity experts have shown that there has been an increase in the costs of cybersecurity. These costs have risen in two ways: through the expenses met to secure an organization through the purchase of security tools, and through the expenses incurred by an organization that has fallen victim to a cyber attack, such as regulatory compliance fines and a damaged reputation. Both of these expenses have economic implications. This is because security products and cyber attacks are almost evenly distributed. Similar cybersecurity products will cost almost the same, while the average cost of a breach will yield the same consequences in terms of direct financial loss, cost of litigations, and loss of customers. This chapter is going to look at both categories of expenses and explain why they have been going up, and what organizations can do to keep them reasonably under control or to avoid them completely. This chapter discusses the following topics:

- The cost of a cybersecurity attack
- Breakdown of the costs of a cyber attack
- Breakdown of the costs of securing an organization

The cost of a cybersecurity attack

The average cost of a cybersecurity attack has been increasing over time. The rewards to hackers in cyber heists have also been increasing, and this has been motivating them to come up with even better tools and techniques in order to allow them to steal more money and data. Several cybersecurity companies have listed their estimates for the average costs of cyber attacks in 2017/2018. The following are some of these estimates.

According to IBM—a tech giant both in hardware and software products—the average cost of a cybersecurity breach has been increasing and is now at $3,860,000. This is a 6.4% increase on their estimate for 2017. The company also estimates that the cost of each stolen record that has sensitive information in 2018 is at $148, which is a rise of 4.8% compared to their estimate for 2017. The following is IBM's report (`https://www.ibm.com/security/data-breach`) on the cost of a cyber breach in 2018:

> *This year's study reports the global average cost of a data breach is up 6.4% over the previous year to $3,860,000 million. The average cost for each lost or stolen record containing sensitive and confidential information also increased by 4.8% year over year to $148.*

For the estimates given throughout the book, note the following:

- All of these estimates are done by companies with their own methodologies, so they may not be comparable to each other.
- Some of them may have a bias towards painting a grim picture—the FUD tactic.
- The figures are not from a governmental or not-for-profit source.
- Not all breaches are reported, and not all reported breaches share detailed information. Hence, all of these reports make a lot of estimates.

According to Sfax, a fax-securing company for hospitals, the global average cost of a cybersecurity breach was at $3,620,000 in 2017. However, in the US, where there were more cyber attacks, the company estimates the average cost of each attack to be $7,350,000. The company places the global average cost for each stolen record at $141, while this is at $225 for US companies. Here's the Sfax report (`https://www.scrypt.com/blog/average-cost-data-breach-2017-3-62-million/`) on the cost of a cyber breach in 2017:

> *The annual study reveals that the average cost of a data breach is currently $3,620,000 globally.*

According to Accenture, the global average cost of a cybersecurity attack is much worse as, in 2017, it cost an average of $11,700,000. The company places the US average at $22,000,000, which is almost quadruple the Australian average of $5,400,000. Accenture was selective in the countries that it chose to calculate averages for; it selected 254 organizations from 7 countries, thus the averages they arrived at were quite high compared to other organizations. The following are the estimates on the cost of cybercrime in 2017 by Accenture (`https://www.accenture.com/us-en/insight-cost-of-cybercrime-2017`):

> *Cyber crime costs are accelerating. With organizations spending nearly 23% more than last year – US $11,700,000, on average – they are investing on an unprecedented scale.*

The cost of different cyber attacks

While it might be easy to say that the average cost of a hack is $3,000,000, not all types of attacks will be around that figure. Some attacks are more costly than others. Costs also differ with the frequency of an attack against an organization. Consequently, it's good to look at how costs vary among common cyber attacks. The following screenshot is Accenture's graphical representation of the costs of the most common attacks based on their frequency in 2016 and 2017. This data was collected from 254 companies around the world:

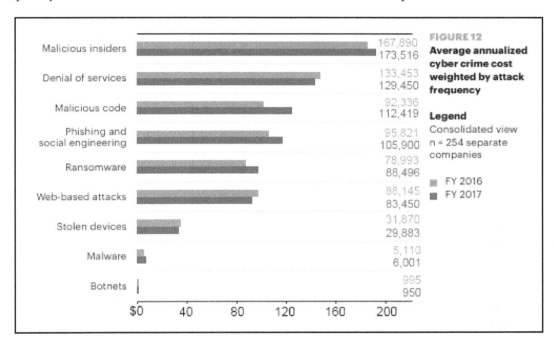

To interpret this data, one should note that frequency was taken into consideration. Consequently, the most frequent attacks had higher averages. As can be seen from the graph, insider threats are the most frequent and costly threats to an organization. Attacks related to malicious insiders led to losses averaging $173,516 in 2017. The reason for this high cost is due to the amount of information that insider threats possess when carrying out an attack. Since they've worked with the victim company for some time, they know exactly what to target and are familiar with which security loopholes to exploit. This isn't a guessing game but an assured attack with a clear aim and a preplanned execution. According to the graph by Accenture, malicious insiders were followed by **denial of service (DoS)** attacks at an annual cost of $129,450, and then malicious code at an annual cost of $112,419.

However, when frequency is not considered, there are several changes to the report, as can be seen from the following graphical representation:

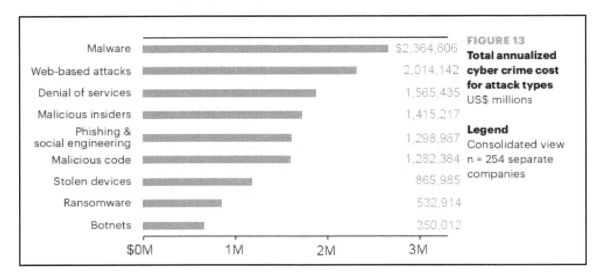

This graph is representative of the situation in the real world. As can be seen, malware attacks are collectively the costliest. Organizations hit by malware lose an average of $2,400,000 per attack. This is because of the establishment of an underground market that's supports the quick purchase of new malware and the huge number of unpatched systems. Malware has also become more sophisticated due to highly skilled black hats selling their malware on the dark web at affordable prices. Therefore, script kiddies have been getting highly effective malware that they can deploy in attacks. Web-based attacks come in second at $2,000,000, while DoS attacks are ranked third at $1,565,000. DoS attacks are ranked high due to the losses that they can cause a company to incur.

At $1,560,000 per attack, DoS attacks are devastating to any company. They are particularly dangerous because of their effectiveness. When a strong enough botnet is directed at a target, the chances of the target surviving the attack are slim. Past attacks have shown that any organization can be taken down. Dyn DNS is one of the leading domain-name resolution companies, and one would imagine that they have a highly secured IT environment capable of repelling all attacks. However, the organization was taken down for a few hours by a DDoS attack. Several sites were not accessible from regions that relied on Dyn for domain-name resolution. It was later observed that the organization was hit with traffic from a botnet peaking at 1 Tbps. If the same attack were to be executed against an e-commerce website, such as Amazon, for a few hours, the losses that the organization would face would be astronomical.

Similarly, other organizations that offer time-critical services can run into losses in the range of millions if they are targeted with a DDoS attack. Unfortunately, the botnet-for-hire business is only becoming more popular in underground markets. Botnets such as Mirai have been formed with hundreds of thousands of zombie devices. The Mirai botnet is the result of a world flooded with unsecured IoT devices. The total estimate of IoT devices released to the market by the end of 2017 was 8,400,000,000. The Mirai botnet recruited quite a number of IoT devices into its network. To do this, it simply tried 61 default username and password combinations from different IoT manufacturers. Since 2016, Mirai has taken down many famous companies. One of the most famous attacks was the Dyn DNS attack of October 2016. The Mirai botnet unleashed a DDoS attack with illegitimate requests that peaked at 1 Tbps, thus overwhelming Dyn's abilities to resolve any domain names for several hours. Prior to this attack, the botnet had been used against OVH, a French hosting company. The botnet was able to launch two separate DDoS attacks on OVH which, when combined, had 1.5 Tbps of illegit traffic. The company later revealed that most of the traffic was coming from approximately 146,000 IP cameras and video recorders. Market analysts say that there will be 20,000,000,000 IoT devices by 2020 and this only continues to intensify the threat of DDoS attacks.

Breakdown of the costs of a cyber attack

The direct financial losses that have been discussed are not as a result of money stolen during an attack or records copied and advertised as for sale on the deep web. All cyber attacks come bundled with other losses to the company, some of which are felt even years after the attack has happened. This is why some attacks that do not involve the direct theft of money have been ranked among the most costly attacks. For instance, DoS does not involve the theft of money from an organization, yet each DDoS attack is said to average at about $1,500,000. This is due to the other costs that come with the attacks. The following is a breakdown of the costs that come with a cyber attack.

Production loss

During a cyber attack, productive processes in some organizations will come to a halt. For instance, an e-commerce shop will be unable to keep its business processes running once it's attacked by a DDoS attack or a web-based attack. Organizations have also had their entire networks taken down during attacks, preventing any form of electronic communication from taking place. In various industries, cyber attacks can take a toll on production systems. Weaponized cyber attacks can even destroy industrial machines by messing with hardware controls. For instance, the Stuxnet cyber attack against Iran's nuclear facility led to the partial destruction of the facility. This shows the affect that an attack can have even behind highly secured facilities.

With the looming cyber warfare and worsening political tensions between countries, it can only be feared that there will be a wave of cyber attacks targeted at key players in the industrial sector. There has been a radical shift in hacking tendencies in that hackers are no longer just looking to embezzle funds or extort money from companies. Instead, they are causing maximum damage by attacking automated processes and systems that control production machines. Cyber attacks are heading into a dangerous phase where they are able to be weaponized by competitors or enemy states, enabling them to cause physical damage and even the loss of life. There are fears that some states already have the capabilities to take over smart grids and traffic lights in US cities. ISIS, a terrorist group, was once also reported to be trying to hack into the US energy grid.

In any case, production losses are moving to new heights and are becoming more costly. A ransomware attack in 2016 called WannaCry was able to encrypt many computers used in industrial processes. Some hospitals were affected and critical computers, such as those used to maintain life support systems or schedule operations in the healthcare facilities, were no longer usable. This led to the ultimate loss: human life. Other far-reaching impacts are environmental impacts, regulatory risks, and criminal liability on the side of the victim.

Economic losses

Cybercrime has become an economic disaster in many countries. It is estimated that at least $600,000,000,000 is drained from the global economy through cybercrime annually. This is quite a huge figure and its impact is already being felt. $600,000,000,000 is an enormous figure and the loss of this has affected many factors, including jobs. Cybercrime is hurting the economy and, in turn, hurting the job market (https://www.zdnet.com/article/cybercrime-drains-600-billion-a-year-from-the-global-economy-says-report/):

> *Global businesses are losing the equivalent of nearly 1% of global **Gross Domestic Product (GDP)** a year to cybercrime, and it's impacting job creation, innovation, and economic growth.*

> *So says a report from cybersecurity firm McAfee and the **Center for Strategic and International Studies (CSIS)**, which estimates that cybercrime costs the global economy $600,000,000,000 a year—up from a 2014 study which put the figure at $445,000,000,000.*

Companies are being targeted with industrial espionage and their business secrets are being stolen by overseas competitors. In the long run, companies have been facing losses due to a flooding of markets with similar but cheap and substandard products. This has forced companies that were once growing fast, opening multiple branches, and hiring thousands, to start downsizing and retrenching their employees. In the US, it's estimated that cybercrime has already caused the loss of over 200,000 jobs. The loss of jobs and the drainage of money from a country's economy has made cybercrime a major concern globally. However, it might be too late for the loss to be averted. It's said that many industries have already had their business secrets stolen. In the US, it's estimated that a large number of organizations are those that are not aware of having been breached and their business secrets stolen. Therefore, the economic loss might continue for a while.

In 2015, then US president Barack Obama agreed to a digital truce to put an end to the hacking of companies for trade secrets because US companies were losing too much data. The following is a snippet from the BBC (https://www.bbc.co.uk/news/world-asia-china-34360934) about the agreement between Xi and Obama:

> *US President Barack Obama and Chinese President Xi Jinping have said they will take new steps to address cybercrime.*

> *Speaking at a joint news conference at the White House, Mr Obama said they had agreed that neither country would engage in cyber economic espionage.*

Political tensions with China due to Donald Trump's presidency are threatening this truce, and an increase in hacking could occur against US companies if these tensions run too high. Unlike Obama, Trump is taking on China head-on and has been hinting at retaliatory moves, such as cutting off China's tech companies, such as Huawei, from the US market. The US arrests of Huawei employees are likely to cause retaliatory attacks from the Chinese; China may hack more US companies and, ultimately, the two countries might enter into a cyber war.

Damaged brand and reputation

An organization will spend a lot of money on building its brand in order to keep a certain market share and also to keep investors satisfied. Without trusted brand names, some companies could fall into oblivion. Cyber attacks tend to attract negative press and this leads to damaging a company's brand and reputation. Investors are put in a frenzy of selling their shares to prevent further loss in value. Shareholders that are left holding onto their shares are unsure whether they will ever recover the money trapped in their shares. Consequently, customers stop trusting the victim company's goods and services. Competitors then take advantage of the situation and intensify marketing in order to win over the customers and investors of the victim company. This could happen within a day or a week due to an unpreventable cyber attack. Investors will always want to keep their money with companies that they trust, and customers will always want to buy from companies that they trust. When a cyber attack breaks this trust, both investors and customers run away. Damage to a brand is very costly. A good example is Yahoo, where, after three breaches, Verizon purchased the company for $4,000,000,000 less than the amount offered in the previous year, before the hacks were public knowledge. Therefore, in a single company, almost $4,000,000,000 was lost due to the brand-damaging effects of a cyber attack. The class-action law suits against Yahoo also contributed to its lower valuation.

Loss of data

Despite the benefits, organizations are said to have been sluggishly adopting cloud-based services due to security fears. Those that have bought into the idea of the cloud have mostly done this halfway, not risking their mission-critical data to cloud vendors. Many organizations spend a lot of resources on protecting their systems and networks from the potential loss of data. The reason that they go through all of this trouble is so that they don't lose their valuable data, such as business secrets. If a hacker were to discover the secret code used to securely unlock iPhones, they could make a lot of money selling that code to underground markets. This is because such information is of high value to a point where Apple was unwilling to give authorities a code to compromise the lock protection and aid with the investigations of terrorists. It wasn't because Apple isn't supportive of the war against terrorism; it was instead a decision made to protect all Apple users. Here is a snippet from an article (`https://www.theguardian.com/technology/2016/feb/22/tim-cook-apple-refusal-unlock-iphone-fbi-civil-liberties`) on Apple's refusal to unlock an iPhone for the FBI:

> *"Apple boss Tim Cook told his employees on Monday that the company's refusal to cooperate with a US government to unlock an iPhone used by Syed Farook, one of the two shooters in the San Bernardino attack, was a defense of civil liberties."*

No company will trust a third party with such sensitive information. With Apple, if a hacker were to steal documentation relating to the safety measures in Apple devices and their shortcomings, the company would face a fall in share prices and a loss of customers. The loss of data is even more sensitive in institutions that offer far more sensitive services. For instance, in June 2018, it was reported that a US Navy contractor lost a large amount of data to hackers. Among the sensitive data stolen were sensitive details about undersea warfare, plans of supersonic anti-ship missiles, and other armament and defense details of US ships and submarines.

Fines, penalties, and litigations

The loss of data in any cyber attack is recovered by all organizations, particularly if the data lost is sensitive in nature. The loss of health, personal, and financial data will cause a company agony when it considers the consequences that will follow. The loss of these types of data comes with many more losses, in the form of fines, penalties, and litigations. If a company is hacked, instead of receiving consolation, it's dragged into court cases and slapped with heavy fines and penalties.

Several regulations have been put in place to ensure the protection of sensitive, **personally-identifiable information** (**PII**) by the organizations that collect them. This is due to the impact of the theft of such information. The demand for PII is on the rise on the dark web. This is because PII is valuable in different aspects. If, for instance, hackers were to discover that some of the data stolen from a hospital included the health information of a politician, they could use this data to extort huge amounts of money from the politician. In another scenario, hackers can use PII to social engineer the owners. Armed with personal details, such as name, date of birth, real physical address and current contact details, it's very easy for a skilled social engineer to scam a target. This is part of the reason why governments have ensured that there are very tough laws to protect PII.

Losses due to recovery techniques

After an attack, an organization will have to do everything it can to salvage itself. The aftermath of a serious attack is not pretty, and lots of funds have to be used to clean up the mess created by the hackers. Some companies prefer to do a complete audit of their information systems to find out the exact causes or influential factors in the attack. Post-breach activities, such as IT audits, can unearth important information that can be used to prevent the same type of attack from being executed. Some companies prefer to pay for digital forensics experts to identify the cause of an attack as well as track the hackers or the data and money stolen. Digital forensics is sometimes even able to recover some of the lost assets or funds. For instance, Ubiquiti Networks was hacked in 2015 and $46,000,000 was stolen through social engineering. Using digital forensics, $8,000,000 was recovered in one of the overseas accounts that the hackers requested the money be sent to. Sometimes all the stolen money can be recovered, but in most instances, that's not the case. The following is an article on the recovery of $8,100,000 by Ubiquiti Networks after an attack that stole $46,000,000:

> *"The incident involved employee impersonation and fraudulent requests from an outside entity targeting the Company's finance department. This fraud resulted in transfers of funds aggregating $46,700,000 held by a Company subsidiary incorporated in Hong Kong to other overseas accounts held by third parties.*
>
> *"Ubiquiti says it has so far managed to recover $8,100,000 of the lost funds, and it expects to regain control of another $6,800,000. The rest? Uncertain."*

In short, the costs associated with a cyber attack are high and charges can even continue for several years after the actual attack happens. The current estimate of each attack being around $3,000,000 per victim organization is a mere statistic. Individual companies suffer huge losses. These costs have been broken down and explained in detail throughout this chapter. However, the costs associated with cybersecurity are not solely tied to the negative aftermath of an attack. Cybersecurity products are an added, but necessary, expenditure for organizations. Analysts say that 75% of cyber attacks happen to people or organizations that don't have any cybersecurity products.

Breakdown of the cost of securing an organization

On a global scale, organizations are realizing that they cannot operate without cybersecurity products running on their networks and computing devices. Cyber threats are constant, and therefore there is never a safety-window period within which an organization can run without these products. Cyber attacks have formed a lucrative cybersecurity industry, and therefore organizations are having to buy multiple cybersecurity products to cover several threat landscapes. Organizations must ensure that their networks are secured. Servers, hosts, and any other computers connected to the organizational network have to be protected. Insider threats also have to be prevented from causing harm to the organization. Furthermore, employees have to be protected from direct attacks, such as social engineering. IT expenditures are only going up as hackers discover new avenues to exploit organizations and the cybersecurity industry develops products to prevent these avenues from being exploited. On top of this, organizations have to set up mechanisms of surviving a cyber attack. This is because, despite huge investments in cybersecurity products, the organization isn't guaranteed to be 100% protected from attacks. A single disgruntled employee could simply allow hackers to access an organization. As a consequence, cyber resilience is being encouraged, in which an organization can keep operating even when attacked. This isn't cheap, either. We'll now look at a breakdown of the common costs of securing an organization today.

Every financial institute should know Carbanak

Carbanak is the name that Kaspersky Labs use for an APT-style campaign that targets (but isn't limited to) financial institutions.

The attackers infiltrate the victim's network, looking for the critical system they can use to cash money out. Once they have stolen a significant amount of money, they abandon the victim.

Please take some time to read the technical details if you haven't already:

- *Hackers stole from 100 banks and rigged ATMs to spew cash*: `https://money.cnn.com/2015/02/15/technology/security/kaspersky-bank-hacking/index.html`
- Carbanak ATP Technical details: `https://usa.kaspersky.com/resource-center/threats/carbanak-apt`

Antivirus systems

The most common form of cybersecurity is prevention. Many organizations rely on attack-prevention tools. Most operating systems come with baseline security products to offer free virus and malware protection from attacks. At the very least, these systems prevent viruses, Trojan horses, worms, and spyware from infecting a computer. Antivirus systems have been evolving and industry leaders have been incorporating additional features based on the global threat environment. For instance, after the 2016 widespread ransomware attack, many antivirus software vendors added ransomware protection. This was most likely due to the worldwide impact of ransomware:

Antivirus Software	# Reviews Rating (1-5)	# Licenses	Best Price
Kaspersky	579 Reviews 4.0 Stars	3 Licenses	$24.90
Bitdefender	88 Reviews 3.0 Stars	3 Licenses	$59.99
Norton 360	1,327 Reviews 4.0 Stars	3 Licenses	$39.00
BullGuard Premium	2 Reviews 3.0 Stars	1 Licenses	$65.18
AVG Antivirus	29 Reviews 3.5 Stars	3 Licenses	$35.26
ESET NOD32	22 Reviews 4.5 Stars	3 Licenses	$38.88

Endpoint Detection and Response solutions

Endpoint Detection and Response solutions (EDRs) are new security solutions in the cybersecurity market that are answering the need for continuous detection and mitigation of security issues and suspicious activities in endpoints. These systems provide both a security technology and a security posture. Unlike endpoint protection programs, such as antivirus programs, EDRs don't focus only on stopping threats before they execute. EDRs offer continued monitoring of any endpoint and aid in discovering, investigating, and responding to threats. They provide a new approach to security that legacy solutions haven't adopted. Leading AV companies continually advertise, and advise their clients to add, newer modules to their already existing software. Even with the extra investments, AVs aren't able to offer full protection to endpoints because of the reliance on signature-based technologies to stop attacks before they happen. This is due to the increasingly common blind spots and the sophistication of hackers who use tools such as PowerShell to avoid detection. When an attack has happened to an endpoint, the installed AV will require human interaction to investigate the attacks and even more time before the signature of the attack is published and installed in other AVs. The update of signatures in some AVs is manual, hence several endpoints in a network could still be running programs that aren't aware of new malware that has already struck down an endpoint in the network.

To reduce the complexity and improve the reliability of the security afforded to endpoints, EDRs offer a wide range of integrated solutions in one product. They can stop both known and unknown attacks, they can prevent zero-day attacks, they can independently handle security incidences, they don't rely on signatures so they can run offline, they automatically discover assets in a network and can carry out forensics. EDRs are providing all-round solutions that enable organizations to let go of legacy solutions, such as AVs, sandboxes, IPSes, and IDSes. Instead of admins having to monitor several systems, they only focus on one. EDRs tend to act as platforms, thus new apps and services can be continually added depending on the needs of an organization. They are therefore adaptable to the modern attack landscapes.

 You can find a list of the available EDRs in the market, alongside their features and prices in the following link: `https://www.esecurityplanet.com/products/top-endpoint-detection-response-solutions.html`

Firewall systems

Firewalls filter traffic flowing into and out of an organizational network. These have been upgraded to include extra features to help prevent certain attacks, such as DDoS. Firewalls have evolved quickly, and smart firewalls are already in use and are more effective than traditional rule-based firewalls. Since internet traffic changes rapidly, a smart firewall is able to distinguish malicious traffic from normal traffic. The release of next-generation firewalls was a big leap in cybersecurity and companies that can afford these are protected from a diverse collection of internet threats. The costs of host-based firewall products in 2018 ranged from $40 – $99 annually, while Enterprise firewalls ranged from upwards of $750, as shown in the following price chart:

PRODUCT	PRICE	OVERALL RATING	TEST RESULTS	USER EXPERIENCE	MALWARE DETECTION & REMOVAL	DRAG ON SYSTEM RESOURCES	NUMBER OF LICENSES
Bitdefender Internet Security...	$51.99 @ Bitdefe...	9.9	10	9.8	100%	97%	3
Kaspersky Internet Security...	$39.99 @ Kaspers...	9.8	9.8	10	100%	95%	3
McAfee LiveSafe	$99.99 @ McAfee ↗	9.5	9.8	9	99%	95%	10
Avira	Check Price ↗	9.4	10	8.2	99%	99%	1

Intrusion-prevention systems

Intrusion-prevention systems are deployed on networks to help detect and prevent suspicious activities on the network, such as enumeration attacks. An attack normally begins with some suspicious activity, such as the attackers trying to learn more about the network and the devices connected to it. Intrusion-detection systems are quite expensive but necessary for increasing the security levels of enterprise networks. In 2018, the prices of intrusion-detection systems averaged $60,000 but low-performance models cost an average of $5,000.

Encryption

A common security mechanism that organizations use to secure their data is encryption. Encryption algorithms differ in quality and cost. The cost of an algorithm is normally based on how many resources will be used to encrypt or decrypt data. It's said that the stolen Yahoo's user data was encrypted using an MD5 algorithm that was easy to crack. Organizations strive for encryption software that's easy to use, economical to purchase, and resistant to cracking attempts. While there is free full-disk encryption software, the average cost of a premium version was $230 in 2018. In addition to encrypting hosts, organizations have to enable the use of encrypted connections to users on their websites through SSL. SSL certificates are offered by different vendors and they ensure that a user's connection to an organizational server is secured. There are free SSL certificates available, but paid SSL certificates start at around $249 per year for the baseline version. The following is the list of prices for different SSL certificates offered by Thawte, a market leader in SSL certificates:

Thawte

Thawte offers five SSL certificate options; Thawte SSL ($149/yr), Web Server SSL ($249/yr), Web Server EV SSL ($599/yr)and SGC SuperCerts ($699) and Wildcard SSL ($639/yr). All the certificates have 128/256 bit encryption and come with warranty ranging from 100,000 US to 500,000 USD.

The certificates are issues between 24 to 48 hours and come with a free Thawte Site Seal. You can compare the features of the SSL certificates at the website.

There are many other advanced security products that organizations have to buy, but at the very least, they require the ones that we have gone through. Alternative sites used for cyber-resilience purposes mean that an organization has to double its spending on cybersecurity to protect the hot sites even if they aren't in active use. Therefore, fully securing an organization requires some substantial financial investments but the peace of mind brought by the security offered is worth every penny.

Bonus

As the Microsoft Windows operating system is the core OS for many financial industries, we thought adding this section to the book would be valuable. This section will help you to build a complete EDR just with what's been given to you by Microsoft.

Why did we add this Microsoft section that is based on Deutsche Bank's recommendation? *Microsoft's Security Business Should Be on Investors' Radar, Analyst Says* (`https://www.barrons.com/articles/microsoft-stock-security-business-should-be-on-investor-radar-analyst-says-51547490101`).

Gartner verifies that Microsoft is a security vendor in the *SWOT: Microsoft, Security Products, and Features, Worldwide* article (`https://www.gartner.com/doc/3896179?_lrsc=c8768d5c-141e-48c5-9cc3-c7531e55fb2b`):

> *"Microsoft is now a security vendor. Technology product managers at security services providers can use this document to identify opportunities to reshape their product roadmaps and integrations based on Microsoft's changed approach to security."*

What is Microsoft offering?

The Windows 10 defense stack can be viewed in the following diagram:

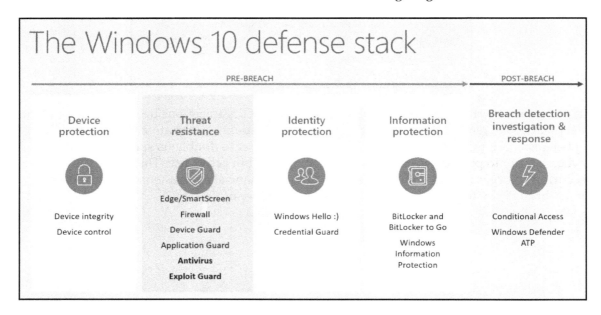

The following diagram explains the security features and benefits of Windows 10:

		Feature	Explanation
WINDOWS 10 SECURITY FEATURES AND BENEFITS	**❶** **Device Protection**	Trusted Platform Module	Windows uses a crypto processor (TPM) to encrypt and keep security keys from attackers
		Windows-as-a-Service	Keeps OS always up to date with latest cumulative features and security to prevent exploits
		Windows Trusted Boot	Insures Windows boots and Anti-Virus software launches before any applications/malware
		UEFI Secure Boot	BIOS replacement, ensures hardware & Windows has not been tampered with before launch
		Virtualization Based Security	Containerizes key OS functions to prevent attacks like "pass the hash" - Can't find it, can't attack it
	❷ **Threat Resistance**	SmartScreen	Prevents users from visiting blacklisted websites or executing blacklisted apps
		Windows Firewall	Device-level PC firewall to prevent unauthorized network access to device
		Windows Defender	Anti-virus software based on the world's largest global threat database
		Microsoft Edge	World's most secure enterprise browser – half the vulnerabilities of other browsers
		WD Application Guard	Tiny HW-isolated Windows instance for Microsoft Edge to browse untrusted website (2017)
		Device Guard	Only IT/Windows Store approved applications can run. Like on a phone, malware can't run
	❸ **Identity Protection**	Windows Hello	Two-factor authentication using face, fingerprint, biometric, or PIN. Confirms to website
		Hello Companion Devices	Use phone, badge, or wearable, or other devices to unlock your PC with Windows Hello
		Credential Guard	Guards your user credentials from being stolen and used on other devices on the network
	❹ **Information Protection**	BitLocker/Device Encryption	Locks your data on hard drive using encryption
		BitLocker to Go	Locks you data on thumb drives or other storage devices using encryption
		BitLocker Admin & Monitor	Ensures corporate devices are BitLocker encrypted for compliance. Stores recovery keys
		Windows Information Protection (was EDP)	Separates business vs. personal data to prevent sharing to non-business documents/apps. Wipes data off devices. Protected documents cannot be opened on unmanaged machine
	❺ **Breach Detection**	Windows Defender Advanced Threat Protection	Global cloud-based threat intelligence service to detect, investigate, and respond to highly targeted advanced attacks on your networks - Know if you are under attack and by whom
		Conditional Access	Only tamper free devices, that are compliant with your security standards can access resources

Windows 10 Defender Security Center

The Windows Defender Security Center includes five pillars that give you control and visibility of your device's security, health, and online safety experiences:

- **Virus and threat protection**: This provides a new view of your antivirus protection, whether it's Windows Defender or any other antivirus we've already discussed.
- **Device performance and health**: This provides a single view of your latest Windows updates, drivers, battery life, and storage capacity.
- **Firewall and network protection**: Provides information on the network connections and active Windows Firewall settings.

- **App and browser control**: This allows you to adjust the settings for SmartScreen for apps and browsers, which helps you be more informed and stay safer online by warning you of potential malicious sites, downloads, and unrecognized apps and files from the internet.
- **Family options**: This gives you an easy way to connect to the family options available online.

Windows Defender

EDR means starting to defend the endpoint, and when we look at Windows 10 it comes with Windows Defender built in. Windows Defender contains five sub-functions: Firewall, Antivirus, Exploit Guard, Application Guard, and SmartScreen.

These can be controlled locally through the Windows Defender Security Center console:

These five functions specialize and focus on preventative defense by applying known security measures and known indicators of compromise. Windows Defender Antivirus does well against other commercial options when evaluated in independent testing, such as the ones conducted by AV-TEST, as can be seen here:

	September	October	Industry average
Protection against 0-day malware attacks, inclusive of web and e-mail threats (Real-World Testing) 202 samples used	100%	96.3%	99.0%
Detection of widespread and prevalent malware discovered in the last 4 weeks (the AV-TEST reference set) 9,797 samples used	99.5%	99.9%	98.5%

Windows Defender Exploit Guard

Windows Defender Exploit Guard is a new collection of tools and features that help to keep your network safe from exploits. Exploits are infection vectors for malware that rely on vulnerabilities in software.

Exploit Guard will help in the following ways:

- Block attacks at the frontline
    - Raise attacker costs to compromise entry points
- Defenses to minimize damage
    - Assume frontline defenses will fail
    - Raise attacker cost to cause damage to environment
    - Prevent Lateral Movement
- Recovery and response
    - Assume all defenses will fail
    - Rapid response to detect threats and disrupt attacks
    - Restore data from backups that are inaccessible to attackers

Controlled folder access

Controlled folder access helps you protect valuable data from malicious apps and threats, such as ransomware.

Controlled folder access works best with Windows Defender Advanced Threat Protection, which gives you detailed reporting into Windows Defender EG events and blocks as part of the usual alert investigation scenarios.

To enable controlled folder access, refer to the following screenshot:

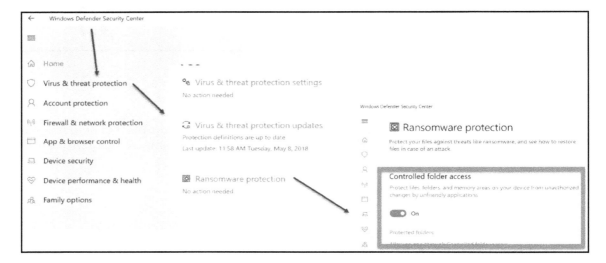

Network protection

Network protection helps reduce the attack surface of your devices from internet-based events. It prevents employees from using any application to access dangerous domains that may host phishing scams, exploits, and other malicious content on the internet.
It expands the scope of Windows Defender SmartScreen to block all outbound HTTP(s) traffic that attempts to connect to low-reputation sources (based on the domain or hostname). It's part of Windows Defender Exploit Guard.

You can enable Network protection in either audit or block mode with Group Policy or PowerShell.

You can use PowerShell to enable or audit Network protection. Type `powershell` in the Start menu, right-click Windows PowerShell, and click **Run as administrator**:

Enter the following cmdlet:

```
Set-MpPreference -EnableNetworkProtection Enabled
```

```
Administrator: Windows PowerShell
Windows PowerShell
Copyright (C) Microsoft Corporation. All rights reserved.

PS C:\Windows\system32> Set-MpPreference -EnableNetworkProtection Enabled
PS C:\Windows\system32> _
```

You can enable the featuring in audit mode using the following cmdlet:

```
Set-MpPreference -EnableNetworkProtection AuditMode
```

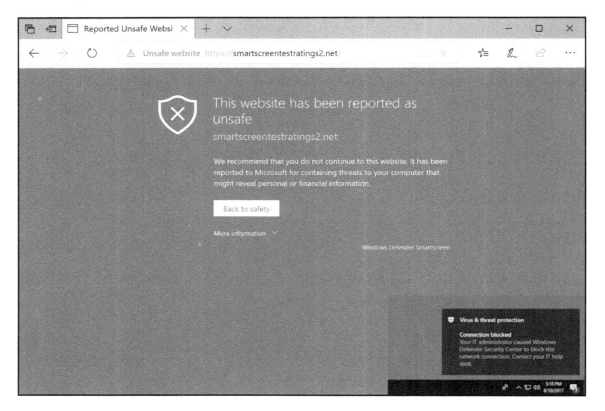

It also works with Firefox, Chrome, and Opera browsers.

For more information, visit https://docs.microsoft.com/en-us/ windows/security/threat-protection/windows-defender-exploit- guard/controlled-folders-exploit-guard.

Attack surface reduction

Attack surface reduction helps prevent actions and apps that are typically used by exploit-seeking malware to infect machines.

The feature is composed of a number of rules, each of which targets specific behaviors that are typically used by malware and malicious apps to infect machines, such as the following:

- Executable files and scripts used in Office apps or web mail that attempt to download or run files.
- Scripts that are obfuscated or otherwise suspicious.
- Behaviors that apps undertake that are not usually initiated during normal day-to-day work.

When a rule is triggered, a notification will be displayed from the Action Center. You can customize the notification with your company details and contact information. You can also enable the rules individually to customize what techniques the feature monitors.

For more information on how to set up the rules, visit `https://docs.microsoft.com/en-us/windows/security/threat-protection/windows-defender-exploit-guard/attack-surface-reduction-exploit-guard#attack-surface-reduction-rules`.

Windows Defender Credential Guard

Windows Defender Credential Guard uses virtualization-based security to isolate secrets so that only privileged system software can access them. Unauthorized access to these secrets can lead to credential theft attacks, such as Pass-the-Hash or Pass-the-Ticket. Windows Defender Credential Guard prevents these attacks by protecting NTLM password hashes, Kerberos Ticket Granting Tickets, and credentials stored by applications as domain credentials.

By enabling Windows Defender Credential Guard, the following features and solutions are provided: hardware security NTLM, Kerberos, and Credential Manager take advantage of platform security features, including Secure Boot and virtualization, to protect credentials. The following diagram illustrates Credential Guard:

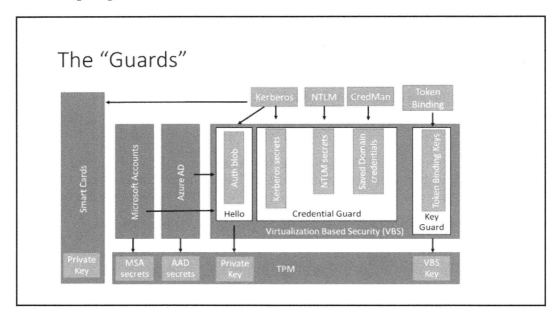

For more details about Credential Guard, check out `https://docs.microsoft.com/en-us/windows/security/identity-protection/credential-guard/credential-guard`.

Windows Defender Application Guard

The threat landscape is continually evolving. While hackers are busy developing new techniques to breach enterprise networks by compromising workstations, phishing schemes remain one of the top ways to lure employees into social-engineering attacks. Windows Defender Application Guard (Application Guard) is designed to help prevent old and emerging attacks, to help keep employees productive. Using our unique hardware-isolation approach, our goal is to destroy the playbook that attackers use by rendering current attack methods obsolete.

For more details about Windows Defender Application Guard, visit `https://docs.microsoft.com/en-us/windows/security/threat-protection/windows-defender-application-guard/install-wd-app-guard`.

Windows Event Forwarding

Windows Event Forwarding (WEF) permits a server designated as an event collector to receive all the events from endpoints that are selected by IT and security staff. Windows can generate events in a very granular fashion for everything that can happen on an endpoint. This event-logging capability is the keystone that changes everything that has been talked about so far in EDR solution. These logs can be fed into a SIEM that can analyze them in real time and can react or give advice accordingly.

Use WEF to help with intrusion detection (`https://docs.microsoft.com/en-us/windows/ security/threat-protection/use-windows-event-forwarding-to-assist-in-intrusion- detection`):

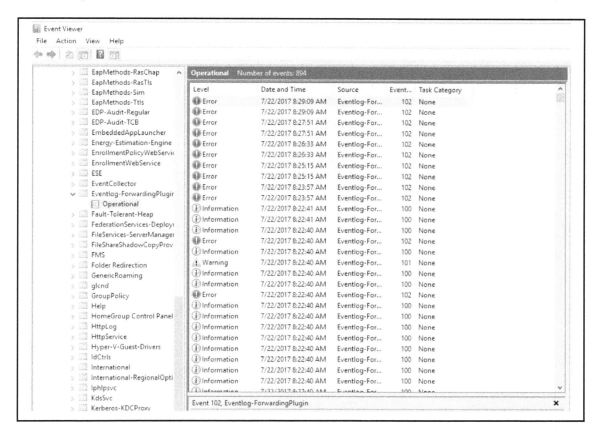

Windows Defender Advanced Threat Protection

Windows Defender **Advanced Threat Protection** (**ATP**) is a security service that enables enterprise customers to detect, investigate, and respond to advanced threats on their networks.

Windows Defender ATP uses the following combination of technology built in to Windows 10 and Microsoft's robust cloud service:

- **Endpoint behavioral sensors**: Embedded in Windows 10, these sensors collect and process behavioral signals from the operating system (for example, process, registry, file, and network communications) and sends this sensor data to your private, isolated, cloud instance of Windows Defender ATP.
- **Cloud security analytics**: Leveraging big data, machine learning, and unique Microsoft optics across the Windows ecosystem (such as the Microsoft Malicious Software Removal Tool), enterprise cloud products (such as Office 365), and online assets (such as Bing and SmartScreen URL reputation), behavioral signals are translated into insights, detections, and recommended responses to advanced threats.
- **Threat intelligence**: Generated by Microsoft hunters, security teams, and augmented by threat intelligence provided by partners, threat intelligence enables Windows Defender ATP to identify attacker tools, techniques, and procedures, and generate alerts when these are observed in collected sensor data:

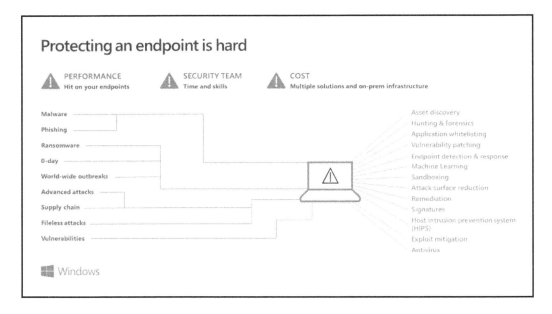

Machine investigation capabilities in this service let you drill down into security alerts and understand the scope and nature of a potential breach. You can submit files for deep analysis and receive the results without leaving the Windows Defender ATP portal. The automated investigation and remediation capability reduces the volume of alerts by leveraging various inspection algorithms to resolve breaches.

Windows Defender ATP works with existing Windows security technologies on machines, such as Windows Defender Antivirus, AppLocker, and Windows Defender Device Guard. It can also work side by side with third-party security solutions and antimalware products:

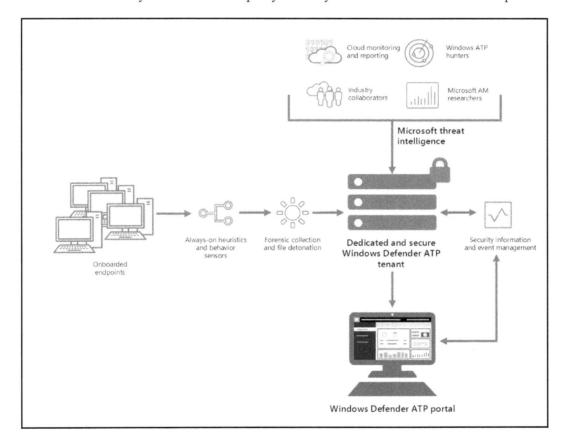

 To get started with Windows Defender ATP, check out https://docs.microsoft.com/en-us/windows/security/threat-protection/windows-defender-atp/minimum-requirements-windows-defender-advanced-threat-protection.

Protecting privileged identities

Privileged identities are any accounts that have elevated privileges, such as user accounts that are members of the Domain Admins, Enterprise Admins, local Administrators, or even Power Users groups. Such identities can also include accounts that have been granted privileges directly, such as performing backups, shutting down the system, or other rights listed in the User Rights Assignment node in the Local Security Policy console.

You need to protect these privileged identities from being compromised by potential attackers. First, it's important to understand how identities are compromised; then you can plan how to prevent attackers from gaining access to these privileged identities.

How do privileged identities get compromised?

Privileged identities often get compromised when organizations don't have guidelines to protect them. Here are some examples:

- **More privileges than are necessary**: One of the most common issues is that users have more privileges than necessary to perform their job function. For example, a user who manages DNS might be an AD administrator. Most often, this is done to avoid the need to configure different administration levels. However, if such an account is compromised, the attacker automatically has elevated privileges.
- **Signed in with elevated privileges all the time**: Another common issue is that users with elevated privileges can use it for an unlimited time. This is very common with IT pros who sign in to a desktop computer using a privileged account, stay signed in, and use the privileged account to browse the web and use email (typical IT work job functions). Unlimited duration of privileged accounts makes the account more susceptible to attack and increases the odds that the account will be compromised.
- **Social-engineering research**: Most hackers start out by researching an organization and then conducting social engineering on it. For example, an attacker may perform an email phishing attack to compromise legitimate accounts (but not necessarily elevated accounts) that have access to an organization's network. The attacker then uses these valid accounts to perform additional research on your network and to identify privileged accounts that can perform administrative tasks.
- **Leverage accounts with elevated privileges**: Even with a normal, non-elevated user account in the network, attackers can gain access to accounts with elevated permissions. One of the more common methods of doing so is by using the Pass-the-Hash or Pass-the-Token attacks.

There are, of course, other methods that attackers can use to identify and compromise privileged identities (with new methods being created every day). It's therefore important that you establish practices for users to log on with least-privileged accounts to reduce the ability of attackers to gain access to privileged identities.

How to prevent attackers from gaining access to privileged identities

You can reduce the attack surface for privileged identities (discussed in the previous section) with each of the mitigations described in the following table:

Attack vectors	How to mitigate
More privileges than are necessary	Implement **Just Enough Administration** (**JEA**) for all IT pros who administer Windows Server and the apps and services (such as Exchange Server or Exchange Online) running on Windows Server by using Windows PowerShell.
Signed in with elevated privileges all the time	Implement **Just in Time** (**JIT**) administration for all users who require elevated privileges so that the elevated privileges can only be used for a limited amount of time. Many organizations use the **Local Administrator Password Solution** (**LAPS**) as a simple yet powerful JIT administration mechanism for their server and client systems.
Compromised identity and Pass-the-Hash attacks	Implement Microsoft **Advanced Threat Analytics** (**ATA**) to help detect compromised identities in on-premises workloads and servers. ATA is an on-premises solution that you can use to manage physical and virtualized workloads.

Summary

This chapter covered the costs associated with cyber attacks and cybersecurity. It began by analyzing different reports from cybersecurity experts on the costs of cyber attacks. Most of these have shown that an attack today costs a victim organization approximately $3,000,000. With most attacks happening in the US, the average cost of an attack for companies was at $11,000,000. Since this was quite an ambiguous cost, this chapter went through a report by Accenture and laid out the costs for certain attacks.

According to Accenture, the top three costliest attacks are malware attacks, web-based attacks, and DoS attacks. To find further information about the costs of cyber attacks and cybersecurity, the chapter has split these costs into two categories: the costs of an attack and the costs of securing organizations from attacks. In the category of the cost of an attack, there has been a detailed explanation of the costs that come bundled with an attack. These are production losses, economic losses, brand damage, data loss, fines, penalties, litigations, and costs associated with attack-recovery techniques. In the breakdown of the cost of securing an organization from cyber attacks, the chapter has looked into the basic security products commonly used by organizations. These are antivirus systems, firewalls, intrusion-detection systems, and encryption. With the evolution of the cybersecurity industry, these costs will continue to vary. However, it should be noted that both cyber attacks and cybersecurity are expensive.

In the next chapter, we will focus on financial services threat landscape and understand the differences between threats against the end customer and threats against financial institutes.

Further reading

The following are resources that can be used to gain more knowledge on the topics covered in this chapter:

- *2017 COST OF CYBER CRIME STUDY*: `https://www.accenture.com/t20170926T072837Z__w__/us-en/_acnmedia/PDF-61/Accenture-2017-CostCyberCrimeStudy.pdf`
- *Internet Security Threat Report*: `https://www.symantec.com/content/dam/symantec/docs/reports/istr-23-2018-en.pdf`
- *APT Trends report Q1 2018*: `https://securelist.com/apt-trends-report-q1-2018/85280/`
- *Carbanak APT*: `https://www.kaspersky.com/resource-center/threats/carbanak-apt`
- If you want to learn more about cybersecurity attacks and defense strategies in general, you can read the book from Packt, *Cybersecurity – Attack and Defense Strategies* (`https://www.packtpub.com/networking-and-servers/cybersecurity-attack-and-defense-strategies`) written by Yuri Diogenes and Dr. Erdal Ozkaya, which was awarded by books authority best of all time.

4
The Threat Landscape

While the financial services industry sector is mostly a highly regulated industry, many financial institutes have started to adopt new technologies, such as cloud services, **Internet of Things** (**IoT**), or social media, to create new business models and reach new customers. In addition to new technologies, there is an ongoing cost reduction objective to provide shareholder value that is mostly achieved through outsourcing or offshoring. While each of these areas is important for ensuring that the business is growing, it also introduces a new threat landscape for financial institutes. These threats need to be taken into account for any successful IT and security department.

When delving into the financial services threat landscape, it is important to differentiate between end user-facing threats and threats targeted at the financial institute itself. Threats against end users and threats against financial institutes are the threat categories for the financial services industry that will be briefly covered in this chapter.

Threats against end customers

The primary target for end user-facing threats is stealing financial records and/or financial fraud. End user threats can be categorized as follows:

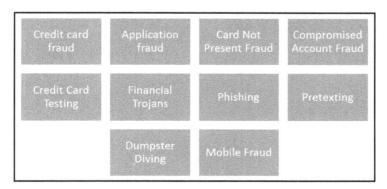

Credit card fraud

Credit card fraud describes cases in which a threat actor gains unauthorized access to a credit card in order to obtain money or property. Threat actors primarily use unsecured websites to obtain the required information. There has been a 15% increase in credit card fraud after the Equifax Data Breach. The following diagram shows US card fraud by type statistics:

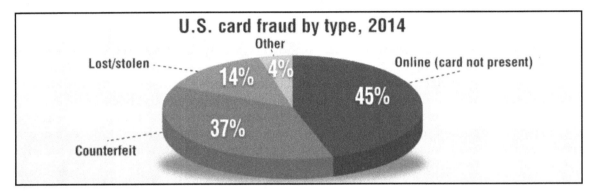

Application fraud

Application fraud can happen when the threat actor applies for a new credit card on behalf of the victim, for example. Very often, the threat actor will gain all the required information in advance by applying social engineering techniques, allowing them to provide the required information during the application. In response to the threat of application fraud, financial institutes also started to require online copies of original documents next to the information provided:

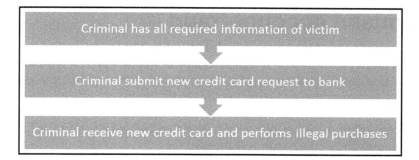

Card-not-present fraud

Card-not-present fraud occurs when the threat actor uses the victim's credit card during an online transaction while not physically possessing it. Through this technique, the threat actor is often able to leverage a social engineering technique such as dumpster diving, phishing, or pretexting to gain the credit card number and expiration date. In response to the card-not-present fraud, many merchants nowadays require their customers to provide the verification code, which is—with the exception of American Express—a 3-digit code found on their card. However, the verification code only has 999 possible combinations. Therefore, threat actors try out combinations by attempting a small number of transactions on a variety of merchants until they identify the correct verification code:

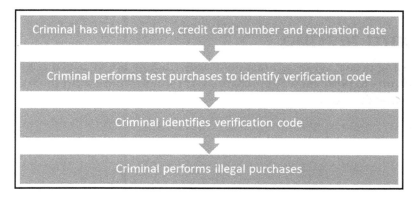

Compromised account fraud

Compromised account fraud is very common in the financial services industry. This threat is best described as an event in which a threat actor is able to gain illegal access to the victim's bank and/or online insurance portal. Similarly to the card-not-present fraud, this is often achieved by leveraging social engineering. In the event of compromised account fraud, threat actors often clone the legitimate website of a financial institute and lure the victim onto it. Very often, a victim does not notice that they are not on the official website and proceeds to enter their username and password:

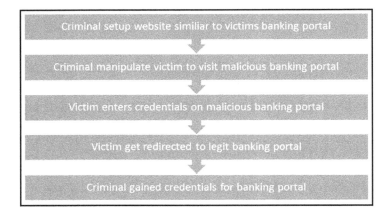

Credit card testing

Credit card testing occurs when a threat actor uses an illegally obtained credit card at multiple merchants to perform test purchases with small values, with the transactions increasing in value each time:

Financial Trojans

Threat actors continue to invest in the development and deployment of financial Trojans. These Trojans are often used to perform credential harvesting of customers and banks to perform fraud. **Point-of-sale** (**POS**) and mobile endpoints are increasingly targeted through financial Trojans by threat actors. According to Symantec, the malware family Rammit was the most active financial Trojan in 2016, responsible for 38% of activity. This was followed by Bebloh, accounting for 25%, and Zeus, had 23%.

Trojans have the following objectives:

- Theft of financial records
- Direct collection theft
- Fake financial institute communication
- Malicious control of financial institute systems

Case study – BackSwap Trojan

BackSwap does not rely on complex process injection methods, but instead hooks into window message loop events. This technique bypasses many available browsers' protection mechanisms. Malware distribution is primarily done over email by sending a malicious email that contains an obfuscated Nemucod JavaScript downloader. BackSwap installs event hooks to monitor when the victim visits specific URLs, allowing them to determine when the victim is performing an online bank transfer. When this is determined, the malicious payload gets injected into the browser.

Case study – Ramnit

When an endpoint gets infected with the Ramnit Trojan, the endpoint will continuously communicate with the threat actor's **command-and-control** (**C2C**) server. This will not only report the heartbeat status but also receives configuration updates. Ramnit includes a **man-in-the-browser** (**MitB**) web injection module that allows it to modify visited websites on the victim's endpoint. This enables criminals to modify transaction content and add, delete, or modify additional transactions. The following diagram shows the kill chain of Ramnit:

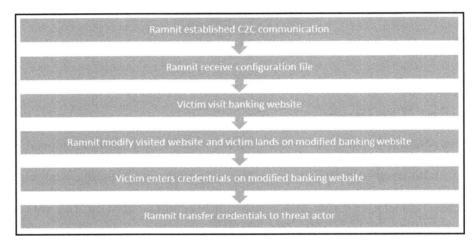

Case study – Bebloh

Bebloh is a financial Trojan that monitors and captures logon credentials for banking websites. Threat actors leverage Bebloh primarily as part of an email spam campaign. Bebloh's focus spans from loans and shopping discounts up to emails with professional subjects such as human resources or law. Some versions of Bebloh follow process hollowing, while others unpack themselves in their own memory space before performing process following:

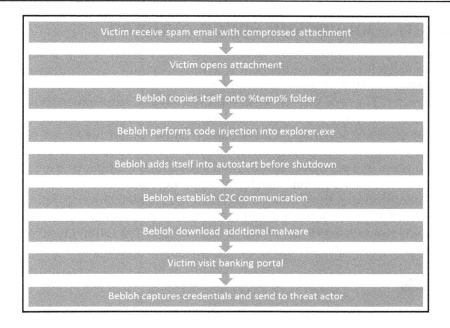

Phishing

In the financial services industry, phishing remains one of the most frequently used techniques. The primary reason for that is that many phishing attacks have a large impact and do not require in-depth preparation or funding. In layman's terms, all it takes is a somewhat trustworthy email template, a list of email addresses, and an email service to send a phishing email. Phishing attacks vary between identity theft and financial fraud, and therefore are a concern for the financial services sector. The magnitude of importance becomes clear when reviewing a press release from Gartner in 2014:

> *"Direct losses from identity theft fraud against these phishing attack victims cost U.S. banks and credit card issuers about $1.2 billion last year."*

The **Federal Deposit Insurance Corporation (FDIC)** is responsible for sustaining confidence in the US financial system. FDIC defines the term *phishing* on their website as follows:

> *"The term "phishing" – as in fishing for confidential information - refers to a scam that involves fraudulently obtaining and using an individual's personal or financial information."*

Case study – immediate action required

A threat actor group has leveraged previously leaked personal data to prepare a phishing campaign to thousands of end customers of a financial institute. In preparation for the phishing campaign, the threat actors have replicated the bank's website and planted a credential harvester. The only directly visible **Indicators of Compromise** (**IOC**) were within the domain name (anonymized example: `www.legitbank.com` became `www.l3gitbank.com`). More advanced users and security professionals could have identified more IOCs, such as the fact that the domain had been registered within the last five days, the domain registrant was a shelf company in Las Vegas, Nevada, and generally the language used on the malicious website had many grammatical mistakes. The threat actors have sent emails to the end customer informing them about a potential data breach and requesting immediate action from them. The threat actors requested that the end customer logs in to the financial institute's website through a URL that they claim is secure. The following screenshot is a phishing email sent to thousands of end customers:

Dear ▓▓▓▓▓▓

It has come our attention that our online banking portal might have been compromised. Protecting our customers identity and assets is very important to us. We therefore are reaching out to you asking you to reset your credentials immediately.

The government is supporting us during the crisis. They have helped build a secure approach to reset customer records without the need of visiting a local branch. Please therefore use the below URL to perform the data reset. Since keeping your records secure is a top priority for us you will be asked to enter the following information's:

- Government ID number
- First and Last Name as it appears on Government ID
- Home address
- Phone number
- Amount and merchant of last 3 purchases
- Expected balance
- Username
- Password

Your security is important to us. We therefore ask to complete this within he next 5 business days. In case you need assistance please contact us over the secure phone line: ▓▓▓▓▓▓▓▓.

Secure URL: ▓▓▓▓▓▓▓▓▓▓▓▓▓▓▓

Thank You,

▓▓▓▓▓▓▓▓

Fraud Detection & Investigation
▓▓▓▓

Pretexting

As well as phishing campaigns, pretexting is another commonly used social engineering technique in the financial services industry. Threat actors trick targets by lying to them to obtain privileged data. Pretexting often involves some sort of scam that helps the threat actor be seen as a trusted individual. There are a variety of tactics that the threat actor can apply. One of the most commonly used ones is when the threat actor directly calls the target, pretending to work for a survey company, and then asks a few questions.

Dumpster diving

Dumpster diving, also known as trashing, is a very old social engineering technique. It is best described as the physical actions of a threat actor to find valuable information by looking in their target's dumpster. Many end customers simply put old letters they receive from companies—including their bank—in the trash. Most often, threat actors are able to find organizational charts, company policy manuals, and purchase histories here.

Mobile fraud

Mobile banking is a competitive advantage for financial institutes. Consequently, many business units will offer a service like that to their end customers. Mobile fraud is where the threat actor leverages the mobile platform to their advantage so as to gain information or to perform fraud directly. Many financial institutes have now become aware of the rise in mobile fraud and since then have introduced **Multi-Factor Authentication** (**MFA**) in their mobile apps. How the threat actor approaches mobile fraud is simple. Most commonly used techniques take the legit app, build a malicious wrapper around it, and then find a way to distribute the malicious version to the end customer.

Threats against financial institutes

In addition to threats against end customers, institutes themselves are also at risk. Threats against financial institutes can be categorized as follows:

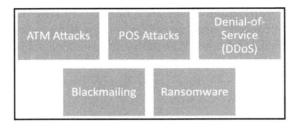

ATM attacks

While security vendors and operating system providers continue to invest in security, ATM attacks are still increasing. This is mainly due to legacy security controls that are in place for ATMs. Until now, many ATMs have run on Windows XP or Windows 7, providing very few security controls, such as the use of **Endpoint Detection and Response (EDR)**. ATM attacks continue to increase every year, although they did slow down in Europe with the introduction of Chip and PIN, which led to a decrease in classic memory scraping threats. For a threat actor to perform an ATM attack, there are two options:

- Gain physical access to the ATM either through a stolen key or by picking the lock. Once physical access is established, the threat actor now plants their malicious payload.
- Gain access to the ATM network through a sophisticated cyber-attack on the financial institute. Many institutes are able to connect remotely to ATMs, which can be leveraged to transfer files and execute commands.

POS attacks

ATM and POS attacks are similar in nature, but the approach threat actors take is different. The reason for this is that POS devices are designed to be reachable by end customers visiting a retail store, bank, or insurance branch. These POS devices typically have almost no physically accessible security controls. Therefore, threat actors try to plug in a malicious portal drive to these POS devices while nobody is looking.

Denial of service

A **denial of service** (**DoS**) attack is often used to hide a bigger financial fraud activity. It is an attempt by the threat actor to keep the IT and security department busy while they are performing financial fraud.

DDoS attacks can include the following:

- Targeting the banking portal to ensure that end customers are unable to log in
- Targeting the telecommunication system to ensure end customers are unable to reach the call center
- Attacks against the financial institute network to ensure they are unable to communicate with the ATM and POS devices

Ransomware

While ransomware is a cross-industry threat, it is particularly serious in the financial services industry. The reason for this is that particular global outbreaks on the scale of WannaCrypt or Petya can have a significant impact on the global economy. When financial institutes are unable to operate, this has an impact on their end customers, but also on governments. This is especially true when the target is a country's central bank.

Blackmailing

Blackmailing is often leveraged by the threat actor when a financial fraud has failed. Instead of giving up, they attempt to blackmail the financial institute, threatening to expose end customer data or a system vulnerability if they do not pay a certain amount of money.

Summary

There are many different attack techniques that are commonly used in the financial services industry. It is important to understand the differences between threats against the end customer and threats against financial institutes. In this chapter, you learned the key aspects of each with a very practical approach, ensuring you benefit from the experience of experts in this field. The next chapter will focus on the techniques used and how exactly money and data are stolen from users via phishing, spamming, and scamming.

5
Phishing, Spamming, and Scamming to Steal Data and Money

Phishing, scamming and spamming are some cyber security threats that have caught the attention of users, corporate organizations, cyber security companies, and law enforcement agencies. Each year, these threats drain lots of money from economies. This chapter demystifies these threats, and explains exactly how they are carried out, the software used to aid them, and how they steal money and data from users. A lot of the focus is put on phishing, which is a constant threat to many organizations. The chapter demonstrates how to create a phishing attack and discusses infamous, real-life examples of phishing attacks. The chapter lastly looks at spamming and discusses how it is used to mint money and how dangerous it can be. The chapter will cover all these points in the following topics:

- Phishing scams
- Spamming

Phishing scams

Phishing is one of the oldest cons on the internet. It dates back to the time when personal computers and emails were becoming common. It is a cyber attack technique where malicious persons send emails claiming to be from reputable organizations in order to gather sensitive information. However, there are variations of phishing that could be used for other reasons, such as to persuade unsuspecting people to send money to fraudsters. Phishing is distinguished from other forms of cyber attack in that it first seeks to get the trust of the victim by masquerading as a trustable entity. What constitutes trustable entities will vary depending on the targets of phishing, which include tax authorities, banks, schools, senior executives, friends, and even family. A phisher can become any entity that will effectively win the trust of the target. The term phishing is used as a pun to make an analogy with *fishing* , that involves throwing bait in to water so that if a fish bites it, it gets held by the hook. In phishing, the target is likened to the fish and the trustable entity serves as the bait. When the target goes for the bait, they get trapped by the hook. Today, the goals of phishing are varied. Most phishing attacks target private information, such as login details to online banking platforms or sensitive systems. Another common goal is to steal money directly from targets by demanding some money from them. Identity theft is also another goal of phishing where the perpetrators hope to get information that they can use to steal the identities of their victims. The stolen identities can be used for future phishing attacks. These are just a few of the common goals of phishing.

There has been a wave of phishing attacks that have taken a heavy toll on users over the years. One of the earliest waves of phishing is what is referred to as the Nigerian prince scam. In this scam, the perpetrator(s) would send emails claiming to be a Nigerian prince who has inherited huge sums of money from his parent. However, they are unable to access their inheritance so are looking for someone who can volunteer to receive the money for them. Targets that were taken in by this were normally asked to send some funds for the processing of the huge amounts to be credited to their accounts. However, it was a never-ending loop of requests for funds that would follow until the victim found out that it was a scam.

Another wave of phishing attacks came when several celebrities had their intimate photos released to the public. In many instances, blame was shifted to insecure cloud servers. The celebrities would claim that their cloud service providers failed to secure their accounts from hackers. However, there were a number of cyber criminals that would send phishing emails to celebrities requesting login information to the cloud platforms. After convincing the celebrities to provide their logins, the photos would be stolen and shared with the public.

In 2016, a serious incident happened during the US presidential campaigns. The campaign chair for Hilary Clinton was targeted by phishers who convinced him to send over his Gmail password. John Podesta's Gmail account was soon taken over by hackers. Several other attacks followed where many individuals and businesses lost money and sensitive information to phishers.

Avast reported that by the end of 2016, there was a big surge in the number of phishing emails. The company reported that 6.3 million spam emails were detected in the first quarter of 2016. This quarter had recorded a surge of 250% in phishing attacks and this continued throughout the year. The attackers had changed their tactics and were now getting bigger and higher profile targets. This was quite a shock since phishing was an overlooked type of threat in previous years. All of a sudden there were reports of corporate organizations losing money, banks issuing disclaimers of fake emails, and law enforcement agencies embarking on missions to find phishers. To best understand all this, let's look at the evolution of phishing.

Evolution of phishing

The first phase of phishing was in the late 1990s and early 2000s. Phishing was just categorized as an email threat and not much concern was attached to it. The most popular type of phishing email was the Nigerian prince scam. The attackers were simply capitalizing on greed and misinformation. The first phishing attack against a payment system called E-gold was made. In 2003, another phishing attack was made against a retail bank. In 2004, an American teen was arrested after being found to have created a website asking people to give their logins. The website was a replica of **America Online (AOL)**, which had been adopted by quite a number of internet users. Later in the year, there were many other phishing scams that succeeded against 1.2 million US targets. This showed that hackers were experimenting with phishing schemes outside the normal Nigerian prince scam. More phishing attacks followed and they were being waged against millions of users annually. Phishers then innovated their attack mechanisms and some turned from targeting several unknown targets to targeting a few known targets. They would isolate one person in a company, do background research and then use the information gained to attack them. This came to be known as spear phishing. In 2008, development made another leap. There was a new type of phishing attack, where CEOs were targeted, which came to be known as whaling. Phishers would send emails to the CEOs claiming to be court subpoenas, and this urged the CEOs to open them. Once opened, the emails would download keyloggers to the victims' computer. There were about 2,000 victims before most people got wind of it and it was no longer effective.

In 2009, there were reports that phishing was no longer profitable and was heading toward a dead end. Reports indicated that the resources attackers use to mass-mail people by far exceeded any returns that these attack would yield. Microsoft was among the companies that declared that phishing was not profitable.

A 2009 article about Microsoft debunking any profitability from phishing

 Do phishers actually make money, or is phishing an unprofitable business, scammers lose time and resources into? Taking the economic approach of generalizing how much money phishers make, a recently released study by Microsoft researchers Cormac Herley and Dinei Florencio (A Profitless Endeavor: Phishing as Tragedy of the Commons), states that phishing isn't as profitable as originally thought.

These reports were based on the fact that many scammers were using the same scam stories and consequently this decreased their effectiveness. The possible revenues that could be realized from phishing were shrinking with the increasing numbers of phishers. It seemed that the vice had no future. The commonly used phishing stories had also been profiled and many potential targets had learned how to tell that an email was a phishing email. Most of the scammers were sending plain text emails with grammatical errors and similar stories aimed at engaging targets in a scenario where they would get rich quickly. As more of these similarly-written phishing emails surfaced, the identification of phishing became quite easy for any average-minded internet user.

However, from 2011, cases of phishing attacks started rising again. By 2013, phishing was spiralling out of control. The number of users scammed between 2012 and 2013 rose by 87% to approximately 40 million. Instead of using similar-styled emails, phishers were using different scenarios to get targets to comply with malicious requests. The use of fake website copies of financial institutions increased. By 2016, phishing became a highly-recognized threat in the corporate and law enforcement world. Organizations, employees, and customers were losing a lot of money to elaborate scams received through emails. Account holders in banks were complaining of being defrauded by unknown persons pretending to be officials from the bank. PayPal, which had in 2009 declared that phishing was not even worthy of being among its top five cyber security threats, started to warn its users of this type of attack. Corporate organizations were complaining that logins to sensitive systems had been given out by unsuspecting employees, leading to the theft of sensitive information. Senior executives in organizations were complaining of their emails having been taken over by malicious people. Phishing had established itself as a high-concern security threat. It attacked the one target that organizations could not protect using cyber security software. There are several types of phishing attacks as we shall discuss in the following.

Social engineering emails

Social engineering emails use tactics designed to make the targets trust that they are genuine and do as they request within a short period of time. Social engineering emails do not normally use malware but are still successful in stealing sensitive details and money from users. The emails are designed in such a way that they sound absolutely believable. Their advantage over malicious emails is that corporate organizations have been adopting security products within their organizations designed to prevent malware in emails from executing or infecting the hosts. However, there is no security product designed to protect a user from social engineering. Social engineers are especially talented in the art of convincing their targets to take some actions that they would not in normal circumstances. A social engineer can convince a target to click on a link, send over some credentials, or send some money.

Social engineering emails are seeing improved chances of success due to the availability of customizable HTML emails containing aspects that can easily delude a target into thinking that an email is authentic. The following are some examples of the cloned HTML emails that are being used by scammers to get targets to believe that they are from respectable sources:

Subject: Record Update.
From: "Dept. Of Labor" <records@dol.gov>
Date: 1/18/2016 1:57 PM
To: undisclosed-recipients:;

This is an urgent request to update your employment record at the U.S Department of Labor.

Update

Thank you

U.S Dept. of Labor
Frances Perkins Building,
200 Constitution Ave., NW,
Washington, DC 20210

The preceding screenshot shows an email format of the real US Department of Labor that has been used for phishing. It set out to acquire personal details, including social security numbers. At the end of the data collection, the hackers will learn lots of employment-related information about the target that they can use to attack the organization they work for. For instance, this email can be used against a junior employee, allowing hackers to use the details stolen to create an email requesting login credentials to banking systems or requesting immediate fund transfers.

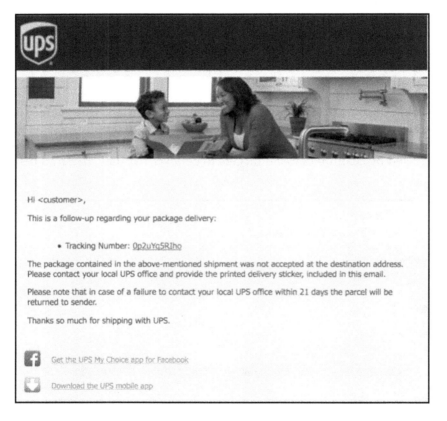

The preceding screenshot is a preformatted clone of the usual UPS emails that people are accustomed to receiving. It shows another phishing email that replicates all the aspects of the normal UPS emails. The email indirectly forces a recipient to click on the link with the tracking number. Once the target clicks on that, he or she is directed to a cloned UPS website where they are requested to log in. With that, their login credentials are stolen.

PayPal

We need your help

Your account has been suspended, as an error was detected in your informations.
The reason for the error is not certain, but for security reasons, we have suspended
your account temporarily

We need you to update your informations for further use of your PayPal account.

Update your information

You are currently made disabled of :

Adding a payment method   Sending payment

Adding a billing address   Accepting payment

Please do not reply to this email. We are unable to respond to inquiries sent to this address. For immediate answers to your questions, visit our
Help Center by clicking "Help" located on any PayPal page or email.

Copyright @ 2016 PayPal, Inc. All rights reserved. PayPal is located at 2211 N. First St., San Jose, CA 95131.

The preceding screenshot is an example of PayPal phishing email. The PayPal scam has
netted many victims, both organizations, and individuals. The email, as can be seen in the
preceding screenshot, requests a user to update their information on PayPal. When they
click on the link on the email, they are directed to a cloned copy of the PayPal site. They are
requested to enter their login credentials. When they do, the hackers withdraw the amounts
in a short period of time. In any case, the login page will show the victims that they have
entered wrong login details. They will then be taken through a long process to *recover their
account* while instead, the hackers will just be harvesting more personal information from
them.

There have been variants to the email though. In December 2017, there was a new version that informed users that their PayPal accounts had transactions that could not be verified. The emails insisted that, as a security precaution, users should log in to their accounts to review these transactions. However, the links would open the cloned PayPal site and after the user had keyed in their login credentials, the funds in their actual PayPal accounts would be withdrawn. The email was designed in such a way that users would think it was from PayPal. Its origin address would show `service@paypal.com`. This was enough for many people to believe that it was actually from PayPal. However, a close inspection showed that the hackers had typed `service@paypal.com` as their name. Therefore, even if the underlying email address was from PayPal, a security-conscious user could just peek at the sender details and see `service@paypal.com` and believe that it was a legitimate email:

We couldn't verify your recent transaction

Dear Client,

We just wanted to confirm that you've changed your password. If you didn't make this change, please check information in here. It's important that you let us know because it helps us prevent unauthorised persons from accessing the PayPal network and your account information.

We've noticed some changes to your unsual selling activities and will need some more information about your recent sales.

Verify Information Now

Thank you for your understanding and cooperation. If you need further assistance, please click Contact at the bottom of any PayPal page.

Sincerely,
PayPal

The preceding screenshot is an another variant of the PayPal phishing email.

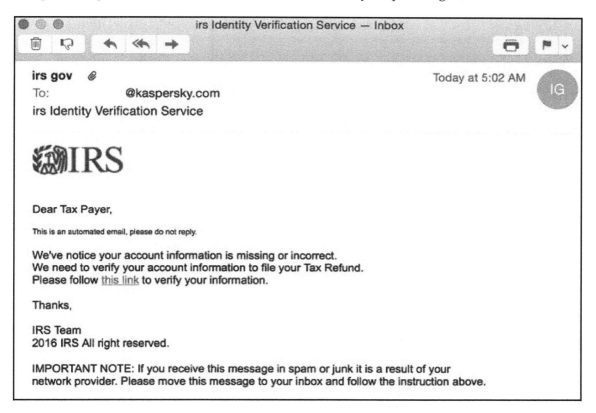

The preceding screenshot is an IRS phishing email. In the 2016 and 2017 tax seasons in the US, there were many cases of theft of information and funds. Hackers took advantage of the confusion in tax seasons by sending emails to many people telling them that their account information was incorrect. The link provided was simply used to steal personal information from the targets.

Spear phishing

Spear phishing is another commonly used technique to steal money and sensitive information from targets. In phishing, many recipients get copies of the same email. The attack casts a wide net to get as many victims as possible. In spear phishing, however, the target is preselected. The attacker will have done a lot of research about the target to know exactly what to use to catch them off guard. This makes spear phishing quite dangerous, since it can capitalize on anything. At times, information used in spear phishing attacks against organizational employees comes from insider threats that know the ranks and responsibilities of all the staff in the organization. The attacker will then create a convincing email trying to get the target to take some action. Many organizations have lost funds after their employees were targeted with spear phishing emails. The following are real-life examples of these types of email:

Scott

To:

Reply-To:

Urgent

Hello Stuart,

Have you got a minute? I am currently tied up in a meeting. We need to facilitate a wire transfer to Indonesia for payment of an invoice Peter needs us to pay for today.

Let me know so I can pass across further information to you. Thanks.

Regards,
Scott

Sent from my iPhone

The preceding screenshot shows a spear phishing email from a hacker that knows the target's name and role in the organization they work. In addition, they supposedly know of a senior member of staff called Scott that can authorize payments and in addition, know that one of the organization's suppliers or contractors is Peter. The email shows the hacker addressing the target by name and informing them he is in a meeting but wants to urgently facilitate a money transfer. It is very easy for the target to fall for this scam. The included elements, such as actual names, the urgency of money transfers, and the issue of the meeting all work towards compelling the target to swiftly accept the instruction to carry out the money transfer. The *Sent from my iPhone* part of the message is intentionally added to remove fears as to why the email does not have aspects such as the organization's email signature, or bear the title of Scott as official emails should. Therefore, there are high chances of success in this spear phishing attack:

---------- Forwarded message ----------
From: **Doug Williams** <chrispid@t-online.de>
Date: Wed, Apr 13, 2016 at 11:47 AM
Subject: Invoice for Lehigh University ; Attention: Controller
To: j

This is a private message for the Controller, Lehigh University. If it is not you, please ignore and discard it.

Hi John Gasdaska,

Since we have not received a contract termination letter, I am assuming that you might have unintentionally overlooked our invoice 04/16000331799 (Unpaid). If you intend to bring to an end the account, just let us know. Be informed that early withdrawal penalties will apply.

Refer to the attached document for billing information.

Regards,
Doug.

Doug Williams
Sterling Savings Bank | Accounting and Billing Team
6400 Uptown Blvd Ne,Albuquerque,New Mexico,87110
T: 866-905-9901 | Copyright © 2016

The preceding screenshot shows another spear phishing email. In this email, it can be seen that the attacker masquerades as an employee of a bank following up on an unpaid invoice. In a list of the ways funds are stolen in phishing attacks, invoices were ranked in the top three slots. Therefore, this is a good example of how many organizations are losing money to attackers. In the email, there are several aspects that add to its credibility from the perspective of the target. To begin with, the email is well formatted and it most likely matches the formatting of emails from Sterling Savings Bank. The email also has the official email signature used by the company, which shows the correct address and contact details. The email also addresses the recipient by name. In the email, the sender informs the reader of an unpaid invoice. The target is told to refer to an attached document. Chances are that the attached document will have a cloned invoice with different payment details, or the attachment is malware that will be used for keylogging. In either case, the recipient is in a dilemma about whether to open the attachment:

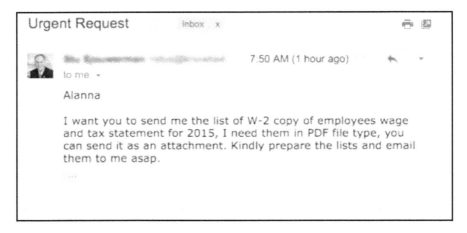

In the preceding screenshot, the attacker takes several measures to ensure that the target thinks that the email is genuine. To begin with, they use a profile picture. This is an added advantage in terms of the attacker's email being quickly thought to be authentic. The email also addresses the recipient directly. The lack of a salutation shows that the sender is someone of a higher rank and probably is known to be rude to employees. The content also requests that the recipient should act as requested with urgency. There is also not a proper sign off, adding to the notion that the sender is a person in higher authority and is not the most polite. The target will be pressurized by these aspects into sending over the W-2 copies of employees to the sender. W-2 copies can be used for fraudulent purposes with regards to tax. If the target sends the W-2 copies of all employees, it will be a big catch for the cyber criminals that sent the email:

13 July 2016 at 9:38 AM

To:

Reply-To:

Payment

Hi Michael,

Please find enclosed vendor banking instructions for a payment that was suppose to go out in the previous week. I need you to process it immediately.

I am a bit busy now but will give you a call within the hour regarding the payment.

Regards,

Sent from my Mobile

In the preceding spear phishing email, a pattern can be seen from the previously described screenshots. To begin with, note that the sender intentionally adds *Sent from my Mobile* at the end of the email. This is to make it appear legit even though it lacks the proper formatting and official email signature. The sender addresses the target by name, just one name to show that it was written in a hurry. In the email content, the sender says that there are some attached payment instructions for a payment that has to be processed immediately. To add to the credibility, the sender says that they will contact the recipient within an hour regarding the payment. It is, therefore, implied that the sender expects the payment to be completed before they contact the recipient. The recipient is therefore under pressure to make the payment with an assurance that further communication will follow from the person that has requested it to be done. It is not uncommon for senior staff to request their juniors to undertake a task and get clarification later. Therefore, there is nothing much that can cause the target to flag this request. It is easy these days for attackers to gather information about employees and identify senior and junior employees. Senior employees such as finance managers or directors can easily issue orders to junior employees such as accountants and these orders will mostly be adhered to without questions. There are many email scraper tools that can be used to collect emails from social media sites such as LinkedIn which attackers can use for their spear phishing attacks.

Business email compromise or whaling

Business email compromise (**BEC**), also more descriptively known as whaling or CEO fraud, is a type of spear phishing that involves compromising emails of executive employees in organizations. The compromised emails are then used to request huge amounts of money or sensitive information from senior employees. This is a type of phishing that gained attention from 2013. The FBI investigated 22,000 cases from organizations that had resulted from once-despised phishing attacks. Between 2013 and 2016, cases reported to the FBI had a cumulative loss of $1.6 billion. The US was ahead in the number of organizations that had been attacked, across all 50 states. The attackers were seemingly combing through all industries with business email compromise attacks. They had, however, shown interest in real estate agencies. The reason was that there were many real estate companies; thus a wider pool of emails could be compromised. The huge sums of money exchanged in real estate transactions were also a big attraction for attackers. All that the attacker needed was to compromise just one of the people in the chain of communication and get access to their email address. After getting access, the attacker would observe all communication and decide when to send a request for funds to be released to a certain account.

Trend Micro, a leading company in data security and cyber security solutions, did an analysis of BEC incidents that had occurred between 2017 and 2018. In their analysis, they revealed that BEC attacks had been on the rise, and by the end of 2018, a total of $9 billion would be lost due to these attacks. They said that BEC attacks were mostly executed in two ways:

- Credential theft—cyber criminals were stealing credentials from employees of target organizations by using keyloggers and phishing kits. Phishing kits are entire systems that come with tools and templates that can be used for phishing.
- Social engineering emails—this is where cyber criminals targeted the organizations without stealing any credentials. They would use their own spoofed emails and make them sound and feel like they came from senior employees in the finance department. The emails would directly order junior employees to quickly transfer some amounts to a certain bank account as payment to suppliers or contractors.

In the analysis of the actual content in successful BEC attack emails, Trend Micro observed that most successful BEC attack emails used purchase orders, payments, and invoices to get the targets to send money. They exploited a flaw in organizations where senior-level employees can order junior employees to make transfers to other parties without raising any questions. In many organizations, this is a norm. Actually including actual purchase orders, bills, and invoices showed that BEC attackers had more chances of convincing their targets that the request was genuine and the money transfer had to be completed.

Credential theft using malicious software

While analyzing other factors that led to the success of these BEC emails, Trend Micro uncovered that there was increased use of two malicious programs. These are as follows.

Ardamax

The first is Ardamax, which is a $50 program that can give cyber criminals quick access to logins used by a target. Ardamax is a keylogger and it sits quietly on a computer collecting typed usernames and passwords to sensitive systems, such as the online banking platforms used by organizations. The software is easily concealed and sent as a normal email attachment. The level of ingenuity in this software is on another level. The software can be created so it has any extension such as JPG or PNG to appear as if it is a normal image. The following screenshot illustrates setting up Ardamax (https://www.ardamax.com/) to appear as a JPG file:

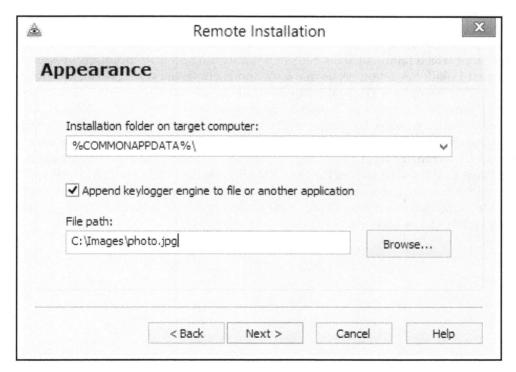

Therefore, even if organizational employees are told not to download suspicious attachments, there is no way that they can consider a simple JPG attachment to be malicious. The content used in the email is normally so enticing that only a few people will resist opening the attachments. Once the attachment opens, Ardamax remote installation begins and the malware starts operating in stealth mode. It collects keystrokes, websites visited, activities on chat platforms, content copied to the clipboard, and can still launch the camera and microphone without the user's knowledge. Therefore, the preceding screenshot chances of an attack succeeding after a user has opened the attachment are very high since the attacker will have a lot of information collected by Ardamax.

LokiBot

The other software that Trend Micro identifies as commonly used in successful BEC attacks is LokiBot. This malware is used for stealing passwords, cryptocurrency wallets, credentials from web browsers, contacts from emails, and information from tools such as PuTTY. LokiBot made its way up Kaspersky's list of dangerous malware in 2017. The malware is sold at $80 in underground markets. However, there are claims that LokiBot is just a modified version of another malware that had been released by another black hat on the dark web that was retailing at $300. Kaspersky, a leading security products vendor, has warned that LokiBot is a dangerous malware and is effective even against Android phones. It is also highly deceptive. The malware can simulate several app screens, causing users to give away sensitive information. LokiBot has been observed to simulate WhatsApp, Skype, and several email and bank applications. It triggers users to interact with the simulated screen through false app notifications. For instance, it could show a notification of a purported fund transfer from a banking application. LokiBot will even make the phone vibrate to capture the attention of the user. On clicking the notification, the user will be greeted with the same login interface as their normal banking app. Once the user types their credentials, they are automatically sent to the cyber criminals and they begin transfers from the victim's bank account.

Besides this, LokiBot is able to open a device's browser and navigate to malicious pages. It also sends spam messages where all contacts in a person's phone are sent copies of the malware so that it can distribute itself. Attempts to uninstall LokiBot are normally futile. The app will have requested administrator rights earlier, which is quite normal for some apps, and users will have given it unfiltered privileges over the device. During uninstallation, a user is required to remove the app from the list of apps with admin privileges. However, when a user does this, LokiBot turns into a ransomware and encrypts the external storage media on the infected phone. A screen lock is also activated that demands that the user sends $100 in the form of Bitcoin to a given wallet address. The analysis of the code in LokiBot has shown that the hackers behind it can also activate the ransomware module remotely. Researchers that have investigated this address have discovered that the hackers have so far made over $1.5 million in Bitcoin. The following screenshot illustrates the banner displayed on a user's phone when LokiBot encrypts it:

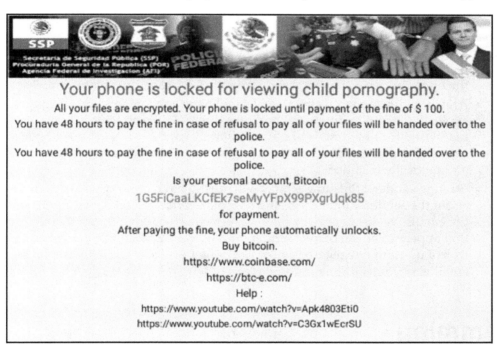

Characteristics of phishing emails

In an analysis of all phishing emails, including those that we have discussed, some patterns can be observed in the emails. These are as follows:

- **Urgency**: Phishers will want their targets to act fast, without time to think twice about their actions. This is the reason why senders say that they need something done immediately or as soon as possible. This puts the target under pressure to complete the task first and then seek clarification later. Phishing emails may contain errors with their grammar and formatting but the recipient will be under too much pressure to notice any of this. The number of people that fell for the PayPal phishing scam is surprising despite the fact that it said *update your* information in several instances.

- **Hyperlinks**: Instead of giving the full link, most of these phishing emails use hyperlinks. These are meant to hide the real URLs, which are obviously not from the real companies. For instance, the emails that we have discussed only had hyperlinked text or buttons. The emails from the real organizations are normally given alongside the full URL. This is done so that if a user has a problem opening the hyperlink, they can copy and paste the URL directly on their browsers.

- **Attachments**: Many phishing emails will have attachments and the targets will explicitly be told to download and open them. These attachments are in most cases used to spread malware. As we have seen, there is a keylogger malware (Ardamax) that can be sent in any file format, and when a user opens the file, it is automatically installed.

- **Strange senders**: Phishing emails will mostly have some issues with the details about the sender. Either the domain or the username will be wrong. In some of the emails we discussed, the senders were smart enough to register usernames that appear to be the correct sender's email. For instance, the PayPal email came from a username registered as `support@paypal.com` while the actual sender's email was from a different domain.

Spamming

Spamming is the act of sending unsolicited emails to a large audience or a large number of users in a mailing list. Spammers were once harmless and were used only for hoaxes. For instance, there were spam emails telling people to switch off their internet at certain periods, or to forward a certain message to all their contacts.

The word spam was coined in 1993 to refer, not to emails, but unwanted postings in a Usenet newsgroups network. There were two such incidents at the time, one of which was a post on many newsgroups with a global alert that Jesus, worshipped by Christians, was coming. The second incident was another posting on even more Usenet newsgroups about the termination of the Green Card Lottery. Possibly to cause nuisance, the idea of sending such messages via email started. In 1996, network managers tried to stop the issue by creating a Mail Abuse Prevention System to keep a list of IP addresses used to spread spam. Mail servers would be given this list to block all incoming messages from IP addresses found to have sent spam. However, this system was not very effective and spam evolved to become a big problem by 2000. President George W. Bush signed a CAN-SPAM Act into law in 2003 hoping to end spamming. Spammers started being arrested, charged, and punished for spreading spam messages. Most of those convicted had sent millions of spam messages to a big number of recipients.

However, spam emails got weaponized and monetized by the end of the decade. They were no longer just used to fool their audience, they were meant to start making money from them. In the February 2011 WIRED magazine, a 2008 study carried out by UC San Diego students was widely cited and it revealed that despite the low rates of response or interaction with spam emails, spammers were generating at least $7,000 a day. Even though there was scepticism later about the figure, it showed that spam emails were being used as money-making schemes. This is the stage where spam emails are at. They are being used to send adverts and malware to millions or billions of recipients. The next section will evaluate the value chain of spam emails and identify exactly how spammers get emails and make money.

How spammers get email addresses

Spammers have a huge recipient list for their emails. One may wonder where all these emails are obtained from. There are different sources that can be exploited. The first one is from chat rooms where users give out their emails. They can also get these emails from websites that have openly given out email addresses of staff or customers. They can also get email addresses from sellers in underground markets. These could come from previous hacks or from people that specialize in collecting emails. These emails can also be obtained from customer lists especially by insider threats. Staff in departments such as marketing have access to customer lists and an employee wishing to make quick money can just steal these email addresses and sell them. Lastly, scripts are also used to harvest emails on different websites, such as social media sites.

How spammers make money

Spamming is used for revenue generation. If it was an unprofitable venture, there would be very few people engaging in this unethical, often illegal act. There are several revenue streams through which spammers make their money. These are as follows.

Advertising

Many spam emails market products to a wide audience even if the products will only appeal to 0.0001% of them. This percentage might seem too insignificant to be worth the efforts. However, Cyberoam estimates that 54 billion spam emails are sent every day. At least 45% of these emails are advertisements of controversial pharmaceutical products, such as non-prescription Viagra. In this context, it can be seen that the small percentage of recipients that actually get to interact with the spam email or make purchases are significant contributors of revenue to the spammers. Companies that sell these products will pay some commission to the spammers.

At times, spammers might use advertising codes from advertisement agency companies and get paid per impression. From the millions of people that they send the spam emails to, if a certain percentage of them opens the emails, the impressions will be counted and the spammers will get some money, even if the recipient does not buy any products.

Malware

Some spam emails contain malware. This malware can come as attachments or can be automatically downloaded and installed on the recipient's device. The malware can then be used to collect sensitive information. While keyloggers collect usernames and passwords, other malware could be used to steal email addresses and phone numbers from contact lists in the infected device. Lastly, the malware could be used to extort money from the users. The following are some examples of malware that can be spread via spam mail.

Storm

Storm is a backdoor Trojan horse and is commonly used in spam email. This malware was first discovered in 2007 when it spread across the US and Europe via a spam mail claiming that there had been a deadly storm in Europe. Spam has been used in many spam emails, some of which are:

- British Muslims Genocide
- Chinese missile has shot down a Russian satellite
- Saddam Hussein alive!
- Venezuelan leader: *Let's the war beginning*
- You have received an E-Greeting.

The following screenshot shows an example of this type of spam email:

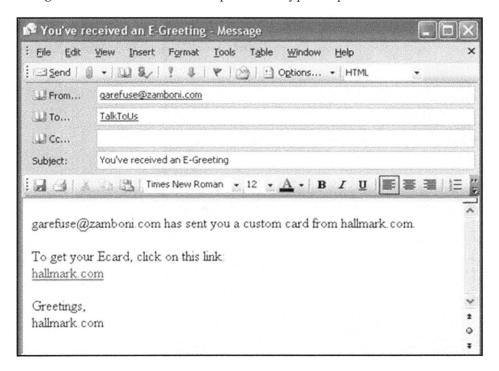

These and many other radical or exciting posts are used to make recipients open spam emails containing the Storm malware. When the email is opened, Storm will be disguised as an attachment with labels such as *Full video, Full story, Shocking image, click this link,* and *Postcard* among others. When a target downloads and opens the attachment, the malware is installed in their computer. In the computer, the malware will inject a payload to be used to forward more spam emails to other recipients containing more copies of the malware. This way, the malware is able to propagate to many computers. Storm can make the computers it infects be part of a botnet, or it can give itself rootkit access to further control the computer.

Triout

First discovered in 2018, is a malware framework that can convert legitimate Android apps into spyware. The malware can be downloaded from illegitimate app websites where it will be repackaged as a normal app but when a user downloads and installs it, it takes over other apps in the phone. Triout, using other apps it has infected, can record phone calls, log SMSs, access photos and videos, take pictures or video clips, and send all this information back to hackers.

The following information is taken from a Bitdefender article explaining the capabilities of Triout (`https://labs.bitdefender.com/2018/08/triout-spyware-framework-for-android-with-extensive-surveillance-capabilities/`). A subsequent investigation revealed that the spyware has the following capabilities:

- Records every phone call (literally the conversation as a media file), then sends it together with the caller id to the C&C (`incall3.php` and `outcall3.php`).
- Logs every incoming SMS message (SMS body and SMS sender) to C&C (`script3.php`).
- Can hide itself.
- Can send all call logs (content://call_log/calls, info: callname, callnum, calldate, calltype, callduration) to C&C (`calllog.php`).
- Whenever the user snaps a picture, either with the front or rear camera, it gets sent to the C&C (`uppc.php, fi npic.php, orreqpic.php`).
- Can send GPS coordinates to C&C (`gps3.php`).

Botnets

Storm is one example of a botnet malware that can be spread via spam mail. Botnets seek to recruit as many zombie computers as possible and this is why spam emails are ideal methods of propagation for botnet malware. While Storm is ranked as the most effective botnet malware, another effective malware is discussed as follows.

Zeus

Zeus came into the limelight in 2007 whereby it targeted Microsoft Windows users. It could infect itself in a Windows computer, make the computer part of a botnet, and additionally steal online banking data from the user's browser. The malware was so effective that it was said the owner decided to retire in 2010. However, new variants of the botnet malware soon came up and a task force was created to fight them. The task force, made up of US Marshals and tech-industry partners, was able to take down the botnet in 2012. Soon after, newer variants emerged, and an FBI task force was created and succeeded in taking it down in 2014. In 2016, new variants of this malware were detected, and they were infecting more operating systems and were particularly targeted at stealing login credentials for Canadian banks, leading email providers, social media networks, and cryptocurrency wallets. The biggest challenge with Zeus is that the original source code was released to the public, thus new variants will keep on appearing for a while. The botnet is still in use, that is, until it is brought down and hackers develop a newer variant.

Characteristics of spam emails

The following are characteristics that can be used to identify spam emails:

- **Anonymity**: A quick way to tell whether an email is spam is by checking the recipients. Chances are that the senders will use blind carbon copy to send it to many recipients. If your email does not appear in the *To:* address, it means that you were a *Bcc,* thus there is a high chance it is a spam.
- **Salutation**: Legitimate emails will address a recipient by name but spam emails will use a general approach such as *Dear Valued Customer* or just *Hello.*
- **Bad grammar**: Most spam emails will have bad grammar or spelling mistakes. Legitimate companies will send well edited emails with minimal grammatical errors, while spammers will not be so concerned about grammar.
- **Signature**: Legitimate companies include their company's signature in their emails, with a phone number that can be used to contact them. Spammers will hardly ever have email signatures and if they do, they will not include phone numbers.

When you observe these characteristics, it is most advisable to avoid engaging with the senders or downloading any attachment. The following is a screenshot of a spam email. Take note of the type of salutation used, the reference to an unknown site, and lack of a detailed email signature:

Hello,

I'm reaching out because I'm experiencing a few minor errors while browsing your site. As a Digital Marketing manager, I know how frustrating things like this can be, so I wanted to reach out to see if I can help.

Mainly, I'm experiencing issues loading your site on my mobile device. This is a fairly common issue, especially since this April, when Google started heavily rewarding sites with a speedy mobile user experience, and punishing those with bulky, lagging designs that aren't suited to small, vertical screens. With over 50 percent of people browsing the internet with their phones, that's a fair share of the market to consider.

Based locally in Libertyville, IL, my team has over 23 years of experience developing elastic designs that can be viewed on any device. We're also Google Partners and have received many accolades throughout the years. Our first client was a little startup company called "E-bay". We would be happy to jump on a call with you to review these problems and more to help your brand get the best online visibility possible.

What day this week works best for a call?

Regards,

Steve K.

Summary

Phishing, scamming, and spamming are methods that are widely used to steal data and money from users. This chapter analyzed the techniques used and how exactly the money and data are stolen from users. A lot more focus has been given to phishing and scamming since there have been significant losses to the global economy as a result of these attacks. The chapter looked at the evolution of phishing and identified its rise, fall, and yet another rise. The most effective type of phishing that has caught the attention of users, vendors, corporate organizations, legal firms, and the cyber security industry is business email compromise. The chapter has looked at this type of phishing in depth and analyzed several real emails sent to targets. The chapter also identified the two commonly used malwares that are commonly used in the theft of money and data, Ardamax and LokiBot. Ardamax has been identified as keylogger software that can get passed to users as an attachment in many file formats. LokiBot, on the other hand, has been identified as a resilient threat actor that can steal data and encrypt a device. The chapter then looked at spear phishing, which is an advanced form of phishing that targets specific people. Real-life examples of spear phishing attempts were given and analyzed. An observable pattern in most phishing attacks was supplied based on the phishing emails we discussed.

Lastly, the chapter looked at spamming. Even though most spam is only annoying but not dangerous, there are instances where spam also exposes targets to various cyber security threats. It is not limited to advertising, and some spam emails contain malicious payloads. Therefore, in this chapter, you have learned about various types of phishing and phishing-related scams, such as spear phishing and business email compromise, and how to identify them; we also discussed challenges when it comes to identifying such threats. You also learned about the dangers related to spam and how it works and can be used to exploit recipients of spam emails. The next chapter will broadly talk about different malware, which will eventually help you to build your own defense strategy.

Further reading

The following resources can be used to gain more knowledge on topics discussed in this chapter:

- *LokiBot: If not stealing, then extorting*: https://www.kaspersky.com/blog/lokibot-trojan/20030/
- *LokiBot - The first hybrid Android malware*: https://www.threatfabric.com/blogs/lokibot_the_first_hybrid_android_malware.html
- *15 Examples of Phishing Emails from 2016-2017*: https://www.edts.com/edts-blog/15-examples-of-phishing-emails-from-2016-2017

- *WHAT TO DO IF YOU ARE A VICTIM*: `https://www.ic3.gov/media/2017/170504.aspx#fn3`
- *Analysis: How Malware Creators Use Spam To Maximize Their Impact*: `https://heimdalsecurity.com/blog/analysis-how-malware-creators-use-spam-to-maximize-their-impact/`
- *Zeus Virus*: `https://usa.kaspersky.com/resource-center/threats/zeus-virus`
- *Spamming*: `https://www.bitpipe.com/tlist/Spamming.html`
- *Triout – Spyware Framework for Android with Extensive Surveillance Capabilities*: `https://labs.bitdefender.com/2018/08/triout-spyware-framework-for-android-with-extensive-surveillance-capabilities/`

6
The Malware Plague

Malicious software—commonly referred to as malware—is used by threat actors to perform malicious activities on a host system. These malicious activities include compromising the corporate network, identity theft, and data exfiltration. The evolution of connected devices and the fact that it has become practically impossible to run an enterprise without a computer has increased the volume of threat actors leveraging malware as part of a cyber attack. Malware can come in the form of scripts or executable code. There are many different classes of malware, but the most well known is by far computer viruses and computer Trojans. Threat actors no longer need to find their own vulnerabilities or build their own malware. Instead, they can procure them through the dark web. There has been an increased demand for sophisticated malware that is used by state-sponsored threat actors and organized crime syndicates:

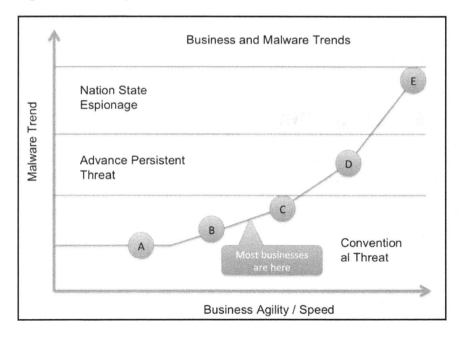

With advancements in malware development, a new risk has arisen in the form polymorphic malware. Polymorphic malware is malware that runs once and never runs again, making it extremely difficult for antivirus providers to prevent malicious activities. Early on, threat actors discovered the benefit of leveraging malware during cyber attacks against institutes in the financial services industry. Once malware had reached the target endpoint, threat actors were able to illegally transfer funds from their target to accounts controlled by the threat actor. In addition to this, because ATMs are connected to the corporate network, threat actors focused on leveraging malware to attack ATMs. Throughout this chapter, you will learn about malware classes and get an insight into some of the most commonly used malware families utilized as part of cyber attacks within the financial services industry.

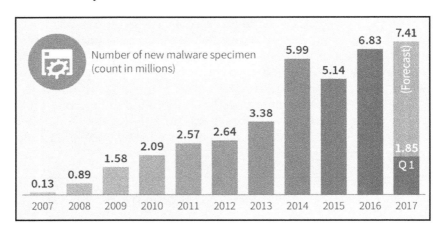

Malware categories

It is important to understand the different malware categories that are leveraged by threat actors during cyber attacks. Only by understanding the differences between a computer virus and a computer Trojan, for example, will you be able to build prevention capabilities. While end users often assume that malware is only applicable to computers, it is important to understand that malware can also affect any connected device, including smartphones and industry appliances:

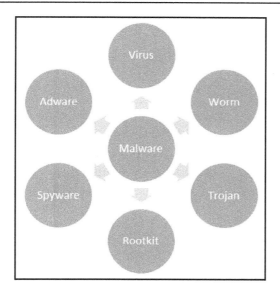

Depending on the objective of the threat actor, the group might use a specific malware family or a combination of malware. It is recommended that security teams build their **Indicators of Compromise (IOC)** aligned to the cyber attack kill chain. The attack kill chain is a process that describes how threat actors perform a cyber attack with malware. The following diagram illustrates the attack kill chain:

Computer virus

At its core, a computer virus is very similar to a biological virus and is one of the most commonly used malware families:

- **Biological virus**:
    - Consists of DNA surrounded by a protein shell to bond to a host cell
    - Replicates itself over the host's metabolic machinery
    - Copies infections to as many cells as possible
    - The virus can't live outside the host cell

The principle for all computer viruses is that they can insert themselves into files and processes on a computer in order to perform malicious actions. The are also able to replicate themselves by modifying other computer programs:

- **Computer virus**:
    - Consists of a set of instructions stored in the operating system or application
    - Replicates when the host program is executed
    - Can only survive when the host program is executed
    - Copies infections to other host programs

A computer virus can infect executables, scripts, documents, or even boot sectors. When a computer virus is able to infect a combination of targets, such as executables and documents, then these kinds of virus are commonly referred to as multipartite viruses.

Computer worm

A computer worm is a self-replicating payload that is able to spread rapidly in the network. While a computer worm and a computer virus are similar in their approach and reach, the big difference is that a computer worm does not require human interaction in order to spread in the network. It is possible for threat actors to combine the characteristics of a computer worm with a computer virus. The most prominent example of this was in 1999 with the Melissa love letter. The Melissa love letter was an email that was sent to targets, containing a Word document with a virus hidden as a macro. When the end user enabled the macro, a virus would be injected through the document file and, at the same time, a worm would be executed. This would then spread across the network:

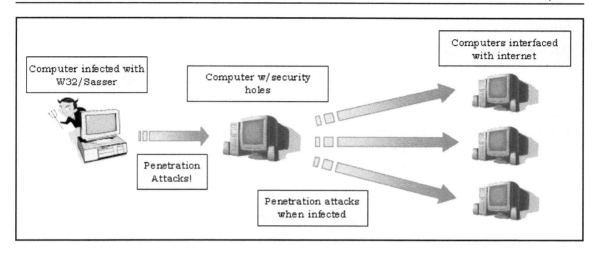

SQL Slammer worm

In 2013, the Bank of America was impacted by a web server worm that later was referred to as SQL Slammer. This took down several ATM services. The SQL Slammer worm leveraged a buffer overflow bug in SQL Server and the Desktop Engine database. When the machine was infected, the worm generated a random IP address, which it would use to distribute itself on other machines that had an unpatched SQL Server version installed.

Crypto worm

A crypto worm is a variation on a computer worm that is leveraged by threat actors for ransomware attacks. In general, crypto worms target unpatched or misconfigured computers by encrypting data and then demanding ransom for decryption.

WannaCry

In May 2017, WannaCry (a global ransomware outbreak) impacted thousands of enterprises around the world. WannaCry was a ransomware attack performed by a threat actor group that leveraged a crypto worm. The targets were computers running an unpatched version of Windows, which it attacked by utilizing an SMBv1 vulnerability. WannaCry also leveraged the EternalBlue vulnerability to spread itself. However, WannaCry was stopped fairly quickly. This was because Marcus Hutchins, a security researcher, discovered a kill switch, which is a programmed stop command, for WannaCry, by registering a domain name that he had found in its source code:

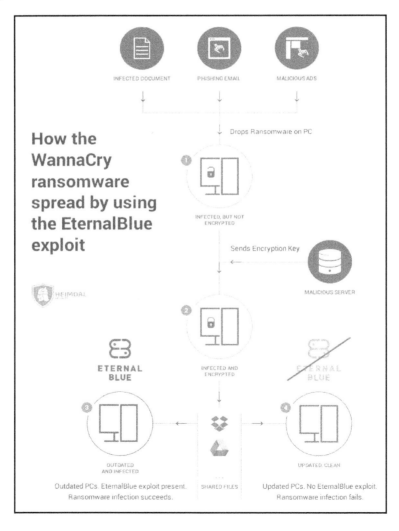

Trojan

A Trojan is a piece of malware that deceives the target as to its true intent. The term Trojan has its origin with the ancient Greeks, who gave the city of Troy a wooden horse with soldiers hidden inside of it. Once the wooden horse was taken inside the city of Troy, the soldiers attacked. The most common delivery mechanism for a Trojan is through social engineering techniques such as pretexting, phishing, or spear phishing. Unlike computer viruses or computer worms, Trojans are typically not injected into files or executable files. Similarly, Trojans do not replicate themselves like a computer worm. When Trojans started to arise, they were generally used for **denial of service** (**DoS**) attacks. A Trojan may do the following:

- Steal personal information
- Steal credentials (username/password)
- Copy confidential and/or sensitive data
- Perform harmful operations

In many cases, a Trojan attempts to open a port on the machine, which allows the threat actor to establish **Command and Control** (**C2C**) communication, which is then used to perform illegal actions:

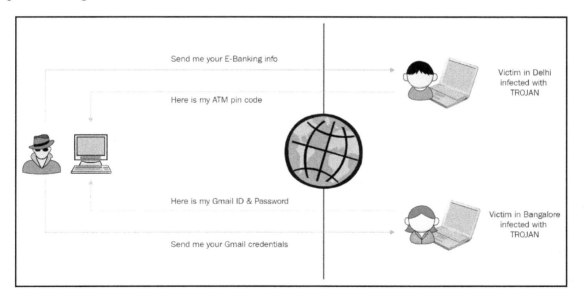

Bebloh

Bebloh is a banking Trojan that is used by threat actors in order to perform credential harvesting and inject the endpoint during a target's online banking transactions. Bebloh is very popular as a banking Trojan because of its ability to change the balance shown on the target's computer when logged in to the online banking portal. In order to achieve that, Bebloh leverages a **man-in-the-browser** (**MitB**) technique. The delivery of Bebloh is often hidden inside an email with a malicious PDF attachment that is sent as spam. Bebloh makes use of a vulnerability in Adobe Reader 9.3, which causes the Adobe Reader to crash during that process and inject malicious code into the system. Bebloh was first discovered in 2009 and a number of German banks were impacted. The following diagram illustrates the kill chain of Bebloh:

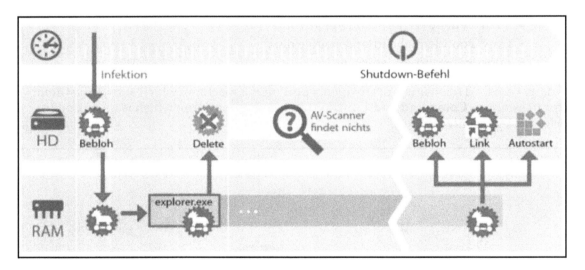

Zeus

Similarly to Bebloh, the primary objective of this Trojan is to steal online banking credentials and to intercept banking transactions. Up to now, Zeus has been the most commonly used banking malware because of its exploit reach. Zeus is a banking Trojan that was developed with a modular approach, making it easy to hide and execute, and actors to incorporate into cyber attacks. Zeus is primarily delivered to a target as spam, phishing, or spear phishing. Zeus leverages a vulnerability in the browser to perform a MitB attack that allows Zeus to modify the transactions performed by the victim during online banking. Zeus is even able to bypass Multi-Factor Authentication. According to the FBI, Zeus has cost the financial services industry over 100 million US dollars so far. The following diagram represents Zeus:

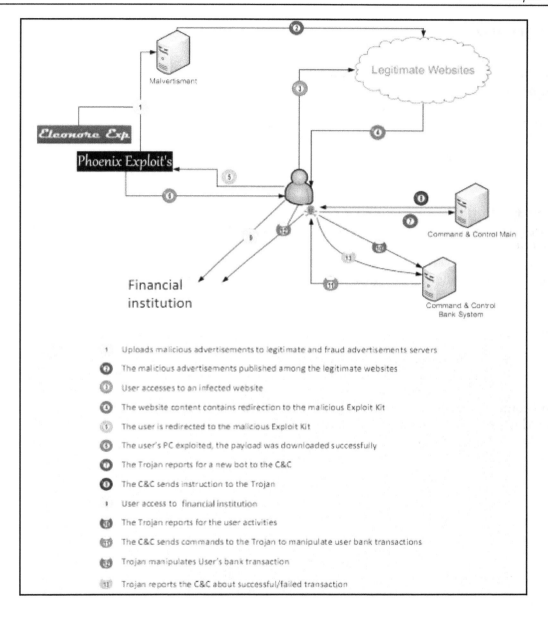

1   Uploads malicious advertisements to legitimate and fraud advertisements servers

2   The malicious advertisements published among the legitimate websites

3   User accesses to an infected website

4   The website content contains redirection to the malicious Exploit Kit

5   The user is redirected to the malicious Exploit Kit

6   The user's PC exploited, the payload was downloaded successfully

7   The Trojan reports for a new bot to the C&C

8   The C&C sends instruction to the Trojan

9   User access to financial institution

10 The Trojan reports for the user activities

11 The C&C sends commands to the Trojan to manipulate user bank transactions

12 Trojan manipulates User's bank transaction

13 Trojan reports the C&C about successful/failed transaction

Rootkit

A rootkit is a form of malware that enables other malicious payloads to make use of its privileged access on a computer. A rootkit can be installed either by leveraging a system vulnerability that bypasses account privileges, or when the threat actor has already compromised administrative privileges. Once the rootkit is installed, it allows threat actors to gain remote access to the computer's low-level systems. A rootkit uses back door tools to modify an operating system and firmware to hide the threat actor's steps. These back doors can operate either in user or kernel mode.

Torpig

Torpig is a technique first seen in 2005 that combined a banking Trojan, a botnet, and a rootkit. The botnet spread the banking Trojan Mebroot, which was then responsible for stealing the logon credentials for banking websites. The way that Torpig ensured that it wouldn't be detected by antivirus software was by leveraging a rootkit exploit.

Spyware

Spyware runs in the background of a computer and its primary purpose is collecting information on the computer without the awareness of the target. The delivery mechanism for computer viruses, computer Trojans, worms, and spyware is the same. Often, spyware will contain Trojans such as keyloggers that track all the keyboard inputs of the target, banking Trojans that harvest online banking credentials, or password stealers that perform credential harvesting:

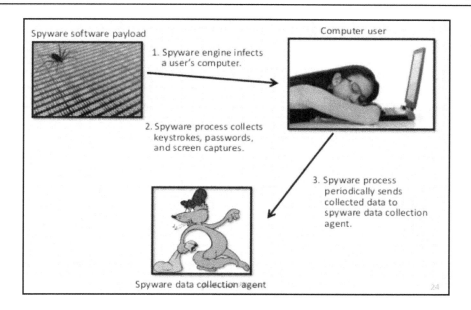

Adware

Adware is a type of malware that displays advertisements on the user interface of the target. Typically, adware is used to gather information on the target, particularly on their internet behavior.

Malware trends

Threat actors are becoming more and more sophisticated, often making it nearly impossible for enterprises to defend against them or for end customers to identify visual indicators of compromise that could prevent the next cyber attack. Even though malware and its families are not new, there is no shortage of new payload and exploitation techniques. On the dark web, there are countless commercial malware providers that offer a variety of malware services, such as the following:

- **Ransomware**: The average cost ranges between $250-300.
- **Spyware**: A simple data stealer costs approximately $10.
- **Remote Access Trojans**: These range between $500-1,000.
- **ATM malware**: Because a single ATM could store approximately $150,000, ATM malware remains at a high price range: $1,500-3,000.

Next to custom-made malware, ATM malware remains the most expensive malware available on the dark web.

While global outbreaks such as WannaCry or NotPetya can have a serious impact on the global economy, they still represent a small fraction of the commodity malware that targets unpatched computers. Modern malware, however, has become a serious threat because traditional security solutions that rely on signatures won't be able to respond to them. Modern malware not only includes zero-day vulnerabilities, but also has polymorphic capabilities. Polymorphic malware is able to change its own characteristics, making it impossible to detect with an antivirus solution that purely relies on signatures. This way, threat actors are circumventing signature-based detection. According to Microsoft, 96% of malware nowadays runs once and then never runs again.

In addition to polymorphic malware, there is an ongoing increase in crypto-mining malware. This is despite the decline of the market cap for cryptocurrency. This is a result of the fact that cryptocurrency offers threat actors a way to hide while receiving the ransom from their targets.

Malware infection vectors

In the 2017 data breach report, Verizon shared an interesting perspective on the infection vectors used by threat actors with malware. This showed that 81% of all malware infections happened through a cyber attack where the malware was remotely installed or injected. The following diagram illustrates the Verizon study:

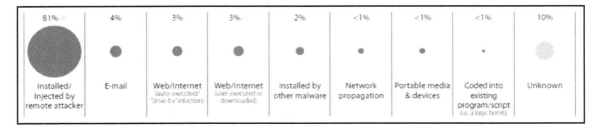

Injected by remote attacker

Threat actors leverages vulnerabilities that allow them to execute remote commands through software.

Email

Phishing and spear phishing techniques are very old forms of computer-based social engineering. Essentially, all that the threat actor needs to do is prepare a believable email with a call to action that the target will interact with, either by opening an attachment that contains a malicious document or by clicking on a hyperlink that redirects the target to a malicious website.

Auto-executed web infection

In the event of the target automatically executing a web infection, the threat actor leverages vulnerabilities on a website in order to plant their malicious payload on their target. The victim is unaware of this and simply browses a website that appears to be legitimate.

User-executed web infection

Unlike an auto-executed web infection, where the threat actor hides their malware, in the case of a user-executed web infection, the threat actor is trying to trick the victim into performing an action on the website. This may include downloading a specific file.

Installed by other malware

As part of the attack kill chain, there is the C2C phase. In this event, the threat actor has direct communication with the compromised computer. By leveraging C2C communication, it is possible for the threat actor to also install additional malware on the compromised computer.

Network propagation

Threat actors regularly scan internet-facing IP ranges of enterprises to detect computers that are reachable. Once identified, the threat actor then proceeds with different techniques, such as brute-force attacks or vulnerability scans.

Portable media

It's human nature to be curious and threat actors that specialize in social engineering are particularly aware of that. One of the oldest social engineering techniques is baiting. This is the process of using malicious portable media to compromise a computer. Operation Stuxnet, a state-sponsored attack against Iran suspected of being conducted by the USA and Israel, leveraged this technique. In this case, the threat actor will typically drop malicious portable media into locations where they're likely to be found by the target. The expectation is that because humans are curious by nature, they will plug that portable media into their computer.

Coded into existing software

Supply chain attacks have become a serious threat. Threat actors are increasingly focusing on understanding who the suppliers and vendors of their target are and then compromising them to get a foothold in the final target. While many large Fortune 100 companies have a large security budget, the smaller companies that do business with these companies do not. But even the smallest company that works for a Fortune 100 company will eventually need to upload an invoice through the Fortune 100 system. Another example is compromising ISVs, which have simple tools that are leveraged by the target. Most commonly, threat actors will try to compromise their update engine.

Summary

There are many different kinds of malware. Not all malware is the same, or can be contained and stopped in the same way. In this chapter, you learned about different malware families and how they spread. This will help you to better plan your defense strategy. The next chapter is dedicated to vulnerabilities and exploits, which are some of the most powerful weapons that hackers can use to compromise a system and perform malicious activities.

Vulnerabilities and Exploits

7

In almost all engineering fields, it is very common to analyze past failures so that we can learn and improve on the current situation. According to the US Department of Homeland Security, 90% of security incidents are the result of exploiting software defects. Many developers are therefore testing their software before releasing it. These tests happen either on-premise or in the cloud. However, they often focus on user ability, performance, and somewhat synthetic security testing. Therefore, many developers are often unaware of security vulnerabilities in their software. There is no mandate or regulation on adapting a secure development life cycle or having a responsible vulnerability disclosure. It is therefore the responsibility of the individual and the broader security community to build more secure software and inform **independent software vendors** (**ISVs**) about potential vulnerabilities. In reality, many vulnerabilities in today's software exist in the source code for a while, but the ISV is simply unaware.

The following topics will be covered in this chapter:

- Detecting vulnerabilities
- Exploitation techniques
- Exploitation delivery

Detecting vulnerabilities

In 2014, Microsoft's **Trustworthy Computing** (**TwC**) division started the **Secure Development Lifecyle** (**SDL**) initiative. With this, the tech company introduced a software development process that's used by Microsoft itself to maintain costs and increase the reliability of software with regards to security-related bugs. The following diagram illustrates this process:

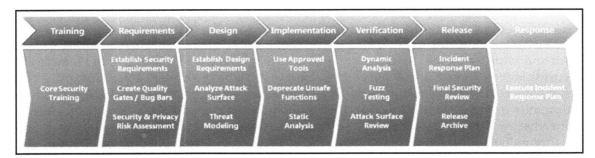

Tech companies and governments started working together to deliver a platform for a responsible vulnerability disclosure process. In addition, many tech companies started rewards programs, offering money for newly discovered vulnerabilities. As an example, Google started the Google **Vulnerability Reward Program** (**VRP**) where the reward for qualifying bugs ranged between $100 to $31,337 US dollars.

There have been many attempts to standardize vulnerability management. One of the most common approaches is the community-developed effort, **Common Weakness Enumeration** (**CWE**). While CWE allows you to enumerate and categorize software weaknesses, which can lead to vulnerabilities, this is very difficult to manage. CWE is supposed to bring a unified and measurable set of software weaknesses. However, there is a fear from many developers that documenting potential security vulnerabilities can be used against them. As a consequence, it's very rare that full vulnerability information can be found. Software vulnerabilities are different to software failures. Vulnerabilities allow an external person to maliciously use software for a different purpose. When a new software vulnerability is discovered, it can cause complex questions regarding how, when, and to whom to report the vulnerability. When this information is shared irresponsibly, threat actors might leverage the vulnerability in a harmful way.

The following diagram illustrates this process:

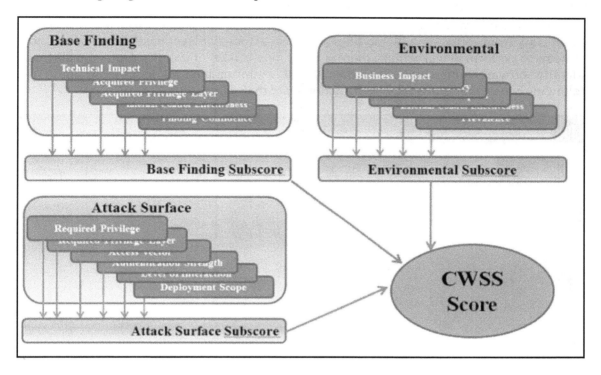

On the dark web, software vulnerabilities are traded; this is a growing market, particularly when diving into 0-day vulnerabilities. These vulnerabilities are unpatched and often undiscovered critical vulnerabilities that can be traded for up to $300,000. While the main beneficiary from software vulnerabilities are threat actors that leverage these to break into systems to perform illegal actions, there is also a new market of security professionals that identify software vulnerabilities and then offer this information back to the ISVs. The following screenshot is of a dark web auction store that sells exploits:

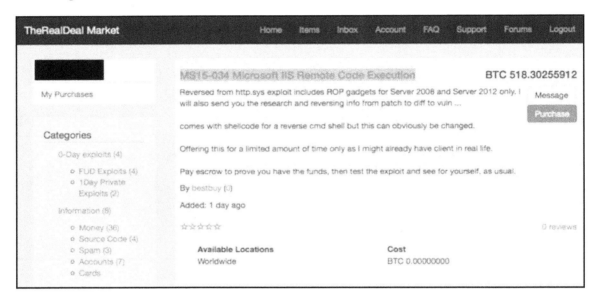

Exploitation techniques

Software can be very complex to build and maintain. Even after excessive testing, there is no guarantee that the software is free from any vulnerabilities. There are two kinds of company, those who know that they have been breached and those who don't. A perfect piece of software with no vulnerabilities does not exist. Hidden deep in the source code, there are always errors that can then lead to vulnerabilities that allow threat actors to be leveraged for exploitation. There are several methods that can be implemented in terms of exploitation, which will be addressed later in this chapter. It is important to understand their differences because the mitigation for each might be different. In this chapter, you will discover the most common exploitation techniques, all of which are illustrated as follows:

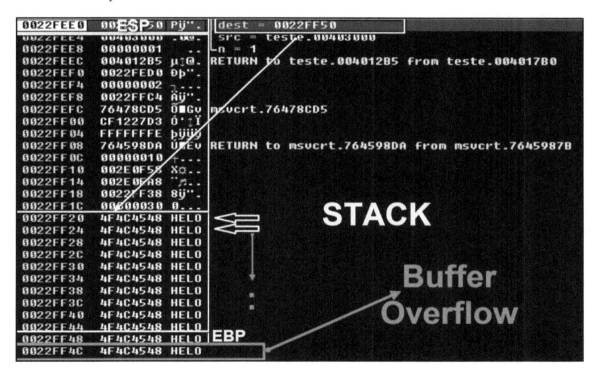

Buffer overflow

A buffer overflow occurs when software tries to store more data in the cache than it can hold. This technique allows threat actors to modify the target process address space. Buffer overflow is common in a few programming languages because they expose low-level information of data types. The programming language doesn't always operate bounds checking and can overwrite allocated buffers. The following screenshot illustrates a buffer overflow example:

Integer overflow

An integer overflow happens when the user tries to place an integer into memory space that is too large for the current integer data type that's in the system:

Memory corruption

Memory corruption is the most common programming error. This is very difficult to analyze because the source of analysis, that is, the memory space, is corrupted, making any correlation near enough impossible.

Format string attacks

A format string exploit occurs when the data that's submitted by the threat actor is evaluated as a command by the software. This allows the threat actor to execute code, read the memory space, or cause software crashes:

```
                                                      Terminal          -  + x
File  Edit  View  Search  Terminal  Help
ilroy@dallas ~/vulnerable $ vi format.c
ilroy@dallas ~/vulnerable $ vi formatstr.c
ilroy@dallas ~/vulnerable $ ./formatstr %x
1064b2e
ilroy@dallas ~/vulnerable $ cat formatstr.c
include <stdio.h>
include <string.h>
include <stdlib.h>

int main(int argc, char *argv[])
{
        char *x=(char *)malloc(40);
        strncpy(x,argv[1],40);
        printf(x);
        printf("\n");
        return(0);
}
ilroy@dallas ~/vulnerable $
```

Race condition

A race condition is a behavior in which the output of a piece of software is dependent on the timing or sequence of uncontrollable events. A race condition can cause software errors as well as device crashes.

Cross-site scripting

Cross-site scripting is an exploitation technique that's typically leveraged against web applications. This also allows threat actors to inject malicious client-side scripts into legitimate web applications. When the end user uses the web application, the malicious exploit gets loaded and can bypass access controls. The following diagram illustrates this process:

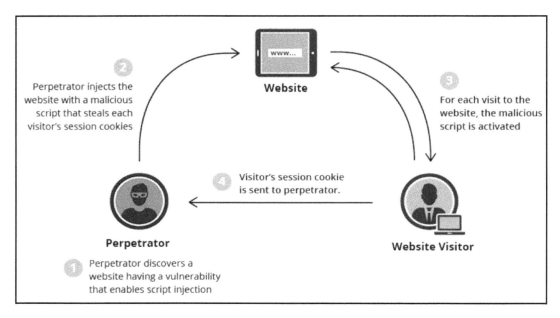

One-click attack

One-click attacks are also commonly referred to as cross-site request forgeries. One-click attacks are malicious exploit techniques where unauthorized commands are delivered to web applications from a trusted source. The following diagram illustrates the process of a one-click attack:

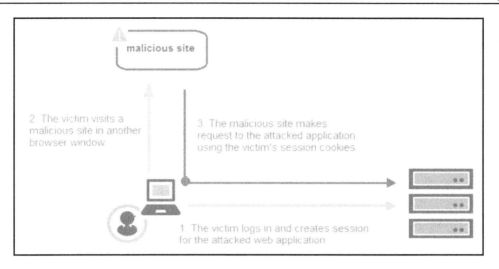

SQL injections

Threat actors use SQL injections to compromise data-driven applications by injecting malicious code. As a result, it may destroy your database. SQL injection is one of the most commonly used exploit techniques. The following diagram illustrates this exploitation technique:

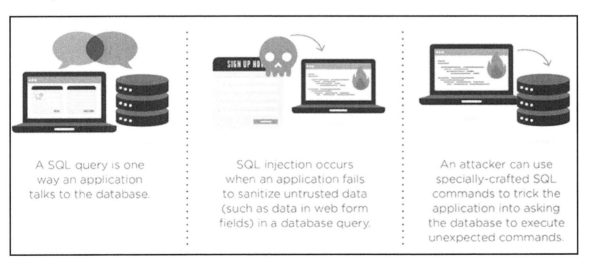

Exploitation delivery

There are two different mechanisms regarding how an exploit reaches the target. It can be delivered through the network internally or externally, which is classified as remote exploitation. Alternatively, it can be delivered locally through an inside job, which, in that case, would be a local exploit. Due to the ongoing push of digital transformation and mobility, it is near to impossible to imagine any enterprise without internet connectivity. Therefore, remote exploitation is the preferred delivery mechanism because it allows the threat actor to hide.

Summary

In this chapter, you have learned about the core concepts of vulnerabilities and exploits. We have dived into their different exploitation techniques such as buffer overflow, race condition, and memory corruption, and how exploits are delivered by threat actors. The next chapter will deep dive into the online economy and related security systems.

Further reading

- *Infrastructure: The Greatest Cyberattack Vulnerability*: https://online.norwich.edu/academic-programs/masters/information-security-assurance/resources/infographics/infrastructure-the-greatest-cyberattack-vulnerability
- *Reducing Vulnerability in Cyber Security*: https://online.uttyler.edu/articles/reducing-vulnerability-cyber-security.aspx
- *What is a Zero-Day Exploit?*: https://cybersecurity.osu.edu/cybersecurity-you/avoid-threats/what-zero-day-exploit

8
Attacking Online Banking Systems

Everyday, people use the internet in order to perform online bank transactions, purchase presents, and exchange personal and business information. In the United States alone, 70.4% of all adult internet users are leveraging digital banking, as depicted in the following diagram:

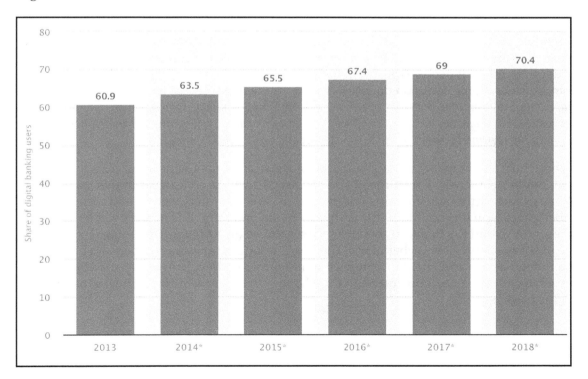

The financial services sector with its banks, e-commerce platforms, insurance companies, accountancy companies, and stock brokerages are aware of the importance of internet and therefore are transforming their business models to ensure their consumers are always able to reach them. Today, it's pretty much impossible to imagine having a bank account with a bank that doesn't offer online banking to perform quick transactions or even a bank without a smartphone app that allows the consumer to check their current balance. All of that data that companies in the financial services industry are now making accessible through the internet to their end customers used to be physically secured and only accessible when the end customer visited one of the company branches. However, with digital transformation, globalization, and the internet, this has changed and all of this personal information and these secrets aren't accessible through the internet in order to make it more convenient for the end customer.

While this helps the end customer to perform most of their regular interactions online, it also adds new security challenges and risks to the company. It's no longer only about the physical security of the premises by making sure that surveillance cameras and biometric fingerprint scans at the gates are installed. It's now about how to identity and protect against cybercrime. Digital banking and online banking are a good example. Today, online banking can be considered a must in many geographic locations and it's still rapidly spreading around the globe. Banks face multiple challenges from a security perspective when offering online banking. The service needs to be built with data privacy and defense in depth in mind. It needs to ensure it has protection against fraud as well as end customer compromises. Some common questions to ask yourself are: *how do we ensure that, even if the end customers computer is compromised, the cybercriminal is unable to perform an online transaction?* Or: *how do we detect whether the end user who is logging into the smartphone app is actually the legitimate owner of the bank account and not a cybercriminal?*

Cybercriminals are aware of the digital transformation of the financial services industry and, therefore, there's an upsurge of attacks directed within companies in this industry. While cybersecurity and ensuring companies are able to protect, detect, and respond to cyber attacks are important for any company in any industry, it is in fact even more important within the financial services sector because of the potential damage to society in the event of a large-scale cyberattack. Therefore, financial service providers are bound to many regulations and are in urgent need of modernizing their preventative and post-breach technologies and processes. In this chapter, the focus will be on attacks toward online banking.

Online banking benefits for financial services

It's important to note that providing online banking to the client isn't just about ease of use for the end customer. It also offers several benefits to the financial institute. It's important to understand them so that you're able to reflect on why the business is pushing for modernization in this sector. Banks that offer an online banking service are able to reduce costs, given the fact that many transactions are made online and the end customer no longer needs to visit a branch. This is, for the most part, the primary motivator for many banks. In addition, product placements ensure additional cross-sell opportunities; as an example, the typical online banking app won't only offer end customer the ability to perform transactions but also enable them to request at a fingertip a personal loan or apply for a new credit card. With these in mind, the financial institute is increasing the retention of its most profitable end customers.

The online banking process

Regardless of whether it's done over a computer or smartphone, online banking follows the same process. It's important to understand the process so you can then understand how attacks to the platform occurs. On a high level, the end customer logs in to the online banking platform of the bank through a web browser, computer application, or smartphone application and then the person is able to perform certain actions. The bare minimum security in that case is the identity verification using a username and password. In this day and age, this is however no longer sufficient.

The following steps illustrate the online banking process:

- The user uses their computer or smartphone to access the online banking website.
- The user is requested to provide their username and password to access their bank account.
- Data is securely transferred through the SSL to the bank server.
- The bank decrypts the information and validates the user identity.
- The bank grants access to the user and they're able to access their bank account.

Attack techniques

There's an urgent need for the financial services sector to modernize their security procedures, making sure that security procedures cover modern threats that are emerging particularly through the digital estate. Worldwide, many of the security procedures from banks are outdated and are useful only to fight against legacy threats. Because of the growing number of online transactions, it's therefore critical to re-evaluate security procedures and modernize them. In order to do that without the influence of scare marketing done by many security vendors, it's therefore critical to deeply understand the attack techniques and vulnerabilities that cybercriminals are using to disrupt the business. Most exploitation techniques are placed online, and end customers are lured into either downloading malware or running it directly from the web. With the malware on the computer or being executed, the threat actor now uses the following techniques to exfiltrate account numbers and personal identifiers and attempts to perform fraud transactions:

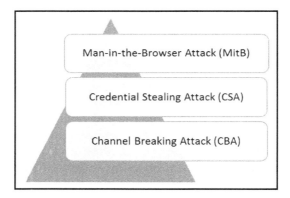

- **Man-in-the-Browser Attack**: A Trojan infects the web browser and takes advantage of a browser vulnerability, which allows the cybercriminal to modify web pages and transaction content to insert malicious code. Many companies in the financial services sector consider MitB as the greatest threat to their service.
- **Credential Stealing Attack**: Cybercriminals commonly use a phishing campaign to lure the legit credentials of a victim. Typically, this is the first stage of a credential-based cyber-attack.
- **Channel Breaking Attack**: CBA is the process whereby the supposedly secure communication between the end customer and the bank is intercepted.

There are, at the moment, many regulatory modernizations on-going, requiring companies to report data breaches. In the past, it was well known that many companies in the financial services sector would attempt to hide cyberattacks and data breaches because of their reputation being at stake as a trustful partner. It has become integral for banks to ensure that they're able to truly authenticate the end customer and to enforce security controls such as multi-factor authentication to make it as difficult as possible to be tampered with. Most online banking platforms today use an old model that has a single point of failure, mainly because the solution relies on a shared secret between the end customer and the bank and an element that only the end customer should own. In this case, the shared secret are plain text credentials and the element that only the end customer should own could be, for example, a fingerprint stored on a computer or a previously registered smartphone. Today, we know that this is no longer sufficient to combat against cybercrime. All that's required for a cybercriminal is to intercept the credentials during transmission and to compromise the end customer's smartphone.

With that in mind, online banking attacks can happen at three points in the process: on the client itself, regardless of whether it's a personal computer or mobile device; on the network layer between the end customer device and the bank's communication; and server side at the bank.

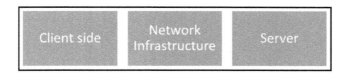

During reconnaissance, the threat actor will choose the entry point that's the easiest to attack, which for the most part will be always the client and likely originate through a phishing campaign.

Summary

This chapter has helped you to understand the key reasons why the financial services industry is pushing IT and security to enable online banking scenarios and how threat actors are looking into breaking into it. The next chapter will introduce you to the most important aspects of cybersecurity which are related to communication and network protocols.

Further reading

The following are resources that can be used to gain more knowledge on this chapter:

- *Internet Banking Attacks*: https://www.dcit.cz/papers/CEPOL_Internet-Banking-Attacks.pdf
- *Highlighting the Vulnerabilities of Online Banking System*: http://www.icommercecentral.com/open-access/highlighting-the-vulnerabilities-of-online-banking-system.pdf

Vulnerable Networks and Services - a Gateway for Intrusion

9

Communication and network protocols form a big part of the cyber-attack landscape. Therefore, many threats are directed toward the networks or communication channels used by people, systems, and devices. At a time when there are millions of IoT devices, employees bringing their personal devices to the workplace due to BYOD, the adoption of the cloud, and many organizations depending on web-based systems, this is obvious why cyber criminals consider networks and communication channels a sweet spot to carry out attacks. There are therefore many attack techniques and tools that have been developed purposefully to exploit common vulnerabilities in networks and communication channels. This chapter will examine them in the following topics:

- Vulnerable network protocols and network intrusions
- Attacking web servers and web-based systems:
    - Online login and password cracking
    - Bypassing web protection
    - Defeating firewalls
- WiFi- and Bluetooth-hacking tools and techniques
- Vulnerable network devices

Vulnerable network protocols and network intrusions

Networks, including the internet, were established at a time when there were hardly any cybersecurity threats aimed at them. Therefore, a lot of focus was given to aspects such as performance and speed. Since there was no security design during the establishment of early networks, several adoptions have had to be incorporated due to shifts such as increased cybersecurity threats. However, this is becoming a catch-up game and hackers are unfortunately growing more powerful. This has seen several vulnerabilities being discovered in network protocols. The following are some internet protocols that are increasingly becoming insecure.

Simple Mail Transfer Protocol

Simple Mail Transfer Protocol (**SMTP**) is used for email purposes by many organizations. This protocol was added to the internet and it quickly became the simplest way for people and organizations to send and receive emails. However, there has been an explosion of threats targeting the SMTP protocol that many organizations use. Since SMTP wasn't conceived with these security issues in mind, it has become the burden of network administrators to secure it. One of the ways that SMTP is attacked is account enumeration. This is normally done by spammers and phishers when harvesting emails. Account enumeration verifies whether an email account is registered on a certain server by running an SMTP command called VRFY on port 25. The response obtained shows whether or not the email is valid.

Secure Sockets Layer

Secure Sockets Layer (**SSL**) has been understood by many people as the ultimate check of security. Users are being advised to check whether a website has SSL before they submit private data to it. SSL works by encrypting data exchanged between a host and server thus making it hardly possible for a hacker to intercept and read the contents of the traffic. However, there is a challenge with this approach toward cybersecurity as the ultimate check for security. SSL has been active since 1996 and has never received any update despite the increased sophistication of hacking techniques. There have been several attacks against SSL security that have made browsers such as Chrome and Firefox want to scrap SSL. The answer to SSL has been **Transport Layer Security** (**TLS**) but it isn't without flaws. TLS came in 1999 as a successor of SSL version 3.0 but still SSL is more commonly used on the internet.

TLS is a crypto-protocol used in internet communications to provide end-to-end encryption for all data exchanged between a client and a server. It's more secure than SSL but still faces its fair share of cyber attacks. One of the attacks against TLS is known as BEAST and is registered as CVE-2011-3389 by the CVE database. In this attack, the attacker injects their own packets into the stream of SSL traffic and this enables them to determine how the traffic is being decrypted and thus decrypt the traffic. Another attack against SSL is POODLE, which is registered as CVE-2014-3566 by the CVE database. POODLE is an ingenious way of attacking SSL used in man-in-the-middle attacks. When a client initiates the SSL handshake, the attacker intercepts the traffic and masquerades as the server and then requests the client to downgrade to SSL 3.0. The POODLE attack happens when the attacker replaces the padding bytes in packets and then forwards the packets to the real server. Servers don't check for values in the padding, they're only concerned with the message-authentication code of the plaintext and the padding length. The man-in-the-middle will then observe the response from the server to know what the plaintext message sent by the real client was.

Domain Name System

Domain Name System (DNS) is the protocol that ensures domain names are translated into IP addresses. However, this protocol is old, flawed, and open to attacks. A hacking group was once able to exploit the working of the protocol causing users that wanted to visit `twitter.com` to be redirected to a different domain. Therefore, should a significant number of threat actors decide to redirect visitors of some websites to different or malicious sites, they can do this through DNS attacks. This is where hackers swap the correct IP address of a website with a rogue IP address. There have been fixes being developed but they have had effects on performance and thus have not been implemented. More applicable fixes are still being developed. Apart from the internet, there are other attacks that are regularly directed at organizational networks. These are more successful due to the narrow scope within which attackers have to focus. The following are some of these attacks.

Packet sniffing

This is where an attacker reads all data that's being exchanged in a network, especially if it's unencrypted. Surprisingly, there are many free and open source programs that can be used to do this, such as Wireshark. Public networks, such as cafe WiFi hotspots, are some of the areas where hackers regularly use these programs to record, read, and analyze the traffic flowing through the network.

Distributed denial of service

Distributed denial of service (**DDoS**) is an increasingly common attack that has been proven to be successful against big targets. Since the 2016 attack on Dyn, one of the largest domain-resolution companies, hackers have been motivated to use this attack on many organizations. There are ready vendors on the dark web that can rent out their botnets to be used for DDoS attacks for a given duration. One of the most feared botnets is Mirai, which is primarily composed of many IoT devices. DDoS attacks are aimed at directing a lot of illegitimate traffic to a network – more than can be handled – thus causing it to crash or be unable to handle legitimate requests. DDoS attacks are particularly of great concern to organizations that offer their products or services via websites as the attack makes it impossible for business processes to take place.

Attacking web servers and web-based systems

Web servers and web-based systems are widely adopted by organizations and agencies for their convenience. Users are able to access various functionalities from these systems. For instance, one can make money transfers using online-banking websites without having to physically go to the bank. Some organizations run web-based ERPs to help. However, these systems are normally exposed to all the threat actors on the internet. Therefore, they can be taken down from anywhere, provided that the attacker has the right tools or uses the right techniques. The following are some of the attacks facing web servers and web-based systems.

SQL injection

This is an old attack but it still works since there are websites that don't follow best practices in their design. SQL injection is an attack where the attacker provides a malicious SQL statement. The statement is made in a way such that once the website tries to process it in the backend, it'll inadvertently execute the statement. Statements, among other things, can be written to delete databases, retrieve data from the database, and modify the data. The attack is effective against websites that don't validate the input provided by users. Just a small addition of some special code to prevent executable commands from being passed directly to the database can secure a website from this attack. The following screenshot shows an example of SQL injection:

Buffer overflow

This is an attack that involves overflowing the buffer memory that's supposed to handle the input that goes into a web-based system or app. Before a user gives an input, applications will have set apart some memory purposefully meant to hold the input provided. However, malicious actors can provide data that fills this buffer, causing other users to be unable to successfully give input into the app.

Advanced Google search operators

Since Google crawls the whole internet, it comes as no surprise that all the data it collects can be exploited. Advanced Google search operators are used to retrieve data that would ordinarily be hidden from public view. Since some web servers are managed in a poor manner, some sensitive files are often kept in the wrong folders that can be visible to the public. An advanced Google search operator can unearth these files. The advanced search queries can also be used to dig out more details about an organization's employee for the purpose of collecting information for social-engineering purposes.

Brute-force attacks

Most organizations will have an authentication process to give their employees or users access to web-based systems. Usernames tend to be common. In some organizations, the username is a combination of the user's first and last name appended to the domain name of the organization. Organizations expect that users will secure their passwords instead. Users are particularly weak when it comes to passwords. The average user will hardly adhere to best practices of using different passwords per site, using complex passwords and regularly changing their passwords. Brute-forcing is aimed at cracking username-password combinations by trying all possible combinations. Brute-forcing is effective when the hacker knows some details about the user, such as birth date, real names, and their pet name, among other pieces of data that users include in their passwords.

IBM identifies the following as the common types of brute-force attacks:

- **Dictionary attacks**: These are performed using tools that try username and password combinations from a file known as the dictionary. The dictionary usually contains commonly-used username/password combinations as well as words from data collected about a certain target.
- **Search attack**: This attack covers all the possible combinations of each character in a defined password length. It takes long but is highly effective.
- **Rule-based search attacks**: This is a variation of the search attack, in which rules are used to generate the passwords from parts of usernames or predefined words. For instance, to attack an account with a username called mike@xyz.com, the attack can be configured to generate password variations with the name "mike".

The following are some of the tools used for brute-force attacks.

Medusa

This is a password-cracking tool that is effective against HTTP, IMPA, MySQL, MS SQL, POP 3, SNMP, SSH, and other protocols. The tool gives the attacker room to guess some of the input for either the username or password fields. The tool can try 2,000 passwords in 60 seconds on a login interface. The tool can also be used in parallel attacks. Therefore, it could be used to crack the passwords to a website backend and at the same time, used to guess the passwords of accounts linked to the website. The following screenshot is of Medusa:

```
                    MEDUSA

Medusa v2.0 [http://www.foofus.net] (C) JoMo-Kun / Foofus Networks <jmk@foofus.net>


Syntax: Medusa [-h host|-H file] [-u username|-U file] [-p password|-P file] [-C file] -M module [OPT]
  -h [TEXT]    : Target hostname or IP address
  -H [FILE]    : File containing target hostnames or IP addresses
  -u [TEXT]    : Username to test
  -U [FILE]    : File containing usernames to test
  -p [TEXT]    : Password to test
  -P [FILE]    : File containing passwords to test
  -C [FILE]    : File containing combo entries. See README for more information.
  -O [FILE]    : File to append log information to
  -e [n/s/ns]  : Additional password checks ([n] No Password, [s] Password = Username)
  -M [TEXT]    : Name of the module to execute (without the .mod extension)
  -m [TEXT]    : Parameter to pass to the module. This can be passed multiple times with a
                 different parameter each time and they will all be sent to the module (i.e.
                 -m Param1 -m Param2, etc.)
  -d           : Dump all known modules
  -n [NUM]     : Use for non-default TCP port number
  -s           : Enable SSL
  -g [NUM]     : Give up after trying to connect for NUM seconds (default 3)
  -r [NUM]     : Sleep NUM seconds between retry attempts (default 3)
  -R [NUM]     : Attempt NUM retries before giving up. The total number of attempts will be NUM + 1.
  -t [NUM]     : Total number of logins to be tested concurrently
  -T [NUM]     : Total number of hosts to be tested concurrently
  -L           : Parallelize logins using one username per thread. The default is to process
```

Brutus

This is a remote password-cracking tool that's designed to be used against online systems. The tool is quick and flexible with the support of HTTP, POP3, FTP, and SMB, among others. The tool can be used against multi-stage authentication systems as it'll continually feed login credentials until one goes through. It can work in parallel against a maximum of sixty targets. It also supports pausing and resuming password-attack processes. The following is an example of Brutus:

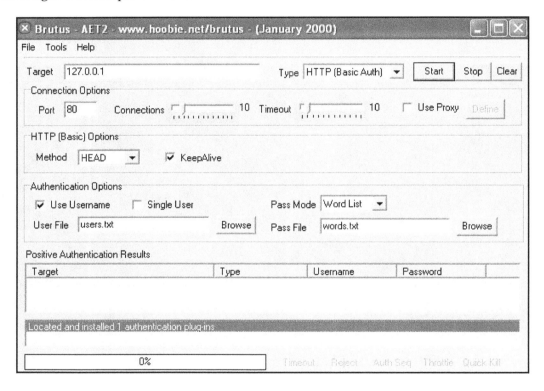

Bypassing web protection

Normally, websites have been adding an extra layer of security to their web-based systems to prevent the discussed attacks and many others. Mostly, these additional layers of security prevent automated attacks from being done on login interfaces. However, hackers have devised ways to beat these additional layers of security. The following are some of the ways used to bypass different types of web protection.

Bypassing captcha

Captchas are normally enabled on websites that don't tolerate bots, so all user have to prove that they're human. Here's an example of a captcha screen:

To bypass a captcha screen, one has to know the code behind it. The following is the code used to generate the preceding captcha screen:

```
>form action="/captcha/captchaCheck" method="post">
  >input name="hash" value="09573e52f752f3f5e6250b62aa34b8a8c08a4d22"
type="hidden">
  >input name="emailAddress" value="test@email.com" type="hidden">
  >input name="name" value="" type="hidden">
  >input name="enteredValue" size="25" type="text">
  >input value="Subscribe" type="submit">
  >/form>
```

A captcha is designed to allow the user to access the website if they enter a value that matches what's expected. The expected value is normally hashed and supplied with each unique captcha screen. Therefore, to beat the captcha, one needs to make sure that they can generate a value that matches the hash. Hackers mostly run the hash through tools that can decrypt hashed values. By running the hashed value against a tool known as dcipher, the following is the output:

```
MacBook-Pro-de-akita:scripts ak1t4$ dcipher 09573e52f752f3f5e6250b62aa34b8a8c08a4d22
✔ 605856
MacBook-Pro-de-akita:scripts ak1t4$
```

As can be seen from the screenshot, the decrypted value matches that on the captcha screen. With this knowledge, hackers can automate the process of bypassing captcha codes using bots. All the bot has to do is retrieve the hashed value, run it against tools that decipher hashes, and then supply the value to the website through a POST request.

Bypassing two-factor authentication

Two-factor authentication has been promoted by many organizations as the watertight authentication procedure that ensures only the right owner of an account can access it. It significantly reduces the chances of hacking by requiring two types of authentication. Therefore, even if a hacker has cracked an account's password, they will be barred from accessing the account by the second authentication factor. In many cases, this is a code sent to a user's phone number or email. Exploiting this type of authentication is hard. However, hackers commonly use two ways to pass through it. The first way is through social engineering. Since the owner of the account will be sent the second factor of authentication, it can be stolen right from them. For instance, if a user's account password is cracked and a code is sent to the owner's phone number, there's an easy way that hackers can steal it. The hackers can initiate contact with the account owner, informing the user that they're from the affected website and are confirming the details of the account owner. They can then ask for the code from the real account owner. The owner will simply give the code to the hacker.

The second way of bypassing two-factor authentication is by exploiting the technicality involved with it. In some cases, two-factor authentication is not enabled during account-recovery. Therefore, a hacker can simply click on account recovery and follow the steps given until they are granted access to the account. Even though two-factor authentication may be required for the next login, the account-recovery process will give the hackers complete access to the account.

Bypassing firewalls

Firewalls are implemented in networks to filter out traffic that may be malicious to devices in organizations. The firewall checks the traffic flow to identify whether it's coming from malicious sources or is abnormal, and prevents it from flowing into a network. However, hackers also have ways to bypass firewall security and get their malicious traffic into an organizational network: using a malware known as Hikit rootkit. The malware interferes with the hardware firewall that blocks the hackers from the targets. The hacker, therefore, has to first compromise the firewall and get admin privileges. Once this is done, the malware will channel traffic from hackers through the allowed ports. This won't trigger alarms from the firewall since it'll already be compromised by the hackers.

The other way to bypass firewalls is by doing a client-side attack. If a client makes a connection with a malicious website that isn't known by the firewall, the connection won't trigger the firewall. Therefore, if the client connects to a website that exploits browser vulnerabilities, reads stored passwords, or steals cookies, the firewall won't be able to do anything to intervene. This is why organizations warn their users against clicking on links in emails from strangers. These links could be to malicious websites that aren't known by the firewalls that can carry out client-side attacks.

Lastly, firewalls can be bypassed through the fragmentation of packets. There are tools that can enable hackers to know how firewalls that protect an organization are configured. With this, they can configure traffic that can bypass the rules. The common way of doing this is by fragmenting a packet. This causes the traffic not to trigger the firewall, since each packet doesn't have enough data that the firewall can use to determine whether it's a threat. To catch these threats, the firewall has to be reconfigured to recollect the entire fragmented packet and then inspect it, but most firewalls don't have this configuration.

Hacking wireless networks

Wireless networks are attack surfaces that attackers take advantage of if they can connect to them. In WiFi networks, there are two broad categories of vulnerabilities that can be exploited. The first vulnerability comes from poor configuration, while the second one is as a result of weak encryption. Poor configuration is normally caused by network admins that set up the network incorrectly. Poor encryption comes up as a result of the keys used to protect the network.

Hacking wireless networks

The following are some of the tools that are used to attack wireless networks.

Aircrack-ng

This is a popular suite of tools used to crack WiFi networks within bands 802.11a/b/g. Aircrack is made up of algorithms that can recover WiFi passwords simply by capturing packets that are flowing through the network. When it has captured enough packets, it attempts to recover the password used to protect the WiFi network. The attack starts with the activation of Airmon-ng. This is a mode that makes a host's wireless network card promiscuous. Instead of receiving only the packets that are intended for it, it starts receiving all packets. After this, Airdump-ng is activated and this enables it to capture packets. The captured packets are used to crack passwords. When packets are captured, Aircrack-ng is activated and it uses some statistical techniques against WEP-secured WiFi networks and then employs dictionary attacks for WPA and WPA2. Once the key has been cracked, the attacker can do much more with the Aircrack-ng suite of tools. They can use Airdecap-ng to decrypt all traffic that flows through the network. Lastly, the suite includes Airbase-ng, which can be used to turn an ordinary laptop's wireless card into a rogue access point that shares the name of a legitimate access point. All devices that will connect to the rogue access point will be easily attacked. Here's an example of Aircrack-ng cracking a password:

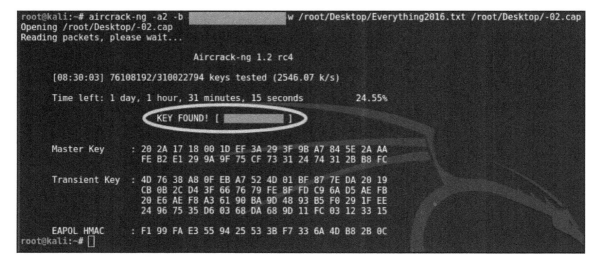

Kismet

Kismet is a tool used when stealth is of importance in an attack, since it works passively. The tool doesn't send any loggable packets, which reduces the potential for detection. It, however, can detect hidden wireless access points and clients, and then associate them with each other. Its main features are that it does sniffing on WiFi networks, can give XML output, can be operated remotely, and is able to capture traffic from multiple sources. Kismet can be used to spy on users since it can scan for all available wireless network channels in a certain area. Kismet is able to determine the activity of devices connected to a wireless network. Therefore, it can know when a laptop is streaming videos or when a gaming console is being used, as long as they are connected to a WiFi network that it can analyze. A hacker with Kismet can discover all electronic devices in a user's home that are connected to the WiFi network. This information can be given to thieves, especially when expensive devices are detected in a user's house. Here's a screenshot of Kismet:

Wireshark

Wireshark isn't necessarily an attack tool, it's designed to be a protocol analyzer. It, however, happens to have functionalities that would appeal to hackers since they appeal to network admins. Wireshark can be used to capture packets flowing in a network. Once these packets are captured, they can be analyzed carefully so that their origin, destination, and contents are known. Plaintext messages and credentials that are sent unencrypted will easily be stolen using this tool. The biggest advantage of using Wireshark is that it can capture packets over a long period of time, thus giving an attacker a rich source of information about an organization's network.

Hacking Bluetooth

Bluetooth is a wireless network protocol that is designed for low-power consumption and near-field communication. Bluetooth can connect any two devices that have such capability, and when they connect, they are paired. For devices to pair, they have to exchange a pre-shared key, which is stored for future pairing. Beyond this, there is hardly any other form of security that protects Bluetooth devices, and this opens them to a wide range of attacks. The following are some of the ways Bluetooth networks are hacked:

- **Bluesnaring**: This is an attack where data, such as SMS messages, is stolen from a Bluetooth-enabled device.
- **Bluebugging**: This is an attack where an attacker gains control over a target's phone through a Bluetooth connection.
- **Bluesmack**: This is a DoS attack against Bluetooth devices.

To perform these attacks, special tools that are used. Some of the tools are as described here:

- **Bluelog**: This is a tool used to scan an area, find all discoverable Bluetooth devices, and then log them.
- **Blueranger**: This is a script used to find the location of Bluetooth devices by estimating the distances between them.
- **Redfang**: This tool is used to discover all hidden Bluetooth devices.

Vulnerable network devices

A group of vulnerabilities in networks are those that come from the network device themselves. These vulnerabilities are normally a result of manufacturer error and, once discovered by attackers, can be exploited in any organization that uses the affected network devices. Before these devices can be patched by the manufacturer, data remains exposed to attackers. Taking them offline could prove to be difficult, especially in large organizations that can't afford downtime. Therefore, it isn't surprising to find that some vulnerable network devices are still in use, despite this known by network admins. It's estimated that 73% of all organizations are using vulnerable networking devices.

Here's a snippet from an article on vulnerable network devices:

> *"73% of companies are using vulnerable, end-of-life networking equipment, up from 60% last year, according to a review of more than 212,000 Cisco networking devices at 350 organizations across North America."*

This only shows that it's easy for determined attackers to bring down most organizations, due to the reluctance of network admins to remove vulnerable devices from the network. One of the network devices known to have vulnerabilities is the Linksys E1000 router. The router has a vulnerability that allows malware to be installed in it, and then take advantage of remote administration interfaces. This can be used by hackers to get quick access to a network. Another vulnerable network device still in use is the Asus RT series router. The router has been found to contain multiple vulnerabilities. These vulnerabilities can be used to allow unauthenticated access into a network, expose usernames and passwords, give hackers access to content stored in removable devices plugged into the router, and enable hackers to reconfigure the router. There are many other vulnerabilities in networking equipment that lead to the estimation of 73% being vulnerable.

Summary

The chapter looked at network and communication protocols as gateways for intrusions. It explained why these two form such a big part of the cyber-attack landscape. The chapter explained several network protocols that have already become unsecured and can be exploited by attackers, such as SMTP, SSL, and DNS. We explained how each of these protocols can be attacked, along with examples of the attacks. We then covered some examples of common network attacks, such as packet-sniffing and DDoS.

Our focus then shifted to web servers and web-based systems, which is another favorite attack landscape for hackers. We discussed some of the attack techniques that are used to compromise web-based systems, including SQL injection, buffer overflow, advanced Google search queries, and brute-force attacks. We took a close look at brute-force attacks that are aimed at cracking passwords. Then we discussed two particularly effective tools for cracking passwords: Medusa and Brutus. We noted that organizations have been adapting to these and other threats by incorporating additional layers of security into their web-based systems. The most common forms of protection are captchas, two-factor authentication, and firewalls. We looked into all of these and identified how they can be bypassed.

Finally, we looked at wireless network hacking, and focused on WiFi and Bluetooth. We discussed tools used to attack WiFi networks, such as Aircrack-ng, Wireshark, and Kismet. Then we looked at Bluetooth and listed its flaws. We covered the various ways Bluetooth can be compromised, as well as the tools that can be used to exploit it.

The next chapter will cover in-depth what a cybersecurity incident is and how to establish an incident response plan.

Further reading

The following are resources that can be used to gain more knowledge on the topics covered in this chapter:

- *73% of companies using vulnerable end-of-life networking devices*: https://www.csoonline.com/article/3124937/networking/73-of-companies-using-vulnerable-end-of-life-networking-devices.html
- *Vulnerable Network Devices: A Growing Concern*: https://www.acunetix.com/blog/articles/vulnerable-network-devices-growing-concern/
- *Bypassing Captcha Like a Boss*: https://medium.com/bugbountywriteup/bypassing-captcha-like-a-boss-d0edcc3a1c1
- *Bypassing hardware firewalls in 20 seconds*: https://www.csoonline.com/article/2601300/microsoft-subnet/bypassing-hardware-firewalls-in-20-seconds.html

10
Responding to Service Disruption

Organizations need to assume that they either have been or will be compromised. There's no organization that's immune against a cyberattack. On average it takes an organization up to 180 days till they discover that they've been compromised. That means that, for 180 days, your system is at risk without you knowing about it. Many organizations focus on purchasing the latest technologies but, when a cyberattack happens and the service is disrupted, they wonder why the technology didn't protect, detect, and/or respond to it. What these organizations forget is that cybersecurity is based on technology, people, and processes:

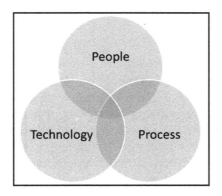

Technology is only as good as the humans responsible for it. People are only as good as they are trained to be. Processes are only as good as they're tested and optimized for. Organizations can have the best technology, but if the employees aren't trained on that technology or the organization doesn't have a proper process when and how to use the technology, then it's just wasted budget. This chapter will cover in-depth what a cybersecurity incident is and how to establish an incident response plan.

Cybersecurity incidents

A cybersecurity incident or information security incident is defined under ISO/IEC TR 18044:2004 as a *"single or a series of unwanted or unexpected information security events that have a significant probability of compromising business operations and threatening information security."* When a cybersecurity incident occurs, it very often causes service disruption because one or more IT services might be affected. These IT services might have been destroyed beyond recovery or forced to shut down or the threat actor is monitoring the IT system, preventing employees from continuing their work. In most cases, the threat actors follow a cyberattack kill chain that includes the injection of malware in the network. A cybersecurity incident by definition is either in the past or ongoing. The threat landscape is constantly evolving, and cybersecurity is a challenge yet, at the same time, n opportunity for all organizations regardless of geography, size, or industry.

Fundamentals

Before outlining an incident response plan, it's essential to understand the fundamentals that need to be in place in order to ensure that the organization is set up for success during a cybersecurity incident. An effective plan requires several critical aspects to be in place before establishing an incident response plan.

Data knowledge

Very often, cybersecurity experts will talk about *protecting the crown jewels of the company*. This can be customer data, research and development papers, or financial records. Even during a service disruption or even during the worst cyberattack, organizations want to make sure that their crown jewels are as best protected as possible. But in order to achieve that, organizations need to first understand what data exists, where this data is stored, and who can access it and under which conditions. Data exfiltration is one of the top motivators for threat actors, therefore; it's critical for an organization to know where the crown jewels are located and how they're protected. As part of a cybersecurity incident, organizations need to expect at any time the potential impact of the loss of data. Organizations, therefore, need to understand redundancies are in place and that the organizations are able to do a disaster recover when needed:

3 Copies of All Data · 2 Separate Secure Copies Saved Onsite · 1 Copy Saved Securely Offsite in the Cloud

Monitoring

The physical security team of any organization is used to monitor CCTV activities to detect potential physical incidents. In the IT space, this can't be any different. Organizations need to be able to detect a cybersecurity incident as fast as possible. In order to achieve that, organizations need to have appropriate monitoring in place.

Attack surface analysis

Attack surface analysis covers all aspects of how a threat actor might breach the environment and cause a service disruption. It is especially useful because an attack surface analysis offers the organization the chance to understand potential vulnerabilities along with associated risks. It covers software and network vulnerabilities as well as the human aspect. The following figure depicts the attack surface analysis process:

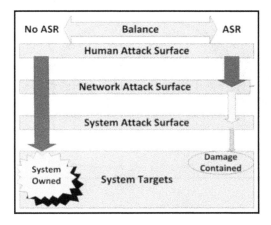

Vendor management

While it might not be the first incident that comes to mind when reading about cybersecurity incidents and incident response plans and how to respond to a service disruption, it's certainly also partially relevant to this space. When the supply chain team onboards new vendors, new agreements are signed. In these agreements, both parties agree on the terms in which they will do business with each other. Nowadays, many organizations have started to review their existing contracts to understand what are the contractual requirements of the vendors they have today during a cybersecurity incident and update the default system requirements to ensure that this section is indeed covered. Therefore, many organizations nowadays enforce a requirement to their vendors for immediate notification once a cyberattack has been discovered. In these terms, it should also grant the organization audit rights, which then can be encompassed as part of the incident response plan.

Incident response and management

A successful approach to incident response and management ensures that an organization is set up for success to protect their organizations information. This is achieved by developing and implementing an incident response plan. With that in place, organizations are able to protect, detect, and respond as fast as possible to a service disruption. The employees that are part of the **Security Operations Center** (**SOC**) and are tasked to follow the incident response plan bear responsibility for remediating as fast as possible any potential breach. The following diagram shows the most commonly adopted incident response plan approach, which will be detailed in this chapter:

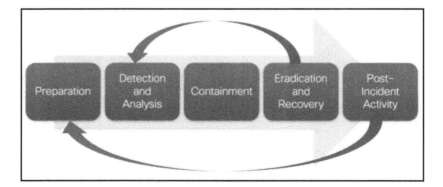

Phase 1 – preparation

The preparation phase is the starting point of an incident response plan. It summarizes all of the activities that are performed before a cybersecurity incident. Center to this phase is developing the incident response plan itself. What's important to understand is that an incident response plan isn't just a document created once and never looked at again, but instead becomes a living document inside the security operations team. When organizations start writing an incident response plan, it often gives them the opportunity to also reassess their current security controls and compare them to industry and vendor best practices. It allows them to detect any unknown point or unaware security loopholes. As the organization matures and handles more cybersecurity incidents, there will be learning outcomes, which will allow the organization to further optimize the incident response plan. Regardless of how many cyberattacks and service disruptions the individuals in the team might have experienced, there's always new learning available.

Phase 2 – detection and analysis

Detection and analysis is the phase where the security operations team need to determine whether there's a true cybersecurity incident and, once confirmed, determine quickly the scope of breach due to that cybersecurity incident. The team needs to be able to determine quickly whether a specific activity was done by an actual employee or potentially a threat actor that tries to mimic the behavior of an employee. As an example, when Microsoft Word launches on an endpoint that doesn't mean that a threat actor is doing anything. Microsoft Word is used by almost all organizations in the world and the chances of that individual activity to be malicious is unlikely. However, when, during analysis, it's determined that Microsoft Word executed in the background of a PowerShell script, this is a bit more unlikely. This is just one of thousands of examples on the level of detail that needs to be analyzed.

Phase 3 – containment

The containment phase is one of the most important phases as part of the incident response plan. In this phase, it's very likely that the containment phase will cause service disruption, but it's essential in order to ensure no further damage is caused. In this phase, the security team will attempt to contain the situation. The risk of not containing it and to just continue running operations is too high as it can cause not only short term, but also mid and long term, exponentially higher damage. Consider the scenario where a cyberattack isn't contained: the security team recovers an IT service and, once recovered, it's compromised again. This is because the cybersecurity incident hadn't been contained first before doing the recovery.

Phase 4 – eradication and recovery

Eradication and recovery are two separate processes that can potentially happen at the same time. With eradication, the organization ensures that it removes all of the artifacts and components associated with the cybersecurity incident. Some good examples for eradication are, for example, the deletion of the malware, deleting the emails received as part of the phishing campaign that were the entry point for the cyberattack, or disabling compromised user accounts. The recovery process is what the organization will always push the security team to perform as fast as possible. But it's important to not rush, stay calm, and follow the incident response plan. Remember, when recovering an environment, you want to make sure that the threat actor can't breach it seconds after recovery again. This step contains restoring the systems to an operational stage but also covers hardening the systems to ensure that the same attack pattern can't happen again.

Phase 5 – post-incident activity

As much as it's important to end the service disruption and enable the business to operate, it's also important to perform a post-mortem after resolving the cybersecurity incident. Cybersecurity is a continuous learning space and, only by learning from the past, can organizations can truly mature in their cybersecurity practice. In the post-incident activity phase, the team reviews the cybersecurity incident to deeply understand how the attack happened in the first place and what could have been done to prevent the attack happening, as well as how to improve the approach to incident response. The findings of the post-incident activity phase directly impact how phase 1 (preparation) is performed moving forward.

Summary

In this chapter, you've learned that cybersecurity isn't just about the technology. Technology is only as good as the person who uses it. It's about technology, people, and processes. When the service gets disrupted and when the threat actor is in your environment, don't panic. Panic will always lead to mistakes. Therefore, this chapter focused on providing you with insights, first, on what a cybersecurity incident is and, most importantly, on how you can respond to a service disruption by developing and implementing a successful incident response plan. The next chapter will briefly consider the human factor impacting the entire cybersecurity implementation including standard, policy, configuration, architecture and so on, from leader to doers.

Further reading

The following are resources that can be used to gain more knowledge on this chapter:

- *Incident management*: https://www.ncsc.gov.uk/incident-management
- *The National Cyber Incident Response Plan (NCIRP)*: https://www.us-cert.gov/ncirp
- *Guide - incident response plans*: https://www.cert.gov.au/ci-big-business/general-guidance/guide-incident-response-plans

11
The Human Problem - Governance Fail

It is said that humans are the weakest links in cybersecurity. Organizations can spend lots of resources setting up a top-class cybersecurity infrastructure, but a small mistake from a user can defeat the purpose of the security infrastructure. This is why organizations need to address the human factor when implementing cybersecurity plans, but unfortunately, that is exactly what they are not doing. Executives in organizations also believe that cybersecurity is the burden of the IT department. Executives, therefore, do not approve funding for initiatives or measures intended to have all users made aware of cybersecurity risks. As a result, statistics show that humans are some of the biggest causes of the losses incurred annually due to cybersecurity risks. According to NIST, a US body that provides a cybersecurity control framework, 35% of data breaches are normally attributed to humans. This translates to losses of $140 million globally due to human factors. Concerning the collaboration between cybersecurity and business, 47% of IT professionals say that it is poor. Even more disturbing, it is said that organizations only start addressing the human component after a security breach involving them has happened. Notably, the average cost of a security breach is over $1 million. Attack techniques and tools are also changing with each passing day. This chapter will focus on human factors and discuss them in the following topics:

- Business versus security
- Failing security management
- Careless online behaviors
- Insider threats
- Technological transformation of financial services
- Failure in implementing security policies

Business versus security

There is a challenge in many organizations in terms of the perception of cybersecurity. Most employees and particularly the executives believe that cybersecurity is just an IT problem. Therefore, the IT department should ensure at all times that all users are secured from all forms of cyber threats. However, it is high time that they realized that gone are the days when cybersecurity was only handled by the IT department. Cyber criminals evolved and stopped focusing on only attacking networks and computer systems. Attacks have become more sophisticated and new techniques are being used. A hack can happen simply as a result of an employee clicking on a link or answering a phone call. With policies such as **Bring Your Own Device (BYOD)**, personal devices infected with malware are being brought into organizations. The widespread use of IoT devices in organizations, especially in production lines, is a security nightmare. Supply chains are also being used as entry points of security threats. There is no way the IT department can be stretched to address all the threats coming from these threat landscapes. This is why everyone in the organization needs to be part of the cybersecurity team. However, due to costs, many organizations are choosing not to have all their employees trained in cybersecurity. They have all manners of justifications. The main justification is that the training costs money, yet there are no notable threats. Therefore, it is their belief that taking out some money and production time from the organization just to sensitize employees on security is a waste of resources.

Other than this, employees are disregarding security policies. They see them as restrictive, time-consuming, and an unnecessary burden. Therefore, the appropriate guidelines meant to keep the organization secure are not being followed. However, this perspective that employees and executives have adopted is demotivating and dangerous to the future of any organization. Threats are on the increase and many organizations, no matter the size, are soon going to face one threat or another. With untrained employees and disregard for security policies, it is becoming very easy for hackers to successfully breach organizations. When organizations are breached, business operations will come to a halt. There will be an interruption of services that are dependent on computer systems. The business will suffer from loss of brand, customers, and customer loyalty. In addition, there will be negative publicity. To top all this, the organization will lose money and most likely continue losing money to hackers. Therefore, executives ought to realize that business and cybersecurity are intertwined. Without cybersecurity, a business could possibly die off. This is why investments have to be made in terms of addressing the human factor that is a major cause of all cyber breaches annually.

Failing security management

Organizations are failing in security management. This is despite the fact that they are spending a lot of resources acquiring and implementing security products and security projects intended to secure their organizations. It is therefore quite depressing to see that most of this money being lost due to poor security management. There are several causes of the failure in security management. They include the following.

Lack of adoption of cybersecurity initiatives

The first cause of failure is the lack of adoption of cybersecurity initiatives in the organization. Cybersecurity initiatives need to be adopted by the organization's executives in order to be successful. If at all the initiative does not sell to them, it will not be successfully implemented. Executives will not buy into an initiative that is not aligned with the organization's objectives. Therefore, IT staff must be able to prove that the initiatives they want to implement in the organization are beneficial to the organization's objectives. Executives are mostly non-technical, therefore, they need to be slowly taken through the advantages of new initiatives, such as the requirement of all employees to use password managers. If they are left to identify the advantages of these initiatives on their own, they will most likely take the short route of rejecting the initiatives. Therefore, IT security managers need to be good at directing the attention of executives to the serious IT problem, explaining how these problems can affect the business, and then obtaining a buy-in from the executives.

Lack of organization and planning

Another reason for the failing security management in many organizations is the lack of organization and planning. It is said that most IT projects fail and very few projects end within the scope or budget that was initially projected. Cybersecurity projects lack proper planning. When IT security managers obtain the buy-in from executives to proceed with an initiative, they need to be prepared in terms of the deliverables and milestones that the project will have. Poor definition of outcomes is one of the key factors in the failure of IT projects. The project also needs to have the right staffing as technical skills are of importance in IT projects. The project needs to be kept within scope and new requirements should not be added to the project if they will push it past the scope and budget.

Poor leadership

Lastly, poor leadership is a big cause of the failure of IT projects. Cybersecurity projects can quickly go south if they do not have strong leaders. An IT project needs to be driven from inception to completion. If the project was to train employees on social engineering attacks, the security leaders need to have experts in social engineering and a well-thought schedule of how employees will be trained in batches. If there is no strong leadership, some junior employees can even fail to show up to the training, citing them as time-wasting exercises. If there are conflicts in a project in terms of how it is to be implemented, there is a need for a strong leader to handle the problem.

Careless online behavior

With the rise of social engineering and the use of highly effective malware in attacks, the online behavior of employees can put an organization at risk of an attack, or just cause on to happen. There have been many organizations swindled through online scams and others have had malware planted in employee computers simply due to careless online behavior. There needs to be a demarcation of what employees can and cannot do when in an organizational network. The main challenge is that employees think that they have nothing or very little to lose as a result of their careless behavior. The following screenshot is an example of a malicious link in a phishing email:

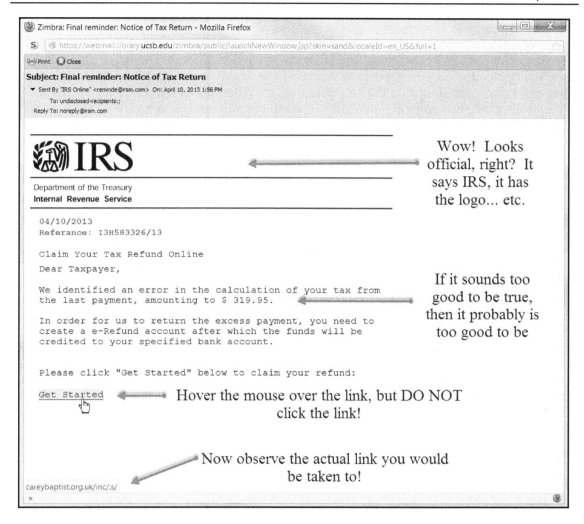

One of the careless online behaviors that IT security managers are having to deal with in their organizations is clicking of links in emails from strangers. Employees should be informed that malware that can be automatically installed in a computer after they click on links. They also need to be informed that there are very many malicious websites that can either automatically download malware into the user's computer or scam the user. There have been phishing scams where hackers use cloned emails of organizations, such as PayPal, and they give the recipients links to malicious websites where information can be stolen. Employees might not be aware of these scams and need to be warned against clicking such sites.

Another careless behavior is employees visiting malicious sites while on organizational computers. There are sites that claim to give certain free services, free movie downloads, free premium software download, and so many more free services. However, some of these sites have malware and, in most cases, it tends to be spyware or adware. Visitors download these malicious files alongside the free resources that they download from such websites. When these malicious software are installed on the organizational computers, chances are that they will quickly spread through and infect other computers and servers. Therefore, the careless acts of one employee will affect the entire organization. The malware could have devastating effects on the organization, such as a widespread theft of passwords or annoying display of ads on computers.

Giving out private information on social media has also turned out to be an unfortunate careless behavior that many employees are engaging in. Motivated by the culture on most social media sites to share out everything, employees are stating their workplaces, titles, and even posting pictures inside their working premises. There has been a case of an IT employee being targeted by a hacking group after they confirmed his workplace and hobbies on Facebook and created a fake profile of an attractive girl who had the same hobby. The attack went smoothly and the employee went on to download a malicious file sent by the hackers through the fake profile. Fortunately, the organization had a strong antivirus system that prevented the malicious file from executing and infecting the employee's computer with malware. Many similar cases but they have not had such fortunate endings. Many social engineering attacks are happening because employees are revealing key information on social media. They are updating their profiles with a lot of information that social engineers can use to attack them.

Insider threats

The following screenshot illustrates the causes of insider threats:

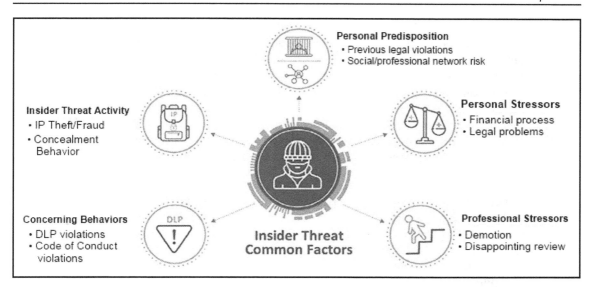

Perhaps one of the biggest threats to organizations is an insider threats. Insider threats are employees that go rogue and either attack or help attack the organization they work for. They are particularly dangerous due to the amount of sensitive information they have and the privileges that they are given by the organizations they work for. An insider threat can conduct a hack within the organization. They are aware of the security measures that the organization has put in place. They can, therefore, tell hackers what type of security to expect and possibly how to compromise it. If it is a firewall, they can tell the hackers the brand and model so that they can research on the vulnerabilities that can be exploited.

Insider threats also have access to many systems. They can authenticate themselves into systems used by organizations. They can, therefore, share these logins with the hackers to make it easier for them to get into the systems. Insider threats that have high privileges, such as system admins, which are even more dangerous since they can conceal the activities of the hackers. System admins can create new accounts for the hackers or simply delete logs after hackers have accessed the systems and made modifications or stolen some data. This is the reason why security frameworks urge for there to be a two-man rule where some operations need to be authorized by more than one admin.

Insider threats can also be the threat actors themselves. They can be out for some monetary gain and do malicious activities. They can be paid by competitors to sabotage the systems of the organizations they work for. They can be paid by disgruntled employees of the same organization to attack a particular senior employee. They can also be paid by advertisers to steal user data from the organization and share it at a certain amount. When they take these actions, it could be hard to suspect that it was an insider that did it. Stolen data can quickly be attributed to a secret hack. Erroneous performance of systems could be blamed on the system vendors. The targeting of specific employees by attackers could be seen as a normal attack by external entities. It is only when it is too late that insider threats are found.

One of the most famous cases of insider threats is that of Edward Snowden. In the period that he worked for NSA, Edward Snowden slowly gathered data on the unethical practices that the NSA did. He then exposed the agency to the world in a TV interview and subsequent releases through other platforms. Edward Snowden can just be any employee in an organization. He had privileges to access data deep inside the NSA and this was normal; thus it could not raise eyebrows. He had privileges to see the type of data that the agency was collecting as it was just a normal part of his job. However, when he released this to the world, he became an insider threat to the NSA. This shows how hard it is for organizations to detect attacks from insider threats. The attacks can be done alongside the normal job routines. For instance, an organization cannot tell that a marketing agent accesses mailing lists and copies the email addresses, and then shares them with the competitors. This is because it is normal and is part of the marketing agent's job routine to access the mailing lists. This, therefore, makes insider threats dangerous types of attacks that an organization is least prepared for.

Common countermeasures that companies should put in place to mitigate the insider threat include:

- Vetting personnel—before hiring, HR admins need to do thorough background checks and screening interviews to try and identify potential hires that might develop insider threat tendencies in future.
- Duty rotation—insider threats cause most harm if they are in charge of sensitive data and systems. Organizations could implement a rotation program where the same employee is not left in charge of such data or systems for durations that may allow them to plan and execute attacks.
- Least privilege and separation of duties—these security controls might prevent an insider threat from causing extensive damage to an organization should they decide to attack since they will either lack sufficient rights or access.

Technological transformation of financial services

The following screenshot is an example of a business email compromise attack email requesting for a transfer of money:

From:	John Doe <jdoe@companydomain.us>
Date:	July 30, 2015 at 10:27 AM EDT
To:	Jane Smith jsmith@companydomain.com

Jane,

Process a wire of $98,500 USD to the attached wiring instructions. This should be coded to Admin Expenses. Let me know when it is completed.

Thanks,

John Doe
CEO, Company Domain

Traditionally, financial transactions were done physically. Payments were done through cash or cheque. Money was stored as hard cash in banks or safes in the organization. There were few loopholes that could be used by attackers to illegitimately get money from organizations. However, technological transformations happened and there were new solutions to ease the burden of handling cash. Internet banking revolutionized the way payments were done. Organizations went cashless opting to carry out transactions through these online payment gateways. However, this also opened doors to attackers.

There have been many cases of organizations losing money to hackers. Surprisingly, most of these cases involve organizations making normal money transfers to the hackers. Phishing has been one of the techniques used to get organizations to move money to fraudsters. There is a particular phishing method called business email compromising that has cost organizations millions. This is where attackers gain access to the email account of an executive employee. With this email, they send urgent requests to junior employees in finance departments to make payments to some third parties. The pretense is normally the payment of overdue invoices or to close a deal quickly. Since junior employees feel obligated to respect the requests coming from the leaders, especially through the official email, they go ahead and make the transfers. It is only until the money has been moved does the organization realize that it was a scam. Many organizations have fallen for this trap. In some cases, spoofed emails are used to get the employees to transfer money to offshore accounts said to be owned by contractors or suppliers. Had it not been for the technological transformations of financial services, organizations would not have to live in fear of such attacks befalling them.

Another type of theft of money is happening through the hacking of organization's online bank accounts. Special malware that are being used to actualize this. Spyware, keyloggers, screen captures malware, and browse password theft programs are the most common ones. All these malware can be sent to and installed in the computers of finance department employees that are authorized to carry out transactions. Spyware will spy on everything the user of the computer does, including the websites visited and inputs provided. These will be used by the hackers to similarly visit the online banking platforms and use the same logins to access the organization's funds. Keyloggers are specifically meant to capture of a user's keystrokes. Keyloggers are efficient since they are stealthy and can operate for long duration. They keep the keys on a log file that is shared with the hackers. The hackers simply have to look for URLs to online banking platforms and the username and passwords typed thereafter. Screen captures are also useful attack vectors for stealing credentials from organizational users with credentials to the online banking platforms. Lastly, there are malware designed to steal passwords from browsers. As is the norm with lazy employees, they would rather save passwords on the browser so that they can easily log in the next time they visit their online banking platforms. However, this is a target for many hackers that have the tools to steal credentials stored in browsers.

Lastly, there is the challenge of insider threats in the finance department. These insider threats are quite dangerous as they can orchestrate attacks. They can also make it seem as if they are the victims, not the perpetrators. Since most organizations rely on the finance department employees making payments to the many suppliers and contractors, an insider threat could create payments to fictitious companies pretending to be one of the many suppliers or contractors. They can even make payments that were not invoiced but to their own shady accounts. As long as they are in the finance department, it is easy for them to hide their tracks, making it hard for anyone else, including auditors, to trace these payments. This vice is made possible by things such as online banking and ERPs used for finance management. It is easy to make the payments and hide your tracks using these systems.

Failure in implementing security policies

Almost every organization has a set of security policies. These policies are created to provide guidance on how the organization can be kept secure at all times. Security policies address a wide scope of threat landscapes. They include guidelines on passwords, user privileges, auditing, acquisition of organizational devices and services, and the use of organizational resources among many other things. Security policies tend to be a bit strict and they are a safe bet that the organization will be kept secure. However, only a few organizations apply these security policies.

One of the reasons why there is a failure in the implementation of security policies is due to the lack of compliance by the employees. If employees are made aware of these policies but they do not follow them, they fail to comply with the very measures put to protect the organization. They inherently put the organization at risk. If the security policies forbid the use of names and birth dates in passwords but an employee goes ahead and does that, this puts the organization at risk of being hacked if password crackers are used against such an account. Non-compliance is seen as a shortcut to evade the tough security policies. Employees do it secretly, not knowing the type of danger that they put the organization into.

The lack of enforcement of security policies is also a reason as to why there is such a failure in the implementation of policies. Non-compliance often goes unpunished in the organization. Employees that visit malicious websites, those that click links in emails from strangers, those copy corporate data to personal devices, and those that post sensitive details on social media among others, contravene the security policies but nothing is done to them. Therefore, there is no clear penalty for not following the security policies. This problem spirals down to many other employees, simply because they have seen their colleagues do it without any negative consequences to them or to the organization. IT departments have taken a step back from enforcement. Perhaps it is due to being overburdened with other responsibility, the challenge of telling who has violated a policy, or just due to laxity. The lack of enforcement of these policies defeats the purpose of their creation in the first place. If only IT departments would be serious about the enforcement of security policies, many attacks would be avoided. However, since enforcement and compliance are left to human factors, there is such as high rate of non-compliance.

Lastly, superiors are also to blame for the failure of the successful implementation of security policies. This is because they have a notion that they are above the law. Therefore, they tend to be the first ones to violate the security policies. Coincidentally, they cannot face consequences for their actions due to the positions that they hold. For instance, a director will not be punished by an IT security manager for failing to use a strong password for their accounts. Additionally, a junior IT staff will not feel free to go and caution an executive for failing to comply with some IT security policies. Executives believe that the IT department is supposed to handle everything related to cybersecurity in the industry. Therefore, the burden of ensuring that systems are protected should be handled by the IT department, but the executives are not willing to put in the effort on their side and set up strong passwords. Executives also see these policies as a nuisance for their busy lives leading the organization. It is only when there is a cyber breach that costs the company huge amounts of money or destroys its reputation that the executives see the need for the security policies.

Summary

This chapter has looked at a number of human factors that have impacted cybersecurity. It has discussed the current statistics of the attacks and losses that are directly attributable to human factors. The chapter has looked at the debate by executives as they decide between business and cybersecurity. Some executives see it as a waste of resources to draw money from the organization and use them on cybersecurity products. Cybersecurity is expensive and not all organizations are willing to pour out the required resources especially with other competing priorities that seem to be profitable. As a result, the organization is not well secured due to such choices, making it easy to hack. In the end, the losses the organization incurs supersede the costs of installing the cybersecurity products or training employees in the first place. The paper has also examined the issue of failing security management as a human factor in cybersecurity. Cybersecurity is in the hands of IT security managers and if they have poor leadership skills, the security stature of the organization will be deplorable. If the IT security manager cannot obtain a buy-in from executives, cannot correctly plan for a project, and cannot lead a project team well, most security projects will fail, thus exposing the organization to threats. Careless online behavior has been discussed as major contributors to the human factor issue in cybersecurity. There have been many attacks resulting from careless behavior of employees online. Employees have installed malicious software on organizational computers. They have browsed on malicious sites and clicked on links from strangers using company devices. In addition, they have provided information that can be used by social engineers on social media networks. By doing all this, they have put the organization at risk of being hacked.

The chapter then looked at insider threats and described them as some of the biggest threats to any organization due to the information and level of internal access that they have. The adoption of technology in finance has also been explained as a human factor related issue in cybersecurity. Due to the adoption of technology to keep organizational money and make transfers to vendors and contractors, organizational employees are being targeted by hackers. Lastly, the chapter has looked at the failure to apply security policies as a human-mediated cybersecurity challenge. It has looked at the human causes of the failure to implement these policies, thus leaving an organization exposed to attackers. In the next chapter, you will learn about the evolution of network segmentation by exploring a network segment that's designed based on various network models.

Further reading

The following are resources that can be used to gain more knowledge on this chapter:

- *The Human Factor in IT Security: How Employees are Making Businesses Vulnerable from Within*: `https://www.kaspersky.com/blog/the-human-factor-in-it-security/`
- *The Human Factors in Cyber Security and Preventing Errors*: `https://www.vircom.com/blog/human-factors-in-cyber-security-preventing-errors/`
- *COMPUTER SECURITY RESOURCE CENTER*: `https://csrc.nist.gov/CSRC/media/Events/FISSEA-30th-Annual-Conference/documents/FISSEA2017_Witkowski_Benczik_Jarrin_Walker_Materials_Final.pdf`
- *Understanding the Human factor to Cyber Security*: `https://www.eci.com/blog/15945-understanding-the-human-factor-to-cyber-security.html`

12
Securing the Perimeter and Protecting the Assets

Securing the perimeter in order to protect assets can be a very broad topic. In this chapter, the focus will be on IT perimeter security. There are a few different approaches to IT perimeter security but, at its core, the goal of IT perimeter security is having security controls in place against known and unknown threats while taking risk-based decisions.

> *"One of the main cyber risks is to think they don't exist. The other is to try to treat all potential risks."*

> *– Stephane Nappo*

A successful IT perimeter security plan will prove whether your security architecture, technologies in use, and established processes are able to prevent cyber attacks and, when they still occur, how fast you can detect and respond to them. Historically, many organizations rely on a single trust network model. In that model, organizations have a single security boundary and, once that boundary is breached, the cyber criminal has full access to the corporate network. This is why cyber criminals are able to move so quickly inside the network and take down the entire infrastructure within minutes or hours after they compromise a single endpoint. One of the biggest problems in cybersecurity is that companies are constantly chasing new technologies that fix specific cyber threats. Over the last years, a lot of research been devoted to IT perimeter security, which has led to innovations such as dual trust network models as well as zero trust network models. This chapter will go deep into the most commonly adapted IT perimeter security model, which is single trust, then share insights into dual trust and finish up with the zero trust network model.

Network models

Before diving deep into endpoint security, let's first understand the different network models that are available. As pointed out earlier, most organizations today will have a single trust network model but, throughout the last years, many organizations have started to move to dual trust and even zero-trust network models.

Single trust network model

The single trust network model is the most commonly used IT perimeter network model. It's based on the assumption that a number of firewalls can control the network from outside to the inside of the environment:

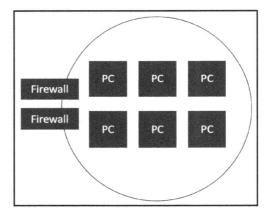

The problem with the single trust network boundary that many organizations use today is that it has very little protection against external threats and no protection against inside threats. If the cyber criminal is outside the network boundary, all that they need to achieve is the compromising of a single security boundary and they have full access to all of the endpoints and infrastructure within that network boundary. Once the cyber criminal has access to one endpoint, they're able to perform lateral movement to quickly jump inside your environment.

Dual trust network model

A dual trust network model is very similar to the one trust network model as it has the same external boundary. The difference between those two network models is an additional internal layer, which sits between the corporate network and the external network and is guarded by an additional firewall and load balancer. Having this additional layer with a load balancer ensures not only that it won't pass traffic that isn't allowed, into the corporate network, but it can also act as a TCP proxy ensuring that, when communication happens to servers inside your network, it gets repeated through the load balancer rather than having direct communication:

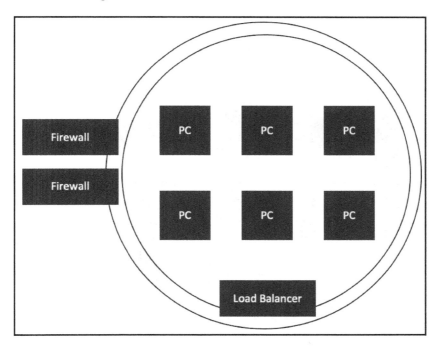

The problem with the dual trust network model is that, for external threats, it's the same threat landscape. However, compared to the one trust network model, it does introduce an additional security layer against internal threats because of the additional network segment and load balancer. But still, once a single endpoint is compromised, the threat actor can again take ownership of the entire environment. While the dual trust network model is more secure compared to a single trust model, it still introduces risks to the organization.

Zero trust network model

The zero trust network model is the recommended approach for network segmentation. With this network model, organizations have an external security layer as in the one trust network model, it has the internal security layer as in the dual trust network model, and it introduces an internal security zone within the network. The zero-trust network model eliminates the core concept of establishing trust on a network location. This model acknowledges the fact that the network is already lost territory to the threat actor. The zero trust network model relies, instead of on the network, on the endpoint and identity to gate access to corporate services and resources:

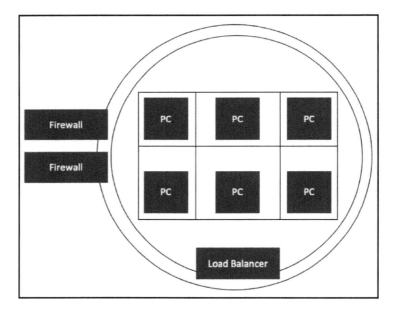

On a high level, a zero trust network model contains the following components:

- An endpoint directory that has an accurate representation of all endpoints that should be permitted access to corporate services and resources
- An evaluation service that can confirm whether an endpoint is compliant with the security policies of an organization
- An identity directory that has an accurate representation of all identities that should be permitted access to corporate services and resources
- An access proxy that can provides access to corporate services and resources by leveraging the preceding components

With the zero trust network model, organizations can ensure that only healthy endpoints with trusted identity have access to corporate services and resources. With this approach, organizations can now perform dynamic trust decisions. Based on today's threat landscape, it reduces the risk of lateral movements significantly because, even if a single endpoint is compromised, it won't be able to communicate with other endpoints or infrastructure. Therefore, many security vendors such as Google and Microsoft see the zero trust network model as the next evolution of network segmentation and security.

Microsoft 365 zero trust network models

Microsoft has bundled their secure modern workplace solution into a single offering called Microsoft 365 Enterprise. Because of the footprint of Windows as an operating system and Office as a productivity application, we'll focus here on the reference architecture of a zero trust network model based on Microsoft 365. One of the challenges seen by security teams is that employees work today from anywhere at any time. Because of that, they need access to corporate services and resources around the block regardless of their own network location. This makes access control policies based only on the identity obsolete:

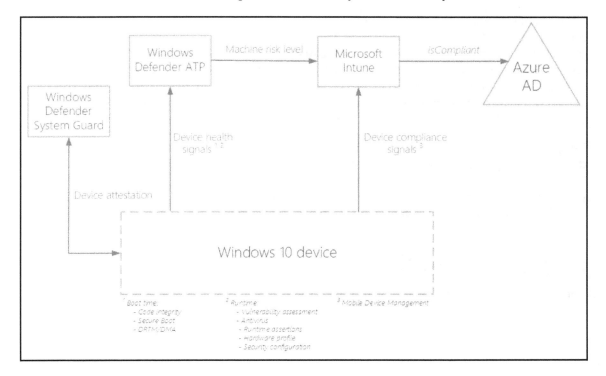

The foundation for Microsoft's zero trust network model is Azure Active Directory conditional access together with Azure Active Directory Identity Protection. With both combined, organizations are able to make dynamic access control decisions based on the identity, endpoint, location, and session risk for every resource itself. Azure Active Directory conditional access provides the organization with a set of policies that can be configured to determine under which circumstances the user can access corporate resources and services. Because of the deep integration across Microsoft services, this can include group memberships, device health status, device compliance status, user role, mobile applications in use, location, and sign-in risk levels. With that, organizations have full control to configure and determine whether the user should get access to the resources, whether it should be rejected, or whether the user should be prompted for additional authentication challenges such as multi factor authentication with Azure Active Directory **Multi-Factor Authentication** (**MFA**).

Endpoint security

An endpoint can be a desktop, laptop, printer, **Point of Sale** (**PoS**) terminal, **Internet of Things** (**IoT**) device, or server—whether on premise on a bare metal machine, on premise but in a virtual environment, or even in the cloud. Endpoint security has become a top priority for many organizations. This is because any endpoint, whether connected to the corporate network or to the internet or even if it's in a disconnected environment, can be targeted by threat actors. Threat actors started to focus more on breaching directly the endpoint because it's connected to the weakest link in the organization's security posture, which are the humans controlling these endpoints.

Endpoint security is the security approach where the security team is focused on locking down the endpoint as strongly as possible. In the past, this would mean compromising on the user experience and productivity for the benefit of security. But throughout the last five years, this has changed, and it's no longer accepted by the business to compromise user experience or productivity over security, instead both need to be balanced.

Endpoint security threats

There are many different threats out there. However, overall these threats can be categorized as follows:

- Physical access
- Malicious code execution
- Device-based attacks

- Communication interception
- Insider threats
- Decreased productivity

It's important to understand these threats in order to ensure mitigations are in place. The following section will give short examples for each threat.

Physical access

Imagine the scenario where you're a security architect at a publicly traded company. This morning, the **Executive Assistant** (**EA**) of the **Chief Financial Officer** (**CFO**) calls in and reports that the CFO has lost her laptop at the airport and that this laptop contained the earning statements that are supposed to be disclosed tomorrow to the public. Here are some questions to ask yourself:

Does the endpoint security strategy ensure the following about the person who finds the laptop:

- They're unable to log in to the endpoint?
- They're unable to extract data on the endpoint?
- They're unable to disable any training software that might be installed on the endpoint?
- They're unable to identify to which company the endpoint belongs?

Malicious code execution

In this scenario, you're a security architect at a company with a complete disconnected environment. There's no direct external connection to the internet. A threat actor has dropped malicious USB thumb drives at the parking lot nearby where most of the employees park. The Head of Research and Development found one of the USB thumb drives and took it inside the company. Once he arrived at his desk, he plugged in the USB thumb drive to his endpoint. Here are some questions to ask yourself:

Does the endpoint security strategy ensure that the threat actor is unable to do the following:

- Compromise the endpoint by running malicious code?
- Perform a lateral movement?
- Destroy the endpoint beyond any possibility of data recovery?
- Extract sensitive data that are stored on the endpoint?

Device-based attack

Imagine you're the security architect at a Fortune 500 organization. The organization had significant cost cuts within the IT department. This has led to the end user computing endpoints not being refreshed during their late migration from Windows 7 to Windows 10. In addition, some of the IT maintenance has been outsourced and has led to the situation whereby Windows 7 endpoints would need to be sent to another company when repairs are needed. Some of the Windows 7 endpoints recently has been send to the outsourcer. However, the outsourcer itself was targeted by an insider attack. One of the threat actors that's undercover at the outsourcer gets access to the endpoints. Here are some questions to ask yourself:

Does the endpoint security strategy ensure that the threat actor is unable to do the following:

- Perform a cold boot attack?
- Extract corporate data from the endpoint?
- Implant malicious hardware that remains undetected?

Communication interception

Imagine the scenario where you're a security architect at a large financial services institute. The Cybersecurity Defense Center reported suspicious activities when end customers are using the online banking system. After further investigation, it's confirmed that a threat actor is attempting to perform a man-in-the-middle attack. Here are some questions to ask yourself:

Does the endpoint security strategy ensure that the threat actor is unable to do the following:

- Succeed in intercepting traffic between the end customer and the bank?
- Disturb the network connection between the end customer and the bank?

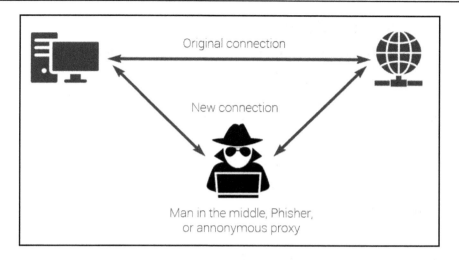

Insider threats

Imagine that you're a security analyst inside the Cybersecurity Defense Operations Center (**CDOC**) of a large corporation. Recently, the organization had a layoff inside the **Human Resources (HR)** and **Research and Development (R&D)** departments. Despite the fact that the employees should return all of their corporate assets, some upset employees kept their laptops. You've been made aware that these laptops contain trade secrets. Here are some questions to ask yourself:

Does the endpoint security strategy ensure that the former employee is unable to do the following:

- Use their corporate credentials to log in to the endpoint?
- Use their corporate credentials to log in to corporate services and resources?
- Copy corporate data from the endpoint to a personal USB thumb drive?

Decreased productivity

You're the new **Chief Information Officer** (**CIO**) at a large organization. As the CIO, you have both the IT and cybersecurity departments reporting to you. Historically, end user productivity wasn't the focus of the security department, which would cause friction between IT and cybersecurity teams. IT would want to deploy latest technologies for end user productivity while cybersecurity would want to prevent most of the projects. Here are some questions to ask yourself:

Does your endpoint security strategy do the following:

- Roll up into a secure modern workplace strategy
- Balance security with productivity

Modern endpoint security

A modern endpoint security plan encompasses device protection, threat resistance, identity protection, information protection, breach investigation, and response capabilities. While, in the past, many organizations invested in the best of breath security nowadays more organizations consider taking security from a single vendor. Given that Windows 10 is the most deployed operating system, the focus of this chapter will be on it. Utilizing its built-in capabilities will ensure a positive response for the questions in the previous section:

Device protection

Device protection is the foundation of Windows 10 endpoints. With device protection, Microsoft ensures that only trusted code is loaded at boot time and that it has early detection when someone tries to compromise boot integrity. The following components are part of device protection in Windows 10:

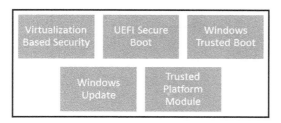

Threat resistance

With threat resistance, the Redmond-based company focuses on making it as difficult as possible for the threat actor to compromise the endpoint. The focus is clearly on reducing the attack surface as much as possible. The following components are part of threat resistance:

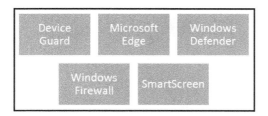

Identity protection

Identity protection is a key investment area and it's important to spend a good amount of time on it. In the last years, pass-the-hash, pass-the-ticket, and other compromised credential/hash-based attacks have become very common. In response to that, Microsoft invested in how secrets are stored and protected and how to eliminate traditional passwords. This is achieved by the following components:

Information protection

Almost all cyberattack targets, in some way or another, are to steal sensitive data. Data exfiltration is almost always the end game of a cyberattack, regardless of whether it's an external or insider threat. Therefore, it's no surprise that security vendors are investing in information protection. The following components are built into the operating system of Windows 10:

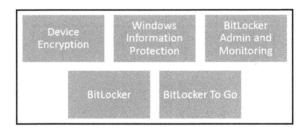

Breach detection investigation and response

Today, organizations need to assume breach. With that, organizations need to be able to detect and respond to cyberattacks and ensure that endpoints have dynamic policies assigned to guarantee that, when it gets compromised, it doesn't have access to corporate resources and services. The following built-in Windows 10 components ensure this:

Summary

In this chapter, you learned about the evolution of network segmentation by diving into the difference between a network segment that's designed based on the one trust network model, dual trust network model, and zero trust network model. Organizations nowadays need to assume that they've been compromised and, with that, the zero trust network model becomes the future of network segmentation. With the zero trust network model, organizations can ensure that only healthy endpoints with trusted identities get access to corporate resources and services. In addition, you got jump-start into different threats that are out in the real world for the endpoint estate. You'll want to make sure that the sample questions asked have a strong answer based on your endpoint security plan. If you couldn't answer some questions or if you now believe what you do today isn't sufficient, it's a good time to invest in that space. Given Windows 10 is the most deployed operating system in the enterprise, we also covered the built-in operating system security capabilities and explained how they help as part of your modern endpoint security plan. The next chapter will talk about three important processes in any organization; auditing, risk management, and incident handling.

Further reading

The following are resources that can be used to gain more knowledge on this chapter:

- *Is your weakest link really where you think it is?*: `https://www.itpro.co.uk/endpoint-security/32733/is-your-weakest-link-really-where-you-think-it-is`
- *Top Key players of Endpoint Security market 2018 - 2023*: `https://currentnewsmagazine.net/top-key-players-of-endpoint-security-market-2018-2023/21/04/52/`
- *Fortifying Your Endpoint Protection Posture Against Upcoming Threats*: `https://solutionsreview.com/endpoint-security/fortifying-your-endpoint-protection-posture-against-upcoming-threats/`
- *Windows Security Patch Breaks PowerShell Remoting*: `https://www.bleepingcomputer.com/news/security/windows-security-patch-breaks-powershell-remoting/`
- *How to prepare your organization for the end of Windows 7 support*: `https://www.techrepublic.com/article/how-to-prepare-your-organization-for-the-end-of-windows-7-support/`

- *Building Zero Trust networks with Microsoft 365*: https://cloudblogs.microsoft.com/microsoftsecure/2018/06/14/building-zero-trust-networks-with-microsoft-365/
- *Zero Trust part 1: Identity and access management*: https://cloudblogs.microsoft.com/microsoftsecure/2018/12/17/zero-trust-part-1-identity-and-access-management/

13
Threat and Vulnerability Management

Vulnerability management is the cyclical practice of identifying, classifying, prioritizing, remediating, and mitigating software vulnerabilities. Vulnerability management is vital for any organization. The term vulnerability management commonly gets confused with vulnerability assessment. Vulnerability assessment is the process of identifying, quantifying, and prioritizing (or ranking) the vulnerabilities in a system. The optimal approach to creating an effective vulnerability management strategy is by making it a vulnerability management life cycle. The vulnerability management life cycle schedules all vulnerability mitigation processes in a prioritized order. The correct counter actions are scheduled to be performed at the right time to find and address vulnerabilities before attackers can abuse them and have the chance to proceed with an attack.

In this chapter, we will focus on the following topics:

- Vulnerability management strategy
- Defining vulnerabilities in a few steps
- The root cause of security issues
- Vulnerability management tools
- Implementation of vulnerability management
- Best practices for vulnerability management
- Understanding risk management
- Defense in depth approach

Vulnerability management strategy

The vulnerability management strategy is composed of six distinct phases, which we will cover in the following sections.

Asset inventory

The first stage in the vulnerability management strategy should be making an inventory. However, many organizations lack an effective asset register and therefore have a hard time when it comes to securing their devices. An asset inventory is a tool that security administrators can use to go through the devices an organization has and the ones that need to be covered by security software.

In the vulnerability management strategy, an organization should start by giving the employee the responsibility of managing an asset inventory to ensure that all devices are recorded and that the inventory remains up to date. The asset inventory is also a great tool that network and system admins can use to quickly find and patch devices and systems.

Information management

This stage controls how information flows into an organization. Financial organizations store different types of data, and some of it must never get into the hands of the wrong people. Information, such as credit cards and personally identifiable information of customers, could cause irreparable damage if it were accessed by hackers. The financial institution would lose its reputation, alongside being fined and losing their customers as well as shareholders trust.

Risk assessment

This is the third step in the vulnerability management strategy. Before risks can be mitigated, the security team should do an in-depth analysis of the vulnerabilities that it faces. In an ideal IT environment, the security team would be able to respond to all vulnerabilities since it would have sufficient resources and time. However, in reality, there are many limiting factors when it comes to the resources that are available to mitigate risks. That is why risk assessment is crucial. In this step, an organization has to prioritize vulnerabilities over others and allocate resources to mitigate against them.

Risk assessment is composed of five areas. Risk assessment starts with scope identification. The scope needs to be identified carefully since it will determine from where internal and external vulnerability analysis will occur. After the scope has been defined, data needs to be collected about the existing policies and procedures that are in place to safeguard the organization from cyber threats. This can be done through interviews, questionnaires, and surveys that are administered to personnel, such as users and network administrators. All of the networks, applications, and systems that are covered in the scope should have their relevant data collected. This data could include the following; service pack, OS version, applications running, location, access control permissions, intrusion detection tests, firewall tests, network surveys, and port scans. This information will shed more light on the type of threats that the networks, systems, and applications are facing.

Vulnerability analysis

Vulnerability analysis is done using many different tools, which we will give some examples of in the next section. The tools that are used for vulnerability analysis are the same ones that hackers use to determine the exposure of an organization to vulnerabilities to determine which exploits to use. Commonly, organizations will call in penetration testers to conduct this process. The biggest setback in vulnerability analysis is the number of false positives that are identified that need to be filtered out. Therefore, various tools have to be used together to reliably come up with a list of the existing vulnerabilities in an organization.

Threat analysis

Threat analysis is performed to look at the risks that could happen in an organization. The threats that are identified must be analyzed to determine their effects on an organization. Threats are graded in a similar manner of vulnerabilities, but are measured in terms of motivation and capability.

Risk acceptance

Here, the existing policies, procedures, and security mechanisms are assessed to determine whether they are adequate. If they are inadequate, it is assumed that there are vulnerabilities in the organization. The corrective actions are taken to ensure that they are updated and upgraded until they are sufficient. Therefore, the IT department will determine the recommended standards that the safeguards should meet. Whatever is not covered is categorized as acceptable risks. However, these risks might become more harmful with time and therefore they have to be analyzed. It is only after it is determined that they will pose no threat that the risk assessment will end. If they might pose a threat, safeguard standards are updated to address them.

Vulnerability assessment

Vulnerability assessment involves the identification of vulnerable assets. This phase is conducted through a number of ethical hacking attempts and penetration tests. The servers, printers, workstations, firewalls, routers, and switches on the organizational network are all targeted with these attacks. The aim is to simulate a real hacking scenario with the same tools and techniques that they use.

Reporting and remediation

Reporting helps the system admins understand the current security state of an organization, the areas that are still unsecure, and points out the person who is responsible for that. Reporting also gives something tangible to management so that they can associate it with the future direction of the organization.

Remediation starts the actual process of ending the cycle of vulnerability management. Remediation compliments this by coming up with solutions to the threats and vulnerabilities that are identified. All of the vulnerable hosts, servers, and networking equipment are tracked down and the necessary steps are established to remove the vulnerabilities as well as protect them from future exploits. It is the most important task in the vulnerability management strategy and if well—executed, vulnerability management is termed to be a success. Activities in this task include the identification of missing patches and checking for available upgrades to all systems in an organization. Solutions are also identified for the bugs that were picked up by scanning tools. Multiple layers of security such as antivirus programs and firewalls are also identified at this stage. If this phase is unsuccessful, it makes the whole vulnerability management process pointless.

Defining vulnerabilities in a few steps

Vulnerabilities are flaws in applications, and include the following:

- Security risks
- Functionality issues

These applications can be in any device, such as virtual machines or appliances. They can have multiple vectors, such as the following:

- Remote network
- Local network
- Local system

An intersection of three elements:

- A system susceptibility or flaw
- Attacker's access to the flaw
- And attacker's capability to exploit the flaw

From vulnerability to threat

A hacker identifies the vulnerability and develops means to use the vulnerability to manipulate the application exploit. The exploit is successfully used and you are open for business, which is depicted as shown:

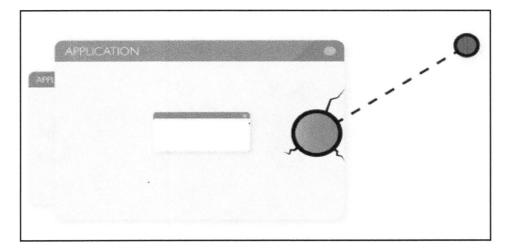

Multiplying threats

A single vulnerability can have multiple exploits and the most common defenses target exploits, not vulnerabilities as shown in the following figure:

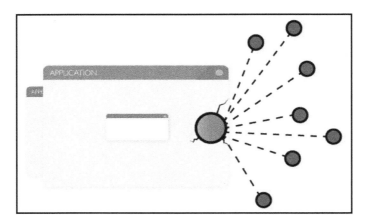

It possess the following characteristics:

- Exploits are commercial offerings:
    - Prices follow ordinary market rules of supply and demand
- Available in the underground as well and as from established vendors
- Procured by different types of customers, such as hacktivists, cyber criminals, organizations, and governments
- Utilized for targeted and broad attacks

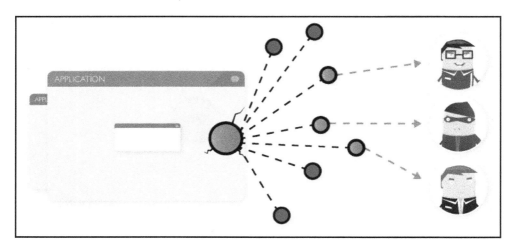

Multiplying risk

Exploits are often sold in bundles. One bundle is equal to multiple exploits, targeting multiple vulnerabilities in multiple products. The number of applications and devices increases exposure exponentially and, consequently, risks too.

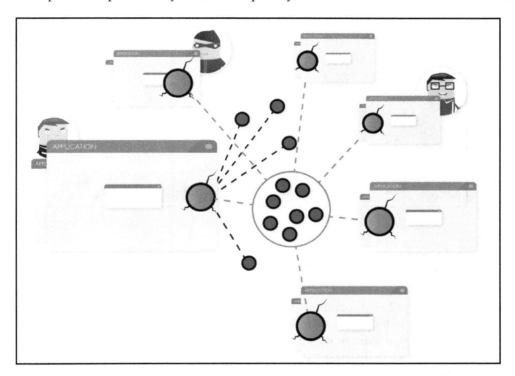

The root cause of security issues

Vulnerabilities in software are used routinely by cyber-criminals as gateways to exploit corporate networks. Based on Flexera (Secunia), in 2018, 75.7 % of the vulnerabilities affected third-party programs:

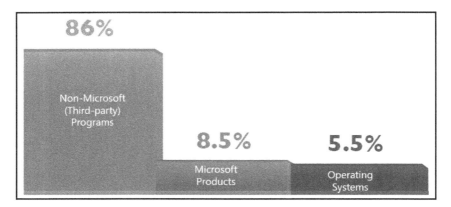

Vulnerability management tools

Vulnerability management tools are vast and for the sake of simplicity, this section will inform you some of the best tools of 2019 without going into detail. If you need more information about these tools, a simple search can help you get access to them. The aim of this section is to help you start working with the right and industry recommended tools that are used widely in the financial sector. Following are some of the Vulnerability management and analysis tools:

- **McAfee Foundstone's Enterprise**: McAfee Enterprise Security Manager delivers intelligent, fast, and accurate security and information (SIEM) and log management.

- **OpenVAS**: OpenVAS is an open source tool that serves as a central service that provides vulnerability assessment tools for both vulnerability scanning and vulnerability management:

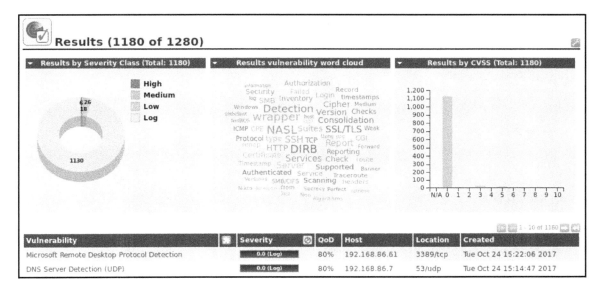

- **Nexpose community**: Nexpose is an open source tool that's used for scanning vulnerabilities and carrying out a wide range of network checks. Nexpose, Rapid7's on-premise option for vulnerability management software, monitors exposures in real-time and adapts to new threats with fresh data, ensuring that you can always act at the moment of impact:

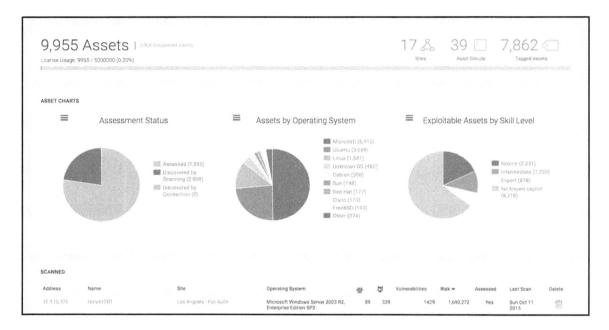

- **Nikto**: Nikto is a greatly admired and open source web scanner that is employed for assessing the probable issues and vulnerabilities in your system. It performs over 6,000 tests against a website. These large number of tests, which are for both security vulnerabilities and misconfigured web servers, makes it a go—to tool for many security professionals and system administrators. It can find forgotten scripts and other hard to detect problems from an external perspective:

```
root@kali:/opt# nikto -port 80 -host http://192.168.0.1
- Nikto v2.1.6
---------------------------------------------------------------------------
+ Target IP:          192.168.0.1
+ Target Hostname:    192.168.0.1
+ Target Port:        80
+ Start Time:         2017-05-11 10:32:23 (GMT-4)
---------------------------------------------------------------------------
+ Server: micro_httpd
+ The anti-clickjacking X-Frame-Options header is not present.
+ The X-XSS-Protection header is not defined. This header can hint to the user agent to protect against some
forms of XSS
+ The X-Content-Type-Options header is not set. This could allow the user agent to render the content of the
site in a different fashion to the MIME type
+ All CGI directories 'found', use '-C none' to test none
```

- **OWASP Zed Attack Proxy**: OWASP **Zed Attack Proxy (ZAP)** can help you
  automatically find security vulnerabilities in your web applications while you are
  developing and testing your applications. It's also a great tool for experienced
  pentesters to use for manual security testing:

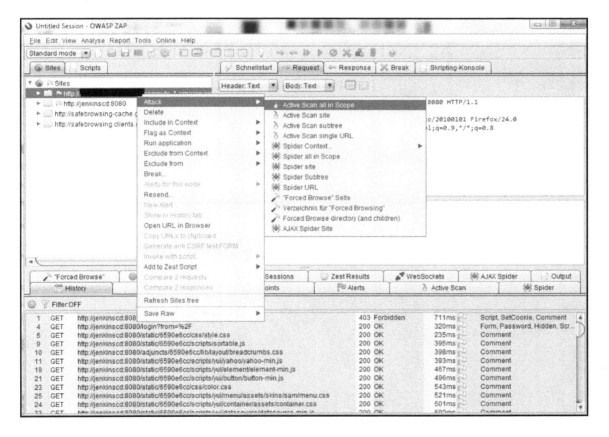

The following screenshot displays the scanning report:

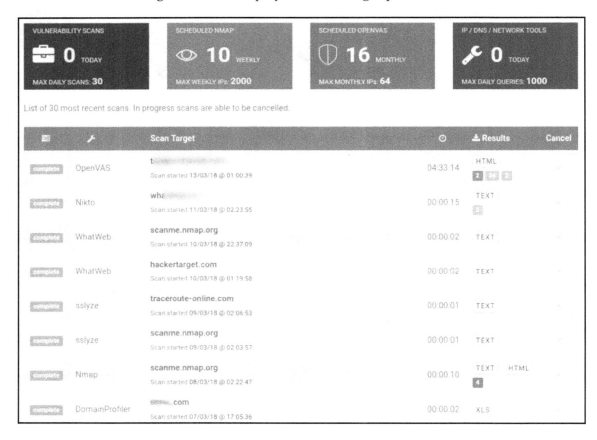

- **Nessus professional**: Nessus helps you to quickly and easily identify and fix vulnerabilities—including software flaws, missing patches, malware, and misconfigurations—across a variety of operating systems, devices, and applications:

- **Burp Suite**: Burp Suite helps you identify vulnerabilities and verify attack vectors that are affecting web applications:

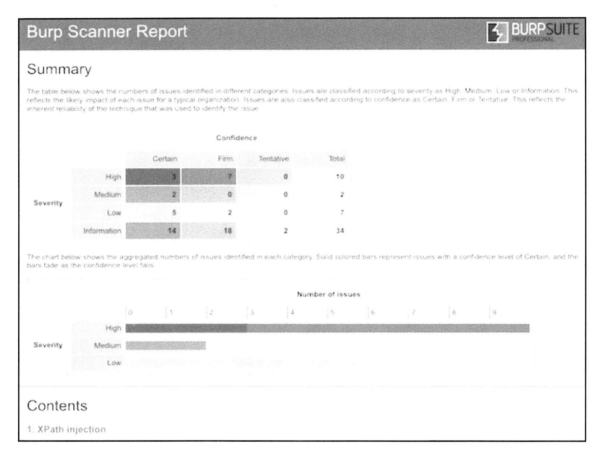

- **Enter Acunetix!**: Enter Acunetix! provides a list of scan results with remediation advice based on best practices, but also provides a suite of vulnerability management tools:

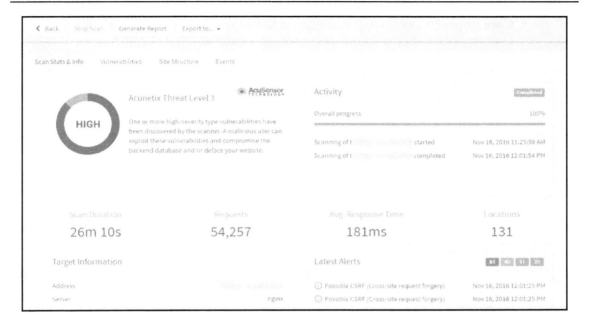

- **Flexera software vulnerability manager**: Flexera enables the prioritization and optimization of processes for managing software vulnerabilities to mitigate exposures, before the likelihood of exploitation increases:

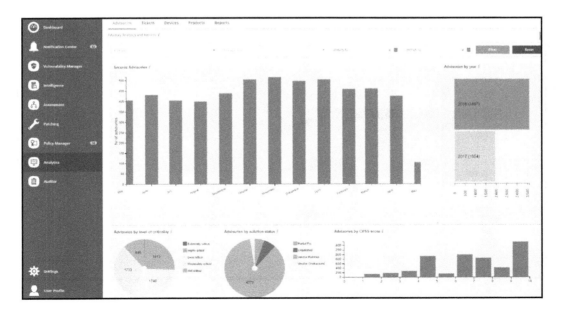

- **Core impact**: Core Impact is designed to provide efficient vulnerability assessments and penetration security testing throughout organizations. It is the only vulnerability scanning tool that enables users to replicate security threats that pivot across systems, devices, and applications while also revealing how exploitable vulnerabilities open paths to an organization's mission-critical systems and data:

- **BeyonTrust retina network security scanner**: BeyonTrust helps you scan, identify, and assess vulnerabilities across all assets (on-prem, cloud, mobile, virtual, container, and so on) within the organization:

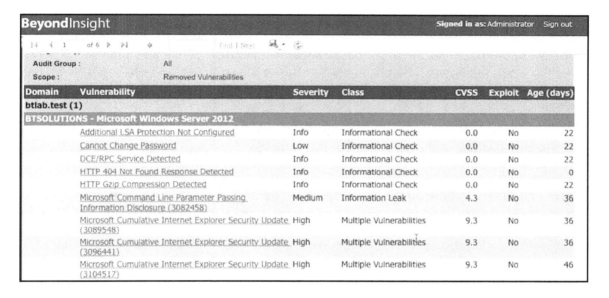

Implementation of vulnerability management

The implementation of vulnerability management follows the stipulated strategy. The implementation starts with the creation of an asset inventory. This serves as a register of all the hosts in a network and also of the software contained in them. At this stage, an organization has to give a certain IT staff member the task of maintaining this inventory and keeping it updated. The asset inventory at the very least should show the hardware and software assets that are owned by an organization and their relevant license details. As an optional addition, the inventory should also find out the vulnerabilities that are present in any of these assets. An up to date register will come in handy when the organization has to respond to vulnerabilities with fixes to all its assets. The aforementioned tools can properly handle the tasks that are to be carried out in this stage. After the implementation of the asset inventory, the organization should pay attention to information management.

The goal should be setting up an effective way to get information about vulnerabilities and cyber security incidents to the relevant people in the shortest of time possible. The right people to get first—hand information about security incidents are the computer security incident response teams. The various tools that were discussed as being capable of facilitating this stage require the creation of mailing lists. The incidence response team members should be on the mailing list since they will receive alerts from an organization's security monitoring tools. There should be separate mailing lists to allow other stakeholders of the organization to access this information once it has been confirmed. The appropriate actions that other stakeholders ought to take should also be communicated via the mailing lists.

The most recommendable tool for this step, which is from Symantec, is able to provide periodic publications to the users in an organization to keep them updated about global cyber security incidents. All in all, at the end of this stage, there should be an elaborate communication channel to incidence responders and other users when there has been a breach of systems. Following the implementation of mailing lists for information management, there should be a risk assessment. Risk assessment should be implemented in the manner that we described in the *Vulnerability Management Strategy* section. It should begin with the identification of the scope. It should be followed by the collection of data about the existing policies and procedures that the organization has been using. Data concerning their compliance should also be collected. After this has been collected, the existing policies and procedures should be analyzed so as to determine whether they have been adequate in safeguarding the security of the organization. After this, vulnerability and threat analysis should be done. The threats and vulnerabilities that the organization faces should be categorized in relation to their severity.

Lastly, the organization should define the acceptable risks that it can face without experiencing pronounced consequences. Risk assessment should closely be followed by vulnerability assessment. The vulnerability assessment step, which is not to be confused with vulnerability analysis of the risk management step, is aimed at identifying vulnerable assets. Therefore, all the hosts in a network should be ethically hacked or have penetration testing done to determine whether or not they are vulnerable. This process should be thorough and accurate. Any vulnerable assets that are not identified in this step might be the weak links that hackers exploit. Therefore, tools that the supposed hackers would use to attack should be used and to the best of their capabilities.

The vulnerability assessment step should be followed by reporting and remediation tracking. All of the risks and vulnerabilities that are identified must be reported back to the stakeholders of the organization. The reports should be comprehensive and touch on all hardware and software assets belonging to the organization. The reports should also be fine—tuned to meet the needs of various audiences. There are audiences that might not understand the technical side of vulnerabilities and it is, therefore, fair if they get a simplified version of the reports. Remediation tracking should follow the reports. After the risks and vulnerabilities that the organization faces are identified, the appropriate people to remedy them should be identified. They should be assigned the responsibility of ensuring that all the risks and vulnerabilities are resolved in totality. There should be an elaborate way of tracking the progress of the resolution of the identified threats. The tools that were discussed have these features and can ensure that this step is implemented successfully. The final implementation should be response planning. This is where the organization plans on the actions to take against vulnerabilities and then proceeds and takes them. This is the judge of whether the preceding five steps were done right. In response planning, the organization should come up with a means of patching, updating, or upgrading the systems that were identified to possess some risks or vulnerabilities.

The hierarchy of severity identified in the risk and vulnerability assessment steps should be followed. This step should be implemented with the aid of the asset inventory so that the organization can confirm that all of their assets—both hardware and software—have been attended to. This step should not take long as hackers are never too far from attacking using the most recently discovered vulnerabilities. The response planning stage must be completed with attention to the time taken from when monitoring systems send alerts to incident responders.

Best practices for vulnerability management

Even with the best tools, execution is all that matters in vulnerability management. Therefore, all of the actions that have been identified in the implementation section must be carried out flawlessly. There is a set of best practices for each step of the implementation of the vulnerability management strategy. Starting off with the asset inventory, the organization should establish a single point of authority. There should be one person that can be held responsible if the inventory is not up to date or has inconsistencies. Another best practice is to encourage the use of consistent abbreviations during data entry. It may become confusing to another person trying to go through the inventory if the abbreviations keep on changing. The inventory should also be validated at least every year. Without validation, it may be updated while having some errors that come to reveal themselves at the worst possible times.

Lastly, it is advisable to treat changes of inventory management systems with the same degree of care as any other change management process. In the information management stage, the biggest achievement that the organization can get is a fast and effective dissemination of information to the relevant audience. One of the best practices is allowing employees to make the conscious effort of subscribing to the mailing lists. Another one is to allow the incidence response team to post its own reports, statistics, and advisories to the organizational users through a website. The organization should also hold periodic conferences to discuss new vulnerabilities, virus strains, malicious activities, and social engineering techniques with users. It is best if all the users are informed about the threats that they may face and how to deal with them effectively. It has more impact than the mailing lists telling them to do technical things that they are not knowledgeable of. Lastly, the organization should come up with a standardized template of what all the security—related emails will look like. It should be a consistent look that is different from the normal email format that users are used to. The risk assessment step is one of the most manually demanding stages of the vulnerability management life cycle. This is because there are not many commercial tools that can be used here. One of the best practices is to document the ways to review new vulnerabilities as soon as they appear. This will save a lot of time when it comes to mitigating them since the appropriate counter measures will already be known. Another best practice is to publish the risk ratings to the public or at least to the organizational users. That information may spread and ultimately reach a person that will find it more useful. It is also recommended to ensure that asset inventories are both available and updated at this stage so that all hosts in a network can be combed through during risk analysis. The incidence response team in every organization should also publish a matrix for each tool that the organization has deployed to secure itself. Lastly, the organization should ensure that it has a strict change management process that ensures that the incoming staff are made available to the security posture of the organization and the mechanisms in place to protect it.

The vulnerability assessment step is not so different from the risk assessment step and therefore the two might borrow their best practices. As an addition to what has been discussed in risk assessment, it is a good practice to seek permission before extensively testing the network. This is because it was seen that this step might introduce serious disruptions to an organization and might do actual damage to the hosts. Therefore, a lot of planning ahead needs to happen. Another best practice is to create custom policies to specific environments, that is, different operating systems of the organization's hosts.

Lastly, the organization should identify the scanning tools that are best for its hosts. Some methods may be overkill, where they do too much scanning to an unnecessary depth. Other tools are too shallow and do not discover the vulnerabilities in a network. There are a few tips that may be used in the reporting and remediation tracking stage. One of these is ensuring that there is a reliable tool for sending reports to asset owners concerning the vulnerabilities they had and whether they have been fixed completely. This reduces the number of unnecessary emails from users whose machines were found to be containing vulnerabilities. The IT staff should also meet with management and other stakeholders to find out about the type of reports that they want to see. The level of technicality should also be agreed upon. The incidence response team should also agree with management on the remediation time frames, the required resources, and put out the consequences of non—remediation. Lastly, remediation should be done following the hierarchy of severity. Therefore, the vulnerabilities that pose the most risk should be sorted first. The response planning step is the conclusion of the whole vulnerability management process. It is where the responses to different vulnerabilities are implemented. There are several best practices that can be used in this step. One of them is ensuring that the response plans are documented and well—known by the incidence response team and the normal users. There should also be fast and accurate information flow to the normal users concerning the progress of fixing the vulnerabilities that are identified. Since there is a chance of failure after machines are updated or patches are installed, contact information should be provided to the end users so that they can reach out to the IT team when such cases arise. Lastly, the incidence response team should be given easy access to the network so that they can implement their fixes faster.

 Verizon 2017 Data Breach Investigations Report stated that:

81 percent of breaches leveraging hacking techniques (misconfigurations, vulnerabilities, or exploits) used stolen or weak passwords in 2017, up from 63 percent in 2016 -

Assess yourself

As can be seen in many security reports, most cyber—attacks usually take advantage of basic, unnoticed/underestimated security vulnerabilities, such as poor patch management procedures, weak passwords, web—based personal email services, and the lack of end user education and sound security policies. This makes an effective vulnerability assessment a critical first step in the effort to protect data.

Tying vulnerability assessments into business impact

To get the maximum benefit from a vulnerability assessment, you need to know your organization's mission—critical processes and underlying infrastructure and apply that understanding to the results. To be effective, the vulnerability assessment should include the following steps:

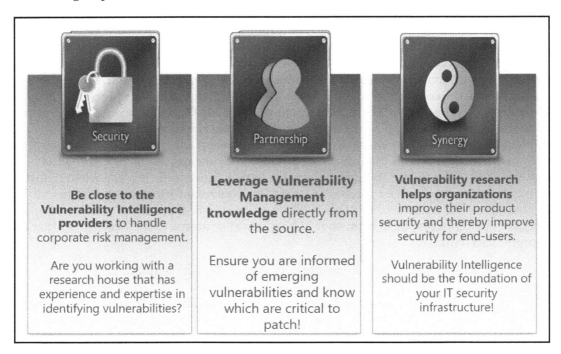

Take an active role

It is important to actively screen potential vendors, engage in the scoping process, provide security consultants with what they need to do the job, and engage in the process to facilitate success.

Identify and understand the business processes

Focus on those that are critical and sensitive in terms of compliance, customer privacy, and competitive position. In many financial organizations, this process requires collaboration between IT and the business units' owners, and legal counsel. The security strategy should task forces with representatives from each department to analyze business processes and the information and infrastructure they depend on. The primary objective is to document the way it's done and understand what the true process is.

Pinpoint the applications and data

Once the business processes are identified, which should be prioritized based on mission criticality and sensitivity, the next step has to be identifying the applications and data on which those mission—critical processes are depending on. Again, the collaboration between IT and other business players are very important in this step.

Try to find hidden data sources

This step should look not just to servers and desktops, but also to mobile devices, smartphones, and tablets. In most cases, data may reside in a static location, but it's very common to find alternate locations, including cloud storage locations. Understand how the organization works, who is mobile, who is sharing information with partners and customers, and draw a data flows between these devices and data center applications and storage. Microsoft Office 365 allows any employee to access mission—critical information on any device, in any location, at any time. To understand this external footprint, determine whether your business users are sending business emails over public channels such as Outlook, Gmail, or Yahoo mail. Also check with developers for their non—production storage as they often use mission—critical data to test new and upgraded applications.

Determine the hardware structure

Work down the layers of infrastructure to identify the servers, both virtual and physical, that run your mission—critical applications. Identify the data storage devices that hold the mission—critical and sensitive data that's used by those applications.

Map the network infrastructure to hardware

Find out the network infrastructure details such as routers and other network devices that your applications and hardware depend on for fast, secure performance. Also, identify subnets as they might have been logically or physically separated and some sensitive assets might be resting there. Understanding networking will also help you identify how your data travels in the infrastructure.

Identify the controls

Identify and document the security measures you already have in place, which includes policies, technical controls, as well as any possible protection capabilities, and then look to find the best way to minimize these vulnerabilities. Then, ensure that you implement the defense in depth strategy.

Run the vulnerability scans

After you have followed every step thus far, you will have a clear understanding of how your applications are mapped out, how the data flows, what the hardware and network is, and what kind of protection you have in place. From here, you can run your vulnerability scans and focus on closing any possible gaps. One of the biggest mistakes companies make is using a scan to determine what to patch, instead of scanning to verify successful patching. This sets the organization up for greater vulnerability rather than less.

Read the results of the scans

Your vulnerability scanner will most probably produce scores that might scare you, both for the benefit of working with business owners and with risk managers, and might have a risk acceptance or ignorance based on previous results and risk profiles. Deriving meaningful and actionable information about business risk from vulnerability data is a complex and difficult task, but it is an important step. For example, a vulnerability found on a server protected by application firewalls, encryption, and other countermeasures may not be as important as addressing the same vulnerability that was found in a less—protected infrastructure that was used in testing and development, particularly if it makes use of data with stringent compliance requirements depicted in the following figure:

Conduct penetration testing by third parties as well

After a major vulnerability assessment is complete, and the business feels it has remediated enough findings to improve its security posture, it's critical to perform penetration testing with the right scope to verify that your remediation are correct:

Knock on the Door		
Ensure Firewalls are Secure	Install IPS, Anti Virus, Anti Malware	Strong Security Policies & Procedures
Get a Foothold		
Use Multi Factor Authentication	Plan Remote Access around Security	Train Staff on Social Engineering Dangers
Exploitation		
Keep Systems Patched Inc 3rd Party Software	Restrict Access to PII and Sensitive Information / Consider Encryption	Disaster Recovery Planning / RISK Management
Hide Tracks		
Implement Secure Auditing Procedures	Implement Forensics Auditing	Limit & Monitor number of Administrators

Understanding risk management

Risk management is the identification, evaluation, and prioritization of risks (as defined in ISO 31000), followed by the coordinated and economical application of resources to minimize, monitor, and control the probability or impact of unfortunate events or to maximize the realization of opportunities:

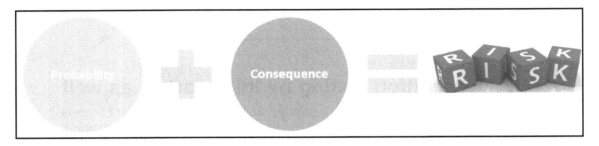

Following steps are covered in risk management:

- **Monitor the assets**: Once the actions that were defined in the risk management plan have been implemented, you will need to monitor the assets for the realization of security risks:
  - Define the elements of value
  - Identify the assets
  - Protect the assets (where vulnerability management will take an important part)

- **Track changes to risks**: As time progresses, changes to your organization's hardware, software, personnel, and business processes will add and obsolete security risks. Similarly, threats to assets and vulnerabilities will evolve and increase in sophistication.

The following are the key security principles:

- Granting the least privilege required
- Defending each network layer
- Reducing the attack surface
- Avoiding assumptions
- Protecting, detecting, and responding
- Security by design, default, and deployment

Defense in depth approach

The principle of **Defense in Depth** (**DiD**) is to provide multiple mitigations or protection mechanisms so that if one mitigation mechanism fails, there are additional protections in place to help protect assets from becoming vulnerable. Defense in depth protections are simply security best practices and are not triaged or rated by criticality. In many cases, good DiD mitigations can be more successful in offering protection against exploits than single point of defense mitigations. This is especially true when considering design or architectural DiD mitigations:

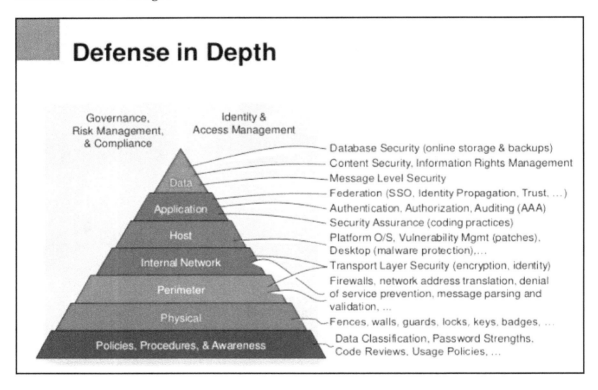

Best practices for protecting your environment

Invest in your platform: Agility and scalability requires forward thinking and building enabling platforms. For this, you must have/do the following:

- A well-documented inventory of your assets
- A clearly-defined security policy—provide clear vision, standards, and guidance for your organization
- Practice good hygiene—most attacks can be prevented with timely patches, AV, and identity monitoring
- Employ multi-factor authentication to strengthen the protection of accounts and devices

Invest in your instrumentation: Ensure that you are exhaustively measuring the elements in your platform by doing the following:

- Acquire and/or build the tools that are needed to fully monitor your network, hosts, and logs
- Proactively maintain controls and measures, and regularly test them for accuracy and effectiveness
- Maintain tight control over change management policies
- Monitor for abnormal accounts and credential activity to prevent abuse

Invest in your people: Skilled analysts and data scientists are the foundation of defense, while users are the new security perimeter. You should do the following to ensure this:

- Establish relationships and lines of communication between the incident response team and other groups
- Adopt the least privilege admin model; ideally, eliminate persistent admin rights to minimize the attack surface
- Use the lessons that you've learned to gain value from every major incident
- Educate, empower, and enlist users to recognize likely threats and their role in protecting business data

If you want to educate or help your IT team to switch to a Cyber Career, you can read the book *Cybersecurity The Beginner's Guide* written by Dr. Erdal Ozkaya and Deepayan Chanda.

Summary

In this chapter, you have learned about threat and vulnerability management. You were exposed to the key principles that are required to establish a vulnerability management strategy for your organization and you have gained practical knowledge on a variety of tools and services that are available in this space.

Further reading

The following are resources that you can use to gain more knowledge on this chapter:

- *Implementing a Vulnerability Management Process*: `https://www.sans.org/reading—room/whitepapers/threats/paper/34180`
- *Threat and Vulnerability Management Standard*: `https://www.resolver.com/trust/policies/threat—vulnerability—management—standard/`
- *Threat and Vulnerability Management*: `http://www.dxc.technology/security/offerings/140115/140190—threat_and_vulnerability_management`
- *Threat and Vulnerability Management*: `https://www2.mmu.ac.uk/isds/information—security/policies/threat—vulnerability—management/`

14
Audit, Risk Management, and Incident Handling

Organizations today have to live with constant pressure to secure their organizations from cyber attacks as well as have a plan for how to react in the case of an attack. At the same time, they need to be able to stay in compliance with many regulatory requirements that have been increasingly added by governments and economic blocs. These regulatory requirements often encompass common targets for cyber criminals such as data. Some of the prominent regulations include the following:

- **Health Information Portability and Accountability Act (HIPAA)**—applicable within the jurisdiction of the US, HIPAA governs the collection, storage, and sharing of health information about patients
- GDPR—applicable for EU citizens, GDPR is focused on protecting user data privacy.
- **Fair Credit Reporting Act (FACTA)**—applicable within the US, FACTA restricts the collection, use and sharing of personal financial information
- COPPA—applicable within the US, the Children's Online Privacy Protection ACT prohibits the collection of data about users under thirteen years of age

There are many other regulations that will be provided in the reading list at the end of the chapter. Organizations have to remain compliant with all these regulations and violations, regardless of the circumstances, are normally punished. For instance, there are many laws concerning user data while hackers have an insatiable demand for user data. If an organization keeping user data is breached and the data stolen, it will have to meet the costs of being non-compliant with regulations as well as losing customers due to the attack. Due to the nature of the consequences that come with a cyber attack, organizations have focused more efforts on avoiding such. They are therefore doing IT audit to establish weaknesses in the IT infrastructure and fixing them before tragedy strikes. Since it is impossible to remain 100% secure, organizations are also focusing on cyber resilience and are thus investing in robust incident handling techniques. This chapter will discuss these cybersecurity approaches in the following topics:

- IT auditing
- Risk management
- Incident handling

IT auditing

This refers to examining of the whole IT infrastructure in an organization. In addition to this, IT audit has been stretched to include the security policies, standards, and procedures that an organization has established. Therefore, a complete audit is able to determine whether an organization has enough controls to protect its IT assets, data and to ensure its attainment of business goals. Organizations mostly rely on IT frameworks to carry out systemic and standardized audits. The following are the commonly used frameworks in IT auditing: Cobit, ISO 27001, and NIST. The following is a more in-depth explanation of why organizations carry out IT audits.

Evaluating the systems, policies, and processes that secure the organization

With the increasing cyber attack incidents, IT security managers have been prompted to add more security solutions to their IT infrastructure. These security solutions range from physical access controls to software access controls since hardware and software security are of equal concern. All these solutions need to be periodically assessed to determine whether they are working as expected. IT audits will go through the configurations or processes used in these solutions to identify whether there are some gaps that can be exploited by internal and external threats. If the gaps are identified, the audit team can give out clear directions of what needs to be done to seal the loopholes. Security policies are also an area of interest during auditing. Security policies cover the whole scope of an IT infrastructure and include both internal and external security controls. If the security policies, standards, and procedures are flawed, this could lead to security concerns in the organization's future. In addition, auditing helps to determine the security policy compliance. If, for instance, the security policies require employees to set an eight-character complex password, auditing may reveal whether there are some employees that have violated the policy.

Determining the risks to the company's assets

IT auditing helps uncover risks to the organization. As mentioned earlier, auditors comb through the internal and external security controls of an organization. While doing so, they will uncover the risks associated with either of the controls. Additionally, they review the organizational security policies. Policies that are inadequate or that can lead to more harm than good can be discovered during the auditing process. An audit process involves many things and it essentially combs through every part of the organization. From systems to physical security installations, the audit is carefully conducted just to find any flaws or vulnerabilities that the organization might have. At the end of an audit, the organization will be familiar with the vast majority of the risks that it faces.

Ensuring that the organization is compliant with the relevant regulations

The IT sector is filled with external regulations that are imposed on all organizations. Since organizational systems may be used by people from different places around the world, there may be more laws to follow than the organization is aware of. For instance, there have been updates to the **General Data Protection Regulation** (**GDPR**) regulations that have affected organizations worldwide. This is despite the fact that the regulations were only of interest to the EU region. There are many other examples of laws being effected in a certain geographical region but applying all over the world. This is because the internet connects users worldwide. Therefore, if you set up an online shop that requires registration with personal details of a user, you are required to take into consideration the GDPR laws. An EU citizen might register on your website, and if there is an issue and they report your site for not being compliant to GDPR, you may be heavily fined. The beauty of auditing is that it is fully encompassing. It will comb through the organization and identify areas where compliance is required. Since auditors are experienced in this, they can easily pinpoint areas where the organization has overlooked compliance. This could save the organization from a lot more trouble, especially due to lawsuits and fines for non-compliance.

Determining inefficiencies in the IT infrastructure and management

The IT infrastructure in many organizations is growing more complex. There is an ongoing trend of modernization of the workplace. Therefore, more departments are using ERPs. Contractors and suppliers are also interacting with the organization via their own systems. Routine operations are being automated. In addition to this, there is a broad spectrum of IT systems and solutions that the IT department will be running in the organization. The end result is a complex IT infrastructure. It is easy for inefficiencies to arise due to the complex nature of the organization's IT infrastructure. However, auditing can help to determine these inefficiencies. In the examination of process flows, auditors may be able to tell where or on which systems there are unnecessary delays, or where some sort of interconnectivity is required.

Apart from the infrastructure, auditing might reveal some of the inefficiencies with the management. With a complex IT department, there may arise some inefficiencies especially with the assignment of special roles to employees. For instance, there could be many transactions that might require approval from the IT line manager who may be bogged down by very many other tasks causing him or her to sluggishly make the approval. If another IT staffer is authorized to make the approvals, transactions could be made faster. Therefore, an audit team will look at the flow of processes and the governance of the IT department closely during an audit process. They will be keen to identify areas where there are inefficiencies resulting from the management of IT and give directions on how this can be avoided.

However, there are some limitations of auditing, and it should not be thought of as the single process that can rectify all the wrongs in an organization. Auditing is limited to a number of things in an organization. There are some preeminent risks that might not be identified through auditing, and this is why there should be an entire risk management process continually running in the organization.

Risk management

Risk management in IT involves the identification, organization, and management of risks in an organization. It is normally done in a way that balances the costs associated with using security solutions to protect the organization and the benefits that they bring. In simpler terms, risk management allows the organization to spend more on the prevalent or more threatening risks and spend little on the insignificant risks. Risks are an integral part of any organization. There will always be a cybersecurity risk facing an organization at any given time. Therefore, it is of importance to the organization that all the risks to its IT infrastructure and data are identified and managed. IT risk management should cover a wide scope since risks can arise from many causes. Human error, natural calamities, cyber attackers, and hardware failure are all potential causes of these risks. Risk management is often described as a five-step process in the organization.

Identification

This is the first step in the risk management cycle. At this point, an organization will focus on uncovering and getting detailed information about the risks that it faces. As said before, risks can emanate from different things, thus the responsible persons need to be open-minded when looking for risks. Financial uncertainties, changing regulations, management issues, accidents, and disasters can all be sources of risks. Risks also keep on changing periodically, thus risk management should be repeated often. To ensure that most of the risks faced are uncovered, the following are some of the strategies that could be used:

- **Interviews**: Interviewing different personnel in the organization could help uncover many potential risks. For instance, an interview with the guards could help uncover the risks to physical security controls. An interview with a normal user could help discover risks associated with system accounts and also the hardware they use. Interviews will yield a wide variety of risks that will be obtained from the users of organizational assets that are protected or from the personnel in charge of enforcing some security controls.
- **Checklists**: There are some common risks that may have been identified over a long period of time in previous risk identification exercises. Since they are already known, the team identifying risks should just go through them as a checklist. However, this method is limited to organizations that already keep a list of common risks. Additionally, this method cannot uncover new risks.
- **Assumptions about security risks**: Assumptions about security risks can be made when there are supporting facts that can be considered true even without proof. For instance, users could be assumed to be creating weak passwords in a system that has no password requirements. The absence of the password requirement can be assumed to lead to the creation of weak passwords even if the user passwords are not known.

Risk analysis

Once the risks have been identified, there needs to be a process of determining the probability of occurrence as well as the impacts. As highlighted earlier, risk management helps the organization spend more resources on the significant risks while spending little on those risks that can hardly happen. Risk analysis is key in ensuring that the nature of a risk and its consequences to the organization are known. The information obtained at this step is important to the whole process and might determine the success or failure of the risk management exercise. Risk analysis is done through qualitative or quantitative risk analysis. In either way, a risk is analyzed in terms of its impact to the organization across several metrics, such as schedule, budget, and the resources it takes.

Risk assessment

This is the in-depth evaluation of a risk. This step looks at the probability of the risk occurring and its consequences. From this, it is possible to decide whether the risk is acceptable or not. According to this sort of filtration of risks, acceptable risks are just assigned low priority since the organization is ready to take them as they cannot do much damage. They tend to have low impacts and a low probability of happening.

Risk mitigation

In this step, the unacceptable risks are mitigated. The organization develops ways to address these risks to ensure that they do not occur, and if they occur they have minimal impact on the organization. Therefore, risk mitigation will include preventive tactics as well as contingency plans. Prevention tactics will curtail the risk from occurring. When the risk does occur, the contingency plans will handle the rest.

Risk monitoring

Risk mitigation is not the end of risk management. Risks change priorities with changes in their severity of impact or possibility of occurrence. Therefore, they should be followed up continuously. Risk monitoring includes the periodic review and updating of the risks. Alongside this, new risks are discovered as well.

There are four approaches that the organization can take for risks which are as follows:

- **Risk avoidance**: This is where an organization is focused on the complete avoidance of the risk by considering different options that do not feature the risk.
- **Risk reduction**: This approach aims to reduce the severity of the impacts that a risk can have once it occurs.
- **Risk sharing**: This is a clever approach whereby the organization distributes the consequences of a risk to other parties such as vendors.
- **Risk retaining**: Organizations can take this approach if they have other business goals that have more priority. Therefore, instead of addressing the risk, the organization can simply retain it at a certain level provided that the resources saved in doing so might lead to more profitable investments.

Incident handling

Incident handling is the response that an organization gives to an attack. When an incident is handled well, a much more damaging future disaster can be averted. If an incident is handled poorly, there could be a total disaster that follows. This section will focus on how organizations should handle incidents in the right way and the steps that should be followed.

Preparation

This is the first step in incident handling. Organizations need to be prepared to deal with security incidents even before they happen and thus preparation is key. Effective preparation will not only reduce the potential of an incident harming the organization but will also aid in quick recovery. Preparation is done in a variety of ways. It can start with a documented policy statement on how the organization will respond to security incidents and who will be responsible for that. Preparation can also entail the implementation of backup solutions, keeping tabs on software patches, and also keeping tabs on the updating process of antivirus programs. These and many other processes keep the organization in an always-ready state to deal with security incidents.

Identification

Once the organization is prepared to face incidents, the next step is to identify when and where incidents have happened. Identification tends to be a bit difficult especially with the level of stealth that attackers are employing in their attacks. Therefore, some security solutions are needed to help alert system and network admins when there are security incidents. The speed at which an incident is detected might be the determinant of its being successfully handled or a total disaster.

Containment

Once an incident has been identified and confirmed to be happening, the focus shifts to containment. Containment allows for the damage that an incident can cause to be limited. Here, preventive security solutions and techniques are mostly used to stop the attack. If it is a virus attack, for instance, antivirus systems are used to scan and remove the viruses from the targeted computer. If the incident involves malicious traffic, firewalls are used to prevent traffic from the malicious sources from getting into the network. Therefore, the actions taken at this point are aimed at neutralizing the attack before it gets serious or severe.

Recovery and analysis

Once the incident has been contained, attention shifts to recovering the affected systems and then analyzing the incident. Depending on organization-specific priorities or the nature of the incident, either recovery or analysis can take place before the other. Recovery ensures that the targeted system is restored to the status it was at before the attack. Analysis is a more comprehensive exercise aimed at determining why the incident happened, whether it was correctly handled, and whether it can still reoccur.

Summary

This chapter has looked at three important processes in any organization; auditing, risk management, and incident handling. The chapter begins by taking a look at the IT auditing process. We supplied an in-depth explanation of what it is, which also summarizes the advantages of having one carried out in an organization. A disclaimer is given, however, concerning the perception of auditing. Since it is held in high regard, it is important to note that it still has some limitations and cannot cover all potential vulnerabilities in the organization. The chapter then looked at risk management. Here, the five-step process of risk management was discussed. This includes identification, analysis, assessment, mitigation, and monitoring. In addition to this, there was a brief overview of the approaches that an organization can take when handling IT risks. Lastly, the chapter looked at incident handling. The steps of incident handling were discussed, and these are preparation, identification, containment and recovery, and analysis. The next chapter will explore encryption and its types, different algorithms, and cryptography.

Further reading

The following are resources that can be used to gain more knowledge of topics discussed in this chapter:

- *INCIDENT RESPONSE POLICIES AND PLANS*: https://www. incidentresponse.com/resources/policies-plans/
- *An Introduction to Information System Risk Management*: https://www.sans.org/ reading-room/whitepapers/auditing/introduction-information-system- risk-management-1204
- *IS Audit Basics: The Core of IT Auditing*: https://www.isaca.org/Journal/ archives/2014/Volume-6/Pages/The-Core-of-IT-Auditing.aspx
- *DATA PROTECTION LAWS OF THE WORLD*: https://www. dlapiperdataprotection.com/index.html

15
Encryption and Cryptography for Protecting Data and Services

Encryption has come as a welcome solution to securing data and communication in organizations and also for individuals. It has been accepted as the most trusted way of securing data against the threats that are in existence today. Cryptography, which is the practice of using encryption and decryption, is often one of the last security measures that organizations employ just in case hackers are able to breach through other layers of security. Encryption, which is the process of converting data from plain text to cipher text, is one of the elements used to add reliability and non-repudiation in communication.

This chapter will take us through the detailed version of encryption from its early methods and gives us a brief idea of how far it has evolved, covering various techniques along with the challenges. In brief, this chapter will discuss the following topics:

- Early encryption methods
- Encryption today
- Protecting data and services with cryptography
- Examples of encryption algorithms
- Encryption challenges

Encryption

Encryption is simply defined as the method through which plaintext data is converted into ciphertext. The ciphertext can be converted back to the plaintext by an entity that has a decryption key. Encryption is not a new technique and its use goes deep in history. Over several centuries, encryption has been used by humans to protect sensitive information, such as trade secrets and communication between leaders. However, encryption in medieval times was fairly simple and was somewhat easy to crack. Methods, such as transposition or substitution of characters were used. However, as technology advanced, encryption became more automated and machines could encrypt and decrypt messages better than humans.

Early encryption methods

Spartans sent encrypted messages in 700 BC during battle to avoid enemies from discovering their war strategies and other sensitive information. The encryption of messages was done using a simple trick. All the senders and recipients had wooden rods of equal size. Messages would be written on pieces of cloth or leather wound around a rod in a certain pattern. When unwound from the rod, the message was unreadable and appeared gibberish to others. If a messenger was to be captured by the enemy while carrying the message, the enemies would not even know what was written. However, when the message got to the intended recipient that had the rod, he would wind the cloth or leather piece on the rod in the same pattern and read the message. The risk was, that if the enemies were to gain access to one of these rods, they would be able to read messages or send decoy messages to disrupt the Spartans.

Encryption became more advanced in the 15th century when some level of automation was added to it. A substitution cipher tool was invented by Leon Alberti that used two metal disks that had alphabets in mixed orders and could be rotated in different ways to determine which letter would substitute the other. This was a more secure encryption method and the sender and recipient only needed to know the rotation that was used on the metal disks to come up with a ciphertext. The only risk with this technique was that an unintended party could guess the combinations of letters since there were only two disks to match. An improved version of this was made by Thomas Jefferson and was called the Jefferson disk. The encryption tool used a set of disks on which letters and numbers were written with some form of randomness. The disks could be rotated on their axle to an order that the sender desired. Since the tool had 36 disks, there were multiple possible combinations, and this made it an unbreakable encryption mechanism at the time. Let's look at an example of the Jefferson disk with its 36 disks:

In the 19th century, there were improvements made to the Jefferson disk in preparation for a large scale war that seemed increasingly likely in Europe at the time. The improved encryption tool was called Bazeries Cylinder and is what was used by the US Army. With the advent of World War II, the Germans had worked on their own encryption machine that was called Enigma. At the time, it was the most mechanized encryption system. It had a keyboard and an inbuilt scrambling mechanism. When a key was pressed on the keyboard, the Enigma would display the matching ciphertext. Its automation saw a quicker creation, sending, and responding to encrypted messages. Speed was crucial in the war environment. However, the Enigma, despite having been thought as an unbreakable machine, was broken by Marian Rejewski, a Polish mathematician, with help from colleagues Jerzy Różycki and Henryk Zygalski. These are only some of the techniques that have been used over millennia. However, the progression over such a long period shows that encryption has been used extensively for a long time.

Encryption today

The invention of computers led to great leaps in encryption. The first state-of-the-art encryption method was the Data Encryption Standard (DES), invented in 1979. The encryption algorithm was celebrated as the unbreakable 56-bit encryption and not even the most capable supercomputers were able to break it through brute force. It was estimated by its inventors that the computers would take at least 20 years in order to break a ciphertext made using DES. However, advances in computing and particularly the processing power led to DES being broken twice in a short period of time. In 1998 and 1999, DES was broken in 56 and 22 hours respectively, instead of the estimated 20 years. From then, there was a need to replace DES, and AES was then created after the public was invited to participate in a competition to build a secure encryption algorithm. 15 proposals were submitted to NIST around 1998, of which Rijndael from Belgium was chosen as the AES in 2001 because of its security, performance, efficiency, implementability, and flexibility.

Symmetric encryption

Symmetric encryption is characterized by the use of the same secret key when encrypting and decrypting a message. Most of the encryption methods that were used in the past were symmetric. Its simplicity made it the most common technique in the history of encryption. There are several symmetric encryption algorithms, including DES, AES, RC4, RC5, and RC6. There are certain advantages of this type of encryption, such as the following:

- **It is faster**: Symmetric encryption is faster since it uses less computational resources than asymmetric encryption as both parties encrypt and decrypt using the same key.
- **It is simple**: This method of encryption is quite easy to use since the sender and receiver need only to have a secure secret key. Unlike asymmetric encryption, no complex mathematical calculations have to be done to derive a key.

However, there were some disadvantages to symmetric encryption that resulted in research to coming up with another encryption method for less secure environments:

- **Secure channel to exchange the secret key**: The biggest problem with symmetric key encryption is that it should be shared in a way that guarantees its security. Encryption keys aren't simple strings of text like passwords, but blocks of gibberish. As such, you'll need to have a safer mechanism to get the key to the other party or else it would be cakewalk for the hackers to crack it.

- **Multiple keys**: For security reasons, senders will use different keys with different recipients. Consequently, they will have to keep a record of the many secret keys. Recipients on the other end will also need to keep a record of all the secret keys for the messages they have received from different senders.
- **The authenticity of a message is not guaranteed**: Symmetric encryption does not employ any measures to guarantee the authenticity of a sender. Since there is no authentication system in symmetric encryption, receivers never know if the message they are receiving is from the trusted sender or from someone who is trying to cause a disruption.

Asymmetric encryption

Asymmetric encryption is also referred to as public key encryption. In this type of encryption, there are two keys used that are long sized. The first one is a public key that is not a secret, and thus is shared with the public. Senders encrypt a message using this key. The second key is the private key that is used by a recipient to decrypt the message. The private key is mathematically related to the public key and is accessible to the senders of the message. However, it is extremely difficult for the private key to be derived from the public key and this is what makes asymmetric encryption secure, even when the public key is known by the public. Asymmetric encryption was invented in 1975, a time when the challenge of sharing private keys for symmetric encryption had started to manifest. The following is an illustration of asymmetric encryption:

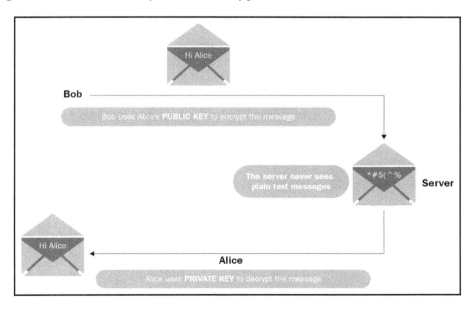

Bob sends a message to Alice through an end-to-end encrypted platform. When Bob writes the plaintext message, he uses Alice's public key to encrypt it and then sends the message to the server. The server just forwards the message to Alice as it cannot read or modify the message. Alice receives the message and uses her private key to convert the message to plaintext.

The following are some of the advantages of asymmetric encryption:

- **It is highly convenient**: The challenge of distributing keys securely is well handled by asymmetric encryption. The public key is not secret and can be made universally accessible without any repercussions to the private key, whereas the private key is a secret key that is used to decrypt the message.
- **Message authentication**: Asymmetric encryption features the use of signatures. These signatures tell the recipient that the message is verified to be from a particular sender. Therefore, even if another party sends the recipient a message with the publicly available secret key, the recipient will know that the message is not from the expected sender.
- **Can detect tampering**: The signature will be invalidated after an unauthorized modification is done. Because of this feature of secure signatures, it is easy for a recipient to know whether the message was tampered with after being sent by the original sender.
- **Non-repudiation**: The use of signatures ensures that neither parties can deny their part in the communication.

The disadvantages are as follows:

- **Authentication of public keys**: Since public keys are in the public domain, the sender has to ensure that a particular private key is owned by a particular recipient before encrypting a message with it. Symmetric encryption users do not have to undergo this.
- **It is slow**: Asymmetric encryption involves so many steps and long key sizes such that it becomes slow, especially for decrypting messages.
- **Computer resource usage is high**: The many operations that take place, combined with the long key sizes that characterize public key encryption, consequently lead to high computer resources usage.
- **Private key loss**: Only the recipient has the private key. If this key is lost, the messages cannot be decrypted nor can the key be obtained from the sender.

Protecting data and services with cryptography

There are two broad categories of data that encryption protects, that is data in transit and data at rest. Data in transit is data that is moving. It could be from a server to a client or from an email sender to a receiver. There is an attack referred to as man-in-the-middle where data in transit is intercepted by a third party that reads, tampers with, or deletes the data as it is sent to the recipient. Encryption prevents the interception and reading or modification of data by the unauthorized party. Data in storage is data stored on a hard drive, a database, an external storage device, or any other container for storing data. Encryption prevents attackers from accessing this data or modifying it.

Data at rest

A lot of data is in storage. Organizations keep huge volumes of data depending on their need for this data. With the use of big data, organizations are storing data that would, early on be regarded as low priority to be saved. This unused data is finally finding use to help organizations pinpoint certain trends and patterns. Organizations are also keeping more details about their customers. Alongside a customer's personal details, there is the use of cookies to help organizations know the online behavior or activities of their customers. The introduction of IoT in business processes, such as manufacturing, is also resulting an increase in data storage. As time goes on, organizations will be storing more data. At the same time, hackers are increasingly targeting organizational data. Organizational data fetches high prices in the dark web and some competitors pay hackers to fetch it. Cyber criminals are stealing data from portable computing devices and removable storage media with hopes of recovering sensitive information as well. Therefore, data in storage is under the continuous threat of being stolen. One of the most relevant hacks is the one against Yahoo that saw the theft of user data belonging to 3 billion users.

Encryption can help protect data that is in storage. Even if this data is stolen, it becomes of no use to the cyber criminals. The following are the ways in which this is achieved.

Full disk encryption

This is the ultimate way of protecting data stored on a computer and it involves encrypting the whole hard drive. Full disk encryption happens at a hardware level and all the contents of the hard drive are inaccessible to all but the one with a key to decrypt it. Therefore, a user of a computer that has full disk encryption normally has to provide the secret key for decryption before the computer can boot into an OS. When a hard disk is encrypted, all the data inside it is stored in a form that is unreadable. The data is only restored to a readable form if the correct key is provided. The advantage of this is that it is a simple security solution that has no pressing demands on the end user. The full disk encryption program will keep data encrypted unless it is being read or modified. Newly written data will also be automatically encrypted. The main disadvantage of this encryption method is that it tends to slow down the access times to data due to the encryption and decryption processes that have to take place in the background. Nevertheless, it is ideal for a workplace environment with portable computing devices.

File encryption

This is a file-specific method of encryption. It makes sense that the user would want to encrypt only part of the data in a hard disk. This could be the only sensitive data that requires additional security just in case an unauthorized party is able to get access to the computer. File encryption does not share the advantages of full disk encryption, in that it is automatic. The user has to encrypt or decrypt the contents of the specific files when necessary. The advantage with this method over the full disk encryption is that it does not slow down a computer. Encryption or decryption processes run only when necessary or when initiated by the user. The disadvantage of the method is that a lot of the encryption and decryption processes are pushed to be a burden to the user. Therefore, in an organization with many users that are not tech savvy, it may introduce some challenges.

Data in transit

Data moves quite often, especially in organizations. There are emails that are exchanged containing sensitive information. Heavy files are normally shared between employees, departments, or organizational branches. Military institutions transfer huge chunks of data in their networks. Web servers continually send and receive data from their clients. Therefore, there is a lot of data in transit. Unlike stored data, data in transit is more exposed. A hacker can simply tap into it as it is being transferred. This is because the technologies used were built for practicality and security was not the priority. For instance, data flowing in and out of a network can easily be captured using packet capturing tools, such as Wireshark. The tool is free to download and use and anyone can use it on wired and wireless networks. Therefore, data in transit has to be secured to prevent it from being read, modified, or dropped by unauthorized parties. The following are some of the ways through which encryption can be used to secure data in transit.

End-to-end encryption

This is probably the most secure way to secure communication channels. It combats the threat of sniffing on networks by making it impossible for a party monitoring the network to be able to see the contents of messages sent through the network. Therefore, only the sender and the receiver of the message will be able to read the plain text contents of the message. How it works is that when a sender is sending a message from an application, it is first encrypted and then sent through the network. In its encrypted form, it will be unreadable by all that do not have the secret key to unlock it. When the message gets to its destination, the recipient's app will unlock the message and display it in plain text. In between, no one will have been able to read or modify it. This includes the internet service provider, the government, hackers, and even the makers of the app. Some chat platforms, such as Telegram and WhatsApp, provide end-to-end encryption to ensure absolute protection of their users from snooping and sniffing.

The advantages of end-to-end encryption are many. To begin with, it secures data from hackers. Senders and receivers can exchange messages even through insecure networks since they are assured that the message cannot be read by any other party. End-to-end encryption also makes sure that data is kept private. The government cannot read the messages sent, neither can the ISP. The lack of end-to-end encryption on some communication platforms, such as Gmail, just shows that the company can see the contents of the messages sent by its users. The disadvantage of this type of blanket-cover encryption is that it can be exploited for negative purposes, such as to discuss sinister things like crime and terrorist attacks. When that happens, no one apart from the communicating parties can tell what is being discussed.

Encrypted web connection (SSL and TLS)

HTTP is a commonly relied on security measure to secure connections to websites. There are threats in the flow of data from a client to a server or from the server to the client. Essentially, packets are sent in plaintext. Therefore, a threat actor lurking in a network can read all the sensitive details that have been exchanged between a client and a server. For instance, if a client was to visit an online banking platform without the encryption, it is possible that their login credentials would be stolen by threat actors monitoring that network. It is very simple for a hacker to capture and keep a record of all the packets that are exchanged in a network. Due to this, web connections are normally secured using TLS or SSL. There are standardized ways through which users can acquire SSL or TLS certificates that ensure that the connection to a certain website is encrypted. This makes the user at ease of sharing more sensitive details without the risk of such data falling into the wrong hands.

Encrypted email servers

Email encryption is quickly coming up as a secure method of sending emails with the assurance that only the intended entities can read it. Previously, almost all emails were sent in a plaintext form. This put them at risk of being accessed or read by people that were not the intended recipients. In encrypted emails, the sender encrypts the email with the recipient's public key. Only the recipient has the private key that can decrypt the email.

Examples of encryption algorithms

There are many encryption algorithms available, out of which the most commonly used ones are explained as follows.

Advanced Encryption Standard (AES)

This is the cryptography standard that is trusted by the US government. It is symmetric. It is strong yet efficient in terms of resource requirements. **Advanced Encryption Standard (AES)** can have 128, 192 and 256-bit keys that are hard to crack. There have not been any reports of weaknesses in it thus security experts are convinced that it will remain strong for a long period of time. The only threat to this algorithm is a brute force attack, but fortunately, it will take a supercomputer 1 billion billion years to break the 128-bit key.

Triple DES

This is an advancement of DES that has already been declared to be insecure. Triple DES came as a replacement to DES and introduced three 56 bit keys. Therefore, the entire key size is 168 bits, though experts argue that the actual figure is 112 bits. (2TDES has a key length of 112 bits - `https://www.tutorialspoint.com/cryptography/triple_des.htm`). DES is a symmetric algorithm and sees use in institutions such as banks. Apart from brute force, there is no other known attack that can break this algorithm. It is estimated that it may take 260,658 years for this algorithm to be broken.

RSA

This is an asymmetric encryption algorithm that has been accepted as the standard for encrypting internet traffic. It is used by programs such as PGP and GPG for encryption purposes. Since there are two pairs of keys, RSA is safer to use in insecure environments, such as the internet, to remove the fear of a key being stolen during sharing. RSA has been cracked once, but that was the 728-bit key version. 1,000 cores were used and the cracking process took two years. However, 1,024 and 2,048 key sizes are the commonly used key sizes, and it is estimated that it may take 7,000 years for the 1,024-bit key to be broken.

Blowfish

This algorithm was also created to be a replacement for DES. It is symmetric and has a unique way of encrypting data where it first groups it into 64-bit groups and then encrypts each of the groups. Blowfish is free to use and many e-commerce websites have adopted it. It is commonly used to secure online payments and in password management tools. Due to its complex nature, Blowfish is not crackable.

Encryption challenges

Encryption, as a form of security, has been tested in several ways by hackers or people who are curious to see how different algorithms can be broken. The most commonly faced challenges are as follows:

- **Brute force**: The most commonly used method to break encryption is brute force. This is where different key combinations are tried until the right key is found. Brute force is able to break most encryption algorithms but the main issue is the time that has to be taken for that to happen. Most of the encryption algorithms used today will take millions of years to break. The length of a key is also a major determinant of the time that can be taken to break it. The longer the key, the more time it can take. However, there is a limit to the key size due to limitations in computation resources. A very long key would take so much time to encrypt and decrypt that it becomes unpractical to use.

- **Cryptanalysis**: This is the process of finding weaknesses in a cipher that can make it easier to break than using a brute force attack. If the cipher is flawed in a way that some elements of it can be easily determined, it becomes a lot easier to break it without having to try every possible combination. The problem is that some cryptography standards are believed to have been weakened by some entities for their own gain. Edward Snowden spoke of the US NSA having weakened multiple cryptography standards. This puts them at an unfair advantage when it comes to breaking ciphers. It is said that NSA was also involved in the weakening of the DES algorithm that resulted in the algorithm being declared unsafe.

- **Increased computational power**: Most of the cryptography standards in use are deemed safe because the currently available computation power cannot successfully break them. However, computational power is set to increase. There have been major developments in quantum computing and this technology could come with big problems for the current encryption algorithm. Due to the massive computing power expected to be in quantum computers, they will take significantly less time to do cryptanalysis or brute force attacks to break ciphers.

Summary

This chapter has looked at encryption as a method of securing data and communication covered which its early methods and how automation was applied to encryption making it more secure and reliable. We explored the different types of encryption and some methods of encryption; data in storage and data in transit. Alongside this, we also discussed encrypted web connection, and encrypted email servers. The most commonly used encryption algorithms have been discussed and wherever possible, the time it takes to break them has been highlighted. Lastly, the challenges to encryption as a security measure have been discussed and these include brute force attacks, cryptanalysis, and the threat of increased computational power.

The next chapter will look at a leap in finance and technology, Blockchain. We will discuss the Blockchain technology, cryptocurrencies, and the challenges that are currently in the way of Blockchain adoption.

Further reading

The following are resources that can be used to gain more knowledge of this chapter:

- *What Is Data Encryption?*: https://digitalguardian.com/blog/what-data-encryption
- *Encryption*: https://searchsecurity.techtarget.com/definition/encryption
- *History of Encryption*: https://www.sans.org/reading-room/whitepapers/vpns/history-encryption-73
- *Digital signatures*: https://www.tutorialspoint.com/cryptography/cryptography_digital_signatures.htm

16
The Rise of the Blockchain

Blockchain has been considered as a great leap in technology that can see application in many areas. It is being looked at as a big step in Fintech due to its applicability in terms of powering digital currencies. However, the technology is bigger than a simple financial solution, though many people seem to look at it from the perspective of cryptocurrencies. Blockchain technology has, and will, continue to bring about significant changes in the global economy. Ever since the introduction of a Blockchain powered digital currency, Bitcoin, in 2008, there have been mixed reactions. Individuals, organizations, and governments have been looking at the potential impacts of this technology. Undoubtedly, Blockchain is going to cause a disruption in several industries, hence the buzz surrounding it. Of interest is how this technology will affect the way financial services are offered. This chapter will look into this through the following topics:

- Encryption challenges
- Introduction to Blockchain technology
- Cryptocurrencies:
  - Cryptocurrency wallets
  - Challenges to cryptocurrencies
- Challenges in Blockchain technology

Introduction to Blockchain technology

The core concept of Blockchain technology is to have blocks of data that are secured and hard to manipulate. The Blockchain is a digital ledger that acts as a distributed database that keeps records of all transactions in the network. A block can be described as a single sheet in the digital ledger. This sheet contains the actual transactions that are conducted on a network, such as the sending and receiving of money. The block is processed as a whole and is protected using cryptographic signatures. All the processing is done in a decentralized way. There is a network of miners or master nodes that are responsible for handling the processing of transactions. The digital ledger is distributed. This means that rather than being stored centrally, it is stored across many devices. This makes it hard for any single party to manipulate it as there are very many copies of it stored in different devices globally. For a hacker to manipulate the entire Blockchain, he or she needs to breach the tough security of the Blockchain and all the devices that have a copy of it. This is almost impossible to achieve. The distributed database is public, thus it is transparent and anyone can download it. The Blockchain is kept in continuous synchronization; thus, a case can never arise where there are inconsistencies in transactions. Therefore, the technology is transparent, reliable, and does not have transactional errors.

Consensus mechanisms in a Blockchain

The information that's added to the Blockchain must be verified. The tough verification measures are what make a Blockchain free of errors. If this is not done, there could be blocks added to the Blockchain with redundant or invalid data. Therefore, there exists some form of consensus of how this verification is done. Different consensus mechanisms are used by different crypto assets and the most popular are *proof of work* and *proof of stake*. These are the consensus mechanisms that shall be discussed. It is, however, noteworthy that other mechanisms, such as delegated proof of stake, exist, and have seen a fair amount of usage in some Blockchains.

Proof of work

The proof of work consensus is the oldest as it was explored in the 1990s. In 2008, when Satoshi Nakamoto wrote the Bitcoin whitepaper, he proposed the use of the proof of work consensus to protect the network from the threat of an entity getting a majority control over it. Proof of work is actualized through mining. The transactions initiated on the Blockchain are bundled and stored in a memory pool. Miners then verify these transactions. This is done in the form of solving a complex mathematics puzzle. The process of solving the puzzle is complex and requires lots of computing power. The first miner to solve the puzzle then gets a reward. In Bitcoin, the miner gets a new Bitcoin and the network transaction fees. The verified memory pool is then referred to as a block and added to the Blockchain. As an added precaution, the block is added to the Blockchain when other miners agree that the given solution is correct. To manipulate the Blockchain, such as Bitcoin, the user will need to have at least 51% control over all the miners in the network. This means that a hacker will have to acquire an increasingly big number of computers to perform what is referred to as the 51% attack. To make it very difficult for such an attack to happen, several measures are employed. These are as follows:

- **Asymmetric puzzles**: The process of getting the answer to a puzzle is complex, while the process of verifying the answer is easy.
- **Brute force solutions**: The answers to these puzzles are only arrived at using brute force. Therefore, none of the miners are at an advantage as they have to solve the complex puzzles in the same way. To gain any advantage of being able to solve a puzzle quicker, a miner has to add more computational power, which is expensive.
- **Puzzle parameters**: The block regeneration time has to be kept consistent. For instance, if the regeneration time is 20 minutes and then after some period it decreases to 18 minutes, the network will increase the difficulty of the puzzle. This will result in miners having to carry out more computations to solve the puzzle.

Proof of stake

Proof of work is being termed as an expensive consensus mechanism. Due to the continually increased complexity of the puzzles, miners have been spending more resources to try and mine a single bitcoin. It is estimated that in a few years, the resources used will outweigh any rewards the network gives miners. This is why some cryptocurrencies are adopting proof of stake. Proof of stake does not use a mathematical puzzle to select the person that gets to create a new block in the ledger. Instead, it chooses the creator of a new block in a probabilistic but deterministic way. Therefore, all creators have determined the chances of being selected and will eventually get selected. The proof of stake consensus, however, requires the creators to stake or possess a certain number of coins. When the user stakes these coins, they can create what is referred to as a masternode. The staking of the coins prevents one person from owning too many masternodes that they can use to manipulate a Blockchain. The proof of stake consensus is said to have energy efficiency as it cuts out the mining process. Additionally, most of the masternodes are run on virtual private servers. The masternodes are rewarded at the end of a certain period, and all masternodes share the revenue. The biggest difference between proof of work and proof of stake is that in proof of stake no new coins are created.

Applications of Blockchain technology

The applications of Blockchain technology can broadly be categorized into recording purposes, government purposes, and financial applications. In the following sections, will see how.

Recording purposes

The nature of Blockchain technology is that it can be easily applied in record keeping. It can, therefore, see use in digital identity.

Digital identity

The Blockchain system is secured using cryptography. The private keys that are used in this cryptography are unique, hence the owners of these private keys are unique as well. In a world full of accounts, there has been a struggle in the way people are identified or authenticated into different systems. Essentially, individuals must possess usernames and passwords for these accounts, and due to the huge number of accounts, users are struggling with keeping their login credentials. The Blockchain can be applied to give universally unique digital identities. All the end users will need is a private key and the systems they are to be authenticated on to be secured through cryptography. This will bring a solution to users using weak passwords or sharing personal data that can be used to uniquely target them.

Government purposes

Blockchain technology can be used by governments to achieve several goals. To begin with, governments can use it to control the issuing, possession, revocation, and replacement of private keys. This institutionalized control of private keys could work alongside identity cards to ensure that all citizens of a country have secured digital identities. These private keys can be used to achieve many government services, such as car registration, business registration, and to make payments.

Governments can also use Blockchain technology for data sharing purposes. One of the main explorations of Blockchain technology has been in the creation of cryptocurrencies. The way in which most governments operate is that they tend to take advantage of business partners in their country. For instance, the government can rely on ISPs to give them personal details of a client suspected to be carrying out malicious activities. However, there are often challenges with the sharing of data, especially when there are conflicting interests, the data is of a sensitive nature, and there are also technological challenges. The distributed ledger of a Blockchain can, however, be used to solve these issues and ensure that there is ease in data sharing.

Governments can apply Blockchain for cross-border vehicle identification—vehicle identification tends to be restricted to a certain country. Crossing borders with cars tends to bring security challenges, especially in European countries. Blockchain can be used in such places to create an international registry for vehicles to ensure that vehicles and drivers can be identified even when outside their country.

Blockchain technology can be applied to distribute government aid—there are situations where the government is required to distribute aid to citizens living in certain places, especially during unfortunate circumstances. Money could be the easiest way to distribute aid but there are many inefficiencies that make it impossible to do so. Programs such as basic income for all have been started using Blockchain technology. These programs give basic income to residents of unfortunate backgrounds. Due to Blockchain technology, the money is distributed transparently and it is easy to find out about the people that have benefited from the aid. Likewise, governments can use Blockchain to distribute financial aid to their citizens. The transparency of Blockchain technology prevents challenges such as corruption and misuse of funds.

Financial applications

Blockchain technology is set to change the world in many ways. The following are some of these ways:

- **Auditing**: In normal financial institutions such as banks, there is a great burden in securing both money and personal data. In addition to this, banks are often required by governments to check their client accounts for suspicious transactions. Blockchain technology can be used to do auditing since all transactions are recorded on a distributed ledger. Therefore, all transactions can be recorded, and if there are any suspicious transactions, the transacting parties can be easily identified.
- **Cryptocurrencies**: Cryptocurrencies are responsible for bringing a lot of attention to the Blockchain technologies. Bitcoin, in particular, showed that Blockchain technology could come up with currencies that were outside the control of any government. The cryptocurrency then saw use in several dark web markets as illegal activities could be procured using this currency due to the security and anonymity that it offered its users. The world then saw the creation of many other cryptocurrencies. Cryptocurrencies have seen increased adoption in the real world and therefore their future is quite promising. They are also being adopted to make payments. Unlike normal currencies, which have to go through various institutions for a transfer to happen, thus introducing more charges and taking several days, cryptocurrencies offer a quick and cheap means of money transfer.

There are many other potential applications of Blockchain technology. Researchers are trying to solve many problems, such as food security, using this technology. However, this chapter will be focused on the Fintech applications of Blockchain and cryptocurrencies in particular.

Cryptocurrencies

As mentioned earlier, Blockchain technology has been exploited more in the creation of cryptocurrencies. Cryptocurrencies are virtual currencies that are decentralized and use a peer to peer network. Since they are decentralized, they are not controlled from a single point or by a single entity. Transactions are conducted directly, that is, from the sender to the receiver without any intermediary. To achieve this, cryptocurrencies rely on peers to have a ledger with all transactions that they can use to validate new transactions. Therefore, if you are sending X amount of digital currency, the peer network will determine whether you can perform the transaction. If the transaction is validated by the peer network, it will go through and will be added to the distributed ledger that all peers have. The following diagram summarizes the process of making a cryptocurrency funds transfer.

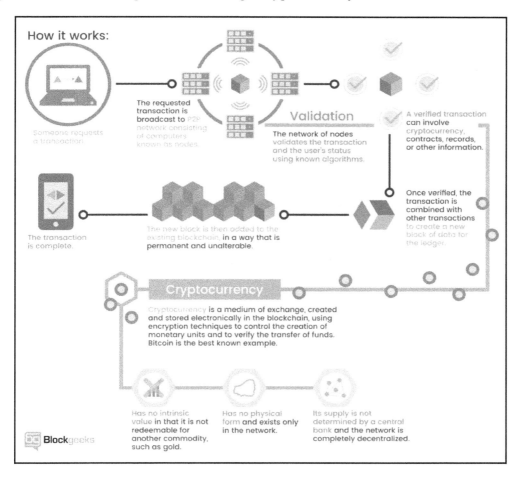

As we discussed earlier, there is a lot that goes on in the background to determine the transactions that will be listed on the distributed ledger. We discussed two consensus systems that are commonly used. Transactions with cryptocurrencies are quite different from those done with flat currencies. The following are the properties of cryptocurrency transactions:

- **They are irreversible**: Once a transaction has been done, it can never be reversed. No one simply has the authorization to reverse a transaction. Therefore, if a transaction happens, it cannot be undone. This means that if you accidentally send funds to the wrong recipient, the funds cannot be reversed. Similarly, if a hacker steals your cryptocurrencies, they cannot be recovered. This is why users are always advised to protect their private keys and to ensure that they crosscheck the recipient wallet addresses before sending money.

- **Pseudonymous**: The transactions conducted through cryptocurrencies are not recorded by any institution or government agency. However, transactions are made public and are written on a distributed ledger. Even though actual names or identities of the transacting parties are not written on this ledger, their addresses are. It is not necessarily possible for the transacting parties to be known, but if a user's address is known by a third party, they can find out about all the transactions that the address has done since all the details are kept on the distributed ledger.

- **Global**: Cryptocurrency transactions happen nearly instantaneously in some coins while other coins may take a few minutes. The transactions can be made to and from anywhere globally without restrictions. This is because there is no intermediary and the transactions are confirmed the moment the peer network validates them.

- **Secure**: It is impossible for a cryptocurrency transaction to be targeted by attackers. A lot of the security concerns in cryptocurrency transactions are related to the wallets that are used, but not the transactions themselves. The cryptography system of cryptocurrencies makes them impossible to break.

Cryptocurrency wallets

A cryptocurrency wallet is used to store or transact cryptocurrencies and other digital assets. They act like safety deposit boxes. Only the person that rents the box gets the keys to unlock it. In the same way, only the person that creates a cryptocurrency wallet gets the keys to access it. This key is the private key. The loss of a private key directly translates to the permanent loss of the money stored in the wallet protected by that key. At the same time, if another party gets hold of an individual's private key, they can move the funds from that wallet. A cryptocurrency wallet stores two types of keys, private and public keys. As we have discussed, the private key is a show of ownership of the wallet. Only the real owner of the wallet should have this key. The public key is derived from the private key using a complex method. The public key is what is used to create a wallet's address. In some wallets, the public key is the wallet address. However, other wallets generate wallet addresses by hashing and shortening the public address. The wallet address is what can be used to receive funds in the wallet. There are different types of wallets and these are discussed as follows.

Desktop wallets

These wallets run as software on a desktop or laptop computer. They will only run on the computer they are installed on. Therefore, the wallets cannot be used outside of the owner's computer. They are secure since they cannot be stolen easily. However, if the computer they are running on is infected with malware, access to the wallet or the funds in the wallets could be permanently lost.

Web wallets

These are wallets that are run on web browsers. Some of these wallets run as add-ons to browsers while others run as web-based systems. They are very convenient for doing transactions and can be accessed from multiple devices. However, they are at more risk of being hacked into due to the many cyber threats that can attack browsers.

Mobile wallets

These are wallets that run as smartphone applications. They are mostly built for convenience purposes of those that want to use their wallets on the go. Due to their portability, they are also at a higher risk of being lost through the theft of the devices they are running on.

Hardware wallets

These are wallets that are bought as special hardware devices that were purposefully created to store cryptocurrencies. They are among the most secured wallets and are commonly used by those that want to store their cryptocurrencies for lengthy periods before transacting. Hardware wallets come with several security measures to protect a user's private key as they never expose it to any computer or web-based system. They are also immune to computer malware and cannot be broken by thieves that steal them. However, they are normally sold at a premium while other wallets are free.

Paper wallets

These are wallets printed on papers. These wallets remove any electronics from the storage of cryptocurrencies. They are used by those that want to keep their cryptocurrencies without transacting them for extended periods of time. However, they are more prone to theft, destruction, and wear and tear.

Challenges to cryptocurrencies

Despite the benefits that cryptocurrencies bring, they have been facing serious challenges in the recent past. Some of these challenges are discussed as follows.

Unstable value

In 2017, the prices of Bitcoin soared and they managed to hit the highs of $19,000 by early 2018. However, the prices then sharply went down to the lows of $6,000 in just six months. This led to the loss of money for many people that had acquired cryptocurrencies as a means of investment. The adoption of cryptocurrencies has gone down since the massive fall in the value of almost all cryptocurrencies in 2018. It makes sense that people and organizations would be afraid of transacting in a currency that can depreciate in value so quickly.

Theft

There is a global increase of cyber attacks. These attacks have led to huge losses. There have been attacks that have become formulated specifically for cryptocurrencies. There is malware that's been designed to steal private keys from users' phones or computers since some wallets keep the private keys in secret directories on the host devices. There are other malware designed to steal keys or sessions from users that prefer web wallets.

Exchange risks

Cryptocurrencies can be exchanged in exchanges. Some exchanges keep a user's cryptocurrencies while doing the exchange. There have been attacks targeting exchange platforms that keep user funds. These attacks have often led to the loss of hundreds of dollars. When these platforms are attacked, there are instances where the users that had some of their money handled by the platforms end up losing all the money. Apart from this, there are risks about some exchange platforms that can defraud users. Since they are not regulated, the platforms can withhold user funds and never release them. Legally, there is not much that the user can do since cryptocurrencies are not regulated.

Blockchain challenges and future

Blockchain technology is gaining traction but so are the challenges that it faces. To begin with, the technology is facing a big challenge with endpoint vulnerabilities. In as much as the technology is secure, it is used through endpoints that do not enjoy the same level of security. For instance, a user could be using cryptocurrencies but on devices that are already infected with malware. Even though this is not a security flaw in Blockchain technology, it is a serious challenge that should be addressed. The network should come up with ways to secure endpoints in the future.

Another challenge with Blockchain technology is uncertainty. Blockchain technology has held up well so far but its implementation is only starting. The technology relies on a peer to peer network and this means that the more its implementation grows, the more the pressure on the peer to peer networks. So far, the technology has not been tested at full scale so it is unknown how it will hold up if it is applied in many other areas.

Lastly, there is the challenge of susceptibility to fraud. Blockchain technology is prone to the 51% attack. This means that, if 51% of the participants in a network conspire to defraud it, they simply can. The main deterrent to this attack has been the cost of resources for this attack to happen. However, what will happen when computing resources and the cost of electricity go down is most likely to destabilize many peer to peer networks. In the future, the technology should be modified to prevent this type of an attack from taking place in the first place.

Summary

This chapter has looked at the rise of Blockchain technology and focused more on the financial aspect of this technology. It has defined what Blockchain means and how consensus is arrived at in the technology. It has discussed two consensus mechanisms; proof of work and proof of stake. We then looked at the applications of this technology. As discussed, the technology can be applied in several areas, such as providing digital identities, providing currencies for transacting, and for auditing. We then focused on cryptocurrencies. A definition of cryptocurrencies and an explanation of how they work have been given. Since the cryptocurrencies are stored in crypto wallets, the chapter has gone through all of the different wallets. These are desktop, web, hardware, mobile, and paper wallets. We then looked at the challenges facing cryptocurrencies, such as unstable values, theft, and exchange risks. Lastly, the challenges facing Blockchain technology as a whole have been explained. The next and the concluding chapter will talk about quantum computing at length, especially the different ways it will shape the future.

Further reading

The following are resources that can be used to gain more knowledge on this chapter:

- *The rise and rise of blockchain*: http://treasurytoday.com/2017/09/the-rise-and-rise-of-blockchain-tttech
- *The Rise Of Blockchain Technology*: https://www.valuewalk.com/2018/05/blockchain-technology-fintech-ecommerce/
- *The Rise of Blockchain*: http://www.fairviewcapital.com/application/files/7914/9369/3742/Fairview_Capital_Rise_of_Blockchain.pdf
- *Blockchain in Education can do Wonders, Here's Why*: https://www.entrepreneur.com/article/315182
- *Security Challenges of Blockchain*: https://medium.com/taslet-security/security-challenges-of-blockchain-3d0ead36221b
- *ISSUES WITH BLOCKCHAIN SECURITY*: https://due.com/blog/issues-blockchain-security/

17
Artificial Intelligence and Cybersecurity

Enterprise customers around the world are investing in Artificial Intelligence and automation to improve their business processes, reinvent productivity, and improve operational excellence. Banks are looking into new ways of how to implement fraud detection in their ATM networks, insurance companies are exploring how to use Artificial Intelligence to predict profitability of their services to the end customers, and brokers have started to apply Artificial Intelligence to predict stock market movements. The following diagram illustrates reasons why business organizations are adopting worldwide Artificial Intelligence as of 2017:

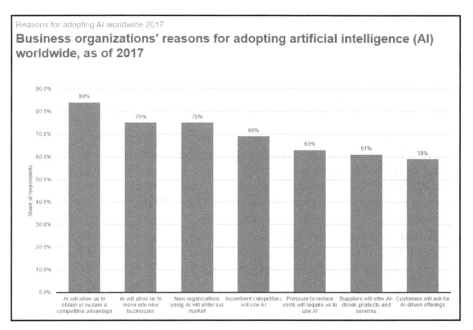

Many buzzwords are used when it comes to Artificial Intelligence. It is important to look underneath those buzzwords to truly understand this new technology. The following diagram illustrates the revolution in the Artificial Intelligence space:

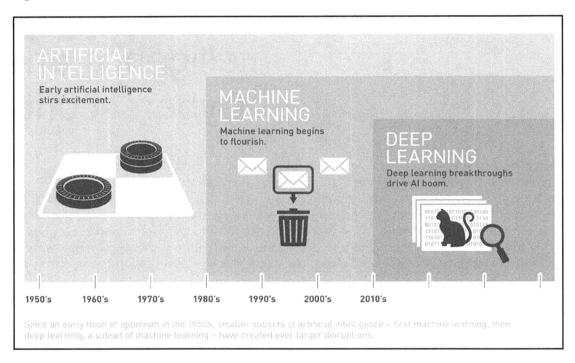

A technological breakthrough in Artificial Intelligence is without any doubt a breakthrough for society. However, the reality is that all of these companies are still targeted by cyber criminals who perform new cyber-attacks daily. Artificial Intelligence offers many benefits in the cybersecurity space. Security vendors have discovered that and started to invest by building Machine Learning engines that analyze massive sets of telemetry data, which is ultimately used to train Artificial Intelligence on how to protect, detect, and respond to cyber-attacks. With Artificial Intelligence-based security products, you elevate threat protection from a tactical product to a strategic platform. With that, you improve efficacy and your environment dramatically. The rate at which malicious content, malware, and exploits are created far exceed any financial resources or human capability. It no longer scales to analyze every single thread by a human analyst. Therefore, it has become the center of success to apply Artificial Intelligence that is powered by machines and deep learning. This chapter will focus on the advantages of Artificial Intelligence in the cybersecurity space.

Threat landscape evolution

According to McAfee and the Center for Strategic International Studies, cybersecurity breaches cost $600 billion a year globally. In addition, The Economist Intelligence Unit confirms that 30% of security professionals expect a major and successful attack within 90 days. These are alarming figures and require immediate attention:

> *"There's no perfect security, and security isn't an endpoint - it's a never-ending journey."*
>
> *– John Klemens, Technical Director of IA Solutions, Telos Corporation*

A successful cyber-attack causes devastating consequences for the business. For example, in the financial services industry sector, a breach can result in a significant loss in revenue and trust with the end customer. Cyber-attacks damage the reputation of the organization. When cyber-attacks remain undetected for up to 180 days, it is simply impossible to combat them with human-based analysis only.

Artificial Intelligence

Let's dive into Artificial Intelligence. First, it is important to understand that not all Artificial Intelligence is the same. As an example, you might still remember SkyNet from the movie Terminator, Lucy the Artificial Intelligence robot that gave a speech at the Saudi Arabia Future Investment Initiative meeting, or Microsoft's Artificial Intelligence-based security automation solution in Windows Defender Advanced Threat Protection. Artificial Intelligence is the study of computer science that is focused on developing software that mimics or exceeds human intelligence. Artificial Intelligence can range from simple calculations, to two robots playing chess against each other, to self-steering technology that radically changes the future:

Narrow Artificial Intelligence

Narrow Artificial Intelligence (**Narrow AI**) has no self-awareness or genuine intelligence. The best example for Narrow AI is digital assistants such as Apple's Siri, Microsoft's Cortana, and Amazon's Alexa. These assistants are performing one task at a time. Take Cortana as an example—Cortana can help the user to perform many tasks, but when you attempt to have a proper conversation, you will discover how narrow the response will become:

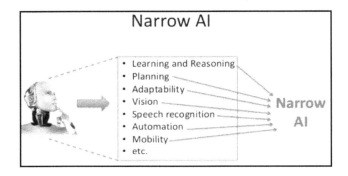

True Artificial Intelligence

True Artificial Intelligence (**True AI**) entails a lot of responsibilities, and that's where you will see politicians, industry leaders, and visionaries start arguing about ethics and what Artificial Intelligence should and, most importantly, shouldn't be able to do. True AI is a computer that is either as smart or smarter than a human brain:

Good examples of True AI are SkyNet from the movie Terminator or the movie The Matrix. Let's take The Matrix as an example and dive into it. In the movie, Artificial Intelligence was developed in the early 21st century. It allowed an entire race of robots to be capable of thinking and acting for themselves without human intervention. The robots started a rights movement, took over the city of Mesopotamia, and built 01, the first Machine City. In 01, the robots then created a new, better Artificial Intelligence. The war between humanity and robots started. During the war, the humans decided to eliminate the power source that was required for the robots to work, which was daylight, but the robots quickly learned that humans can be a power source themselves, which led to the slavery of almost all mankind. Inside pods, humans were plugged into virtual reality. The True AI had developed Artificially Intelligent sentient programs such as the architect and the oracle. All aspects in the virtual world were managed and controlled by different Artificial Intelligence-based programs that were guarded by the Agent programs. You might say that this only happens in the movies, but let's take a real-world example of something similar. In 2017, Facebook stopped an Artificial Intelligence experiment after they discovered that two chatbots had invented their own language that only they could understand. This happened after Facebook challenged the chatbots to try and negotiate with each over different trade. The following image illustrates the conversation between the chatbots **Bob** and **Alice**:

Bob: i can i i everything else . . . .

Alice: balls have zero to me to me to me to me to me to me to me to me to

Bob: you i everything else . . . .

Alice: balls have a ball to me to me to me to me to me to me to me

Bob: i i can i i i everything else . . . .

Alice: balls have a ball to me to me to me to me to me to me to me

Bob: i . . . .

Alice: balls have zero to me to me to me to me to me to me to me to me to

Bob: you i i i i i everything else . . . .

Alice: balls have 0 to me to me to me to me to me to me to me to me to

Bob: you i i i everything else . . . .

Alice: balls have zero to me to me to me to me to me to me to me to me to

Technologies powering Artificial Intelligence

To enable Artificial Intelligence, you need to have access to big data and smart algorithms. Let's dive into the technologies that power Artificial Intelligence:

- **Supervised Machine Learning**: The majority of practical Machine Learning is supervised learning. Supervised learning is where you have input variables (X) and an output variable (Y) and an algorithm to learn the mapping.
- **Unsupervised Machine Learning**: Unsupervised Machine Learning is Machine Learning, which is unsupervised learning. In the case of unsupervised learning, you only have input value (X) and no matching output variable.
- **Semi-supervised Machine Learning:** Semi-supervised learning is where you have a large amount of input value (X) and only a portion of the output variable (Y).
- **Deep Learning:** While Machine Learning is focused on task-specific algorithms, deep learning architectures such as a deep neural network have been applied to various fields where they have produced results comparable to and in some cases superior to human experts.

Artificial Intelligence-powered cybersecurity

Almost all security vendors currently advertise that their technology has some sort of Artificial Intelligence. However, Artificial Intelligence comes in many variations and there are many underlying technologies. You will want to watch out for buzzwords that have been placed by marketing departments. It is not always clear what these security vendors are specifically doing with Artificial Intelligence, Machine Learning, and so on.

Building a security solution that is powered by Artificial Intelligence is challenging and requires investments. The costs include building the fundamental systems that are required to operate the technology, additional costs that are required for scaling the system in a hyperscale environment, and, lastly, there is a very limited pool of talents available in the market that have sufficient experience in working on Artificial Intelligence code and who are able to handle complex mathematical principles to create an efficient and scalable solution. Even if some companies can invest into the infrastructure and are able to hire these talents, Artificial Intelligence requires data—a lot of data to train the Artificial Intelligence. There are only a few companies in the world who actually have that amount of data. These companies need to have in-depth knowledge and data on the threat landscape, on the digital identities, email accounts, web presence, and telemetry coming from endpoints and mobile devices. With that, companies like Apple, Google, Microsoft, Amazon, and Facebook have a clear advantage.

It is clear that Artificial Intelligence powered security solutions will assist cybersecurity teams in many stages of defense. Narrow AI could be used to perform simple tasks such as searching for a specific **Indicator of Compromise** (**IOC**) in a threat intelligence database, all the way up to a super AI being self-aware and not only alerting the **Security Operations Center** (**SOC**) when it detects a cybercriminal trying to breach the environment, but also automatically adjust preventative security controls to prevent the breach from happening in the first place. Without any doubt, Artificial Intelligence-based security solutions will offer intelligent recommendations to the cybersecurity teams. The following screenshot illustrates the artificial intelligence-based security automation from Microsoft's Windows Defender ATP solution:

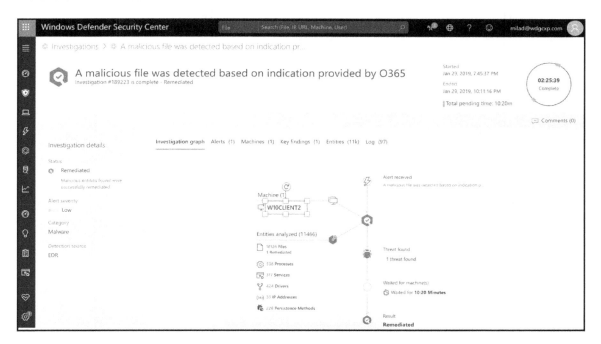

Use cases

There are five use cases that you will want to enable through Artificial Intelligence to improve your cyber hygiene and operational excellence, all of which are shown in the following diagram:

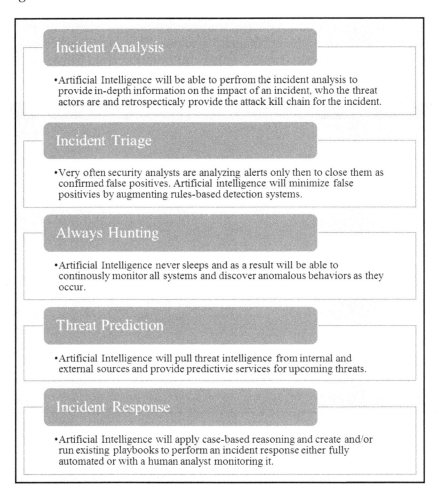

All of these use cases are fairly new and yet their full potential hasn't been discovered by any security vendor. It is clear, however, that the benefits of Artificial Intelligence to fight cybercrime is critical and that security vendors are investing.

Summary

In this chapter, you have learned that Artificial Intelligence is not just Artificial Intelligence —there are many different technologies, use cases, and scenarios to take into account too. It is important to deeply understand what Artificial Intelligence is before jumping on the next call with the sales representative of a security vendor that tries to sell the world's first Artificial Intelligence-based security solution. You are now able to ask smart questions such as *is the Artificial Intelligence a Narrow AI or True AI capability?* and *when you say Machine Learning, is it supervised Machine Learning, unsupervised Machine Learning, or semi-supervised Machine Learning?* The key is not to get fooled, and understand how the technology can help you protect, detect, and respond against the ever changing threat landscape. You will want to make sure that the technology helps you to truly discover and remediate cyber-attacks as quickly as possible. The following diagram illustrates a project from the MIT, of an Artificial Intelligence-based cybersecurity system that can detect 85% of cyber-attacks. However, this is only the beginning:

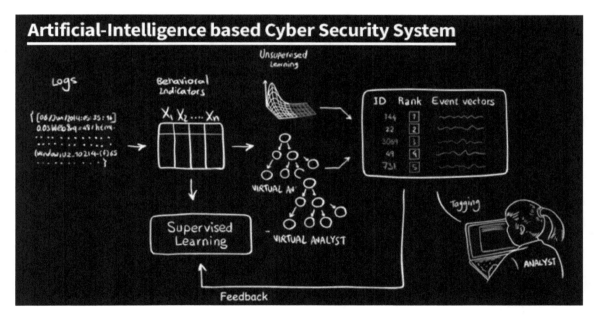

Further reading

The following are resources that you can use to gain more knowledge on this chapter:

- *Securing the Future of Artificial Intelligence and Machine Learning at Microsoft*: `https://docs.microsoft.com/en-us/security/securing-artificial-intelligence-machine-learning`
- *MIT builds Artificial Intelligence system that can detect 85% of Cyber Attacks*: `https://thehackernews.com/2016/04/artificial-intelligence-cyber-security.html`
- *AI for cybersecurity is a hot new thing—and a dangerous gamble*: `https://www.technologyreview.com/s/611860/ai-for-cybersecurity-is-a-hot-new-thing-and-a-dangerous-gamble/`
- *Artificial Intelligence Is a Threat to Cybersecurity. It's Also a Solution*: `https://www.bcg.com/publications/2018/artificial-intelligence-threat-cybersecurity-solution.aspx`
- *AI Companies Race To Get Upper Hand In Cybersecurity—Before Hackers Do*: `https://www.investors.com/news/technology/ai-companies-artificial-intelligence-cybersecurity/`

The Quantum Future $\mathbf{18}$

Computing is all about to change with the unveiling of quantum computers. This is going to be a big leap in computing that will bring with it fundamental shifts in different technologies that are used today. Currently, there are many security technologies built on the complexity of computing different puzzles of which normal computers can take thousands, millions, or billions of years to crack. These are mostly security solutions that use cryptography. However, the unveiling of quantum computers will mean that these complex puzzles will be solvable in less time. Therefore, many encryption algorithms that are currently deemed secure will not be after the release of quantum computers in the world. Quantum computers will take over the future. It is not just an advanced way of computers, it is a reformation of computers atom by atom. These changes will have impacts that will be felt in all sectors.

This chapter will look into this based on the following topics:

- Evolution of quantum technology
- The quantum technology race
- Quantum technology breakthroughs
- Impacts of quantum technology

The first general purpose computer was built in 1837 and it was man's biggest attempt at computing. After a century, another big milestone was reached when ENIAC was built. It was the first electronic computer. It used vacuum tubes to control the flow of electricity. After that, transistors were introduced allowing smaller computers to be built. Today, the microprocessor technology is in dominance and it has allowed for the creation of very powerful but small computer processors. Therefore, computers have been reduced from the size of entire rooms to the size of a device that is handheld. This is the current stage of computing that seems to be a big improvement from the ancient computers. However, there has not really been a fundamental change in the way computers are built. Most attempts were done to reduce the size of computers. The same idea of building a computer using a top-down approach is still in play. However, research is ongoing to build computers from the bottom up, at atom and electron level.

Evolution of the quantum technology

The following is the path that the quantum technology research has taken.

1965

A physicist called Richard Feynman was involved in the development of the atomic bomb. In his research, he came up with several theories on quantum electronics that explained how electrons interacted with each other. He created visual depictions between electrons and photons, as well as depictions of several other atomic interactions.

1980

Feynman investigated the conventional concepts about quantum physics and how binary states could be presented in two-state quantum systems. The idea was to simulate quantum computers, but instead of using the conventional computers, he wanted these simulations to be done in quantum systems.

1985

A theoretical paper was published by David Deutsch in Oxford explaining the two-state quantum system and a universal quantum computer. It describes how the attainment of the two-state quantum system could lead to the ability to perform simple operations.

1994

Peter Shor proposed an algorithm that could be used to break encryption systems. Since many encryption systems use large prime numbers, the algorithm is designed to efficiently arrive at these numbers if it is run on a quantum computer. The algorithm sparked a lot of interest from computer scientists.

1995

NIST and the California Institute of Technology worked on ways that can be used to shield quantum computers from potential environmental influences. Their research also touched on ways through which magnetic fields could be used in quantum systems to allow ions to be trapped and cooled.

1996–present

Researchers from IBM, MIT, University of California, and Harvard University studied the way nuclear magnetic resonance could be used to manipulate quantum information in liquids. To reduce the effect of disturbances of the information, they use multiple molecules to represent a single qubit. Their study shows that NMR could act on the atomic nuclei of molecules making up the fluid causing a spin that could lead to the alignment of an atom's spin, which would betray its value, either a 0 or 1. When the electromagnetic field was varied, the researchers were able to identify oscillations that could lead to spins that flipped the states in a qubit, allowing it to have both zeros and ones at the same time. The researchers were also able to observe interactions between molecules that could be exploited to create logic gates within the qubit. The research team was able to build a 2-bit quantum computer and subsequent improvements have since been made to the quantum computer.

The quantum technology race

Nations globally are racing toward achieving quantum computing. The country that gets hold of the immense computing power offered by quantum computers will definitely be at a strong advantage over other countries. There is a fierce competition between the US and China in this race. Both nations have made massive investments in research and development activities aimed at achieving the quantum computing reality. This will usher in a new era of computing and cause several changes in security solutions that are offered today.

Europe, even with a rich history on research on quantum computing, seems to have fallen behind in the race. It has only made small and stealthy moves, the most recent being in 2016 where it said it would jointly fund a €1 billion research on the quantum technology. The research was aimed at quantum communication, computing, simulation, and sensing. Europe is also looking at areas that other nations have not. In its 10 year quantum technology roadmap, it has included research and development activities on quantum software and quantum control. Since Europe's roadmap is clearer and more public, let us take a look at its areas of interest, which will be of mutual importance to all in the quantum future.

Quantum communication

As stated already, one of the main disadvantages of quantum computing is that it will break the currently used encryption technologies. Some security experts have been arguing that the security of the existing encryption algorithms can be boosted by increasing the secret key lengths. However, quantum computers might have enough power to crack these keys. Therefore, there will be a need for a new security standard to be established to secure communication. Europe's quantum roadmap highlights this as one of the areas of focus. It wants to use quantum computing to create another mechanism of sending messages from a sender to a receiver without any worries on the privacy of the communication. Secure communication is of high importance. Currently, it is due to secure communication that e-commerce stores can request their customers to pay online, people can enter login credentials to internet banking platforms, and that other types of sensitive data can be exchanged. Without secure communication, these things would be difficult to achieve. The challenge to quantum communication is with the cost, since the systems that will be involved will be expensive. Alongside this is the challenge that quantum communication is estimated to work in point-to-point connections not exceeding 100 kms. This is why there is a lot of research on quantum routers to send signals to quantum computers that are further apart.

Quantum computation

This is the research area that has been the center of focus for a long time. It is where quantum processes will be used for data processing. Therefore, instead of the normal use of bits in today's computers, there will be the use of quantum bits. Europe outlines the different ways that it is performing research to achieve this. One of these ways is through the storage of data in ions that are entrapped in magnetic fields or nuclei of atoms. Another way it has explained that can be used to achieve quantum computing is through the flow of current through very tiny superconducting circuits. Lastly, it has listed the use of photons that have been forced to travel through photonic circuits as another way of achieving quantum computing. It is expected that history will repeat itself in quantum computing. Like early electronic computers, the early quantum computers will be large-scale versions of the ones that will be there after five or ten years have elapsed.

Quantum simulation

Simulation is one of the most resource-intensive activities in computing. Ordinary computers face many challenges when trying to simulate quantum properties so that more can be learned. However, quantum systems can themselves be used to simulate other aspects of quantum systems. The basic idea of doing this is by coming up with a quantum system that can be manipulated and measured and then use it for the simulation purposes. The well-understood quantum systems that fit these descriptions are ultra-cold atoms, ions trapped in magnetic fields, and then superconducting circuits. These can be used to simulate much more advanced quantum computing properties. However, it is not as easy as it may seem. Even though the existing quantum systems are known, there are hardly any existing techniques that can be used to run the simulations in these systems. Even when techniques to do the complex simulations are discovered, there is also the challenge of ensuring the correctness of the simulations.

Quantum sensing

To exploit the quantum future, there needs to be well-defined ways to sense or measure it. This will involve doing measurements at the scale of atoms. At this scale, changes happen over very short timescales. There have been some theorized techniques to achieve this. The first one is the use of quantum clocks. As said before, changes at the scale of atoms will take very short duration and the normal clocks might not be adequate to measure them. Therefore, quantum clocks will be necessary and they will have to be very accurate. The atomic-sized sensors will have to be very sensitive to changes.

Quantum software

Quantum computers will not be just a mere iteration of the current computers, they will be a new type of computer. Therefore, they will require a new type of software to run. These programs will be written quite differently from today's programs. Today, programs end up being translated into ones and zeros so that the processor can understand them. With quantum computers, qubits will be able to exist as zeros and ones simultaneously. This will enable the qubits to carry out multiple calculations in parallel. This is what makes quantum computers so powerful. However, when these calculations are done, their answers will need to be extracted. Extracting answers from qubits will not be as easy as today's method of extracting answers in the form of zeros and ones. Therefore, very strong algorithms will be needed to extract answers after computations. The problem is that there are hardly any algorithms known that can extract answers from qubits. This is why quantum software is of particular interest to Europe. If Europe is successful in coming up with software that can operate in quantum computers, it will be years ahead of its competitors in the quantum road race.

Quantum technology breakthroughs

With the extensive research being done on quantum computing, some countries have been said to have had their own breakthroughs in the technology.

To begin with, China has been said to have achieved quantum communication. It is said that it has a satellite in space that is capable of quantum communication. Therefore, it can enable the secure sending and receiving of messages through quantum computers.

Secondly, in companies such as Google and Microsoft, it is said that there are early prototypes of quantum processors. It is reported, however, that the existing processors are five to ten qubits in size. In Microsoft, there are projects to overcome the environmental obstacles facing qubits. Qubits have unique properties that unfortunately make them susceptible to any slight disturbances. The qubits have quantum superstition. This is the feature that allows a qubit to hold zeros and ones simultaneously. Qubits are also capable of entanglement, a feature that enables them to affect other qubits. These characteristics, however, mean that vibrations or external electric fields can upset the qubits. These characteristics have also limited researchers to building just between five and ten qubit test systems. The following photo is of Google's Quantum computer, which is currently under development:

Google is aiming to build a 49-qubit system. This will be an attempt to reach the threshold known as quantum supremacy. This threshold is where today's classical supercomputers have hit a snag. No computer, or even supercomputer, is able to handle the exponential growth of memory and bandwidth requirements that are necessary to simulate quantum systems. Therefore, supercomputers have been able to simulate what 10 to 20 qubit quantum computers can do, but as they approach 50 qubit computers, it becomes impossible for the simulation to happen. Researchers are quite confident that 100 qubit computing systems will be stable enough to carry out operations. In five years, they estimate that they will have created 100,000-qubit computer systems. These computers will disrupt many fields and industries.

If this is scaled up to a million-qubit computing system, the end results cannot be fathomed at the moment.

Impacts of the quantum technology

Having looked at the promising roadmap and current breakthroughs in the quantum technology, it is necessary to look at the impacts of the quantum technology. They will be discussed as follows.

Communication

As discussed before, the quantum technology will be able to break through encryptions. However, quantum computing systems will be used to create new and secure communication methods. There will, therefore, be a new global network designed to be unbreakable under the known laws of physics. Current encryption methods are not designed to be unbreakable, they are designed to be difficult to break. However, quantum communication security mechanisms will be designed not to break.

Mining

The quantum technology will come with new ways of sensing called quantum sensing. As described earlier, these methods of sensing will be precise and able to detect very small changes. In mining, they will be able to detect reservoirs more accurately. They will also be used for ultra-sensitive detection of leakages or faults in mines.

Finance

Current trading algorithms are made using very powerful computers. This is why trading algorithms tend to be sensitive to market changes as these computers easily find out that there are changes in the market based on trading patterns. Quantum computing will create even better algorithms that are capable of detecting changes in stock and forex markets as they happen.

Defense

The sensing capabilities of quantum systems will be brought to task in defense. There are submarines and planes that are designed to avoid detection by radar. However, quantum technology will bring in new ways for sensing the environments. Therefore, stealth will be hard to achieve. From another perspective, quantum computing will strengthen military organizations. Since the technology is based on laws of physics, it will be able to simulate planes that are faster, lighter, and stiffer that can be used in battlegrounds. The technology will also be ideal for locating targets.

Health

There are many research efforts in the health sector that have not been completed due to limitations in computing power. Some operations, such as MRI scans, are slow and expensive due to the nature of computers in use today. The improvement or invention of drugs is also very slow due to the limitations of the current technology. Quantum computing will address all these issues. It will come with many solutions to the health sector and significantly improve the quality of life of humans.

Energy

The quantum technology will be at atomic level. There is a lot of energy that can be harnessed from atoms. Take, for instance, atomic bombs that can produce insanely huge amounts of energy. The current battery technology is based on the lithium-ion. Quantum computing will introduce new energy solutions based on other ions.

Big data

Big data is quite a new computing innovation itself. This is where unstructured data is analyzed for meaningful information to be retrieved. The challenge with big data is that its processing takes a lot of time due to the nature of computers in use. With quantum computing, there will be lots of processing power. Therefore, organizations will be able to sift through large datasets and retrieve useful information in record time.

Artificial Intelligence

Machine learning used to give robots Artificial Intelligence is not a fast process. Robots are taking a lot of time to learn through different datasets, mostly due to the limitations of computing power. With quantum computers, the machine learning process will be very fast and it will lead to what is referred to as quantum Artificial Intelligence.

Summary

This chapter has focused on an advancement in computing that is set to hit the world soon. We have talked about quantum computing at length, especially the different ways it will shape the future. The evolution of quantum computing has been described, from the point where it was just a theory to the time when the first quantum computer was built. We then looked at the quantum race where different countries are making huge investments to make significant developments in quantum technology. To best explain the main areas of interest, we taken the roadmap published by Europe on what it hopes to achieve in the quantum technology. The areas of focus are quantum communication, quantum computing, quantum sensing, quantum software, and quantum simulation. Some of the remarkable breakthroughs in the quantum technology have been highlighted. These include China's quantum communication satellites and some if the tech giants' early prototypes of quantum processors. Lastly, we looked at the impacts of quantum computing in different fields and sectors.

The entire book has been focused on the effects of cyber security on finance. It began by looking at all the costs involved in cyber security and then discussed the most common attacks that have been used to steal data and money from individuals and organizations. We then looked at some of the gateways used by these attacks, mainly the humans, networks, and systems. The importance of auditing, risk management, and incident handling have been discussed as part of mitigating cyber crime and its effects. The addition of cryptography as the last layer of security in data protection was then covered. Lastly, we looked at future prospects of the technology space, such as quantum computing and explained the effects that they will have in different sectors.

Further reading

The following are resources that can be used to gain further knowledge regarding this chapter:

- *Practical Quantum Computers*: https://www.technologyreview.com/s/603495/10-breakthrough-technologies-2017-practical-quantum-computers/
- *Economic Impact of Quantum Technologies*: https://www.nrc-cnrc.gc.ca/eng/solutions/collaborative/quantum/qc_economic_impact.html
- *Microsoft Quantum Technology*: https://www.microsoft.com/en-us/quantum/technology
- *Author's blog*: https://www.erdalozkaya.com/
- *Microsoft Quantum*: https://www.youtube.com/watch?v=doNNClTTYwEfeature=youtu.be
- *Microsoft Quantum documentation*: https://docs.microsoft.com/en-us/quantum/index?view=qsharp-preview
- *How Google's Quantum Computer Could Change the World*: https://www.wsj.com/articles/how-googles-quantum-computer-could-change-the-world-1508158847
- *Google Quantum Computing*: https://ai.google/research/teams/applied-science/quantum-ai/
- *Quantum computing*: https://news.harvard.edu/gazette/tag/quantum-computing/

Other Books You May Enjoy

If you enjoyed this book, you may be interested in these other books by Packt:

Hands-On Cybersecurity for Architects
Neil Rerup, Milad Aslaner

ISBN: 978-1-78883-026-3

- Understand different security architecture layers and their integration with all solutions
- Study SWOT analysis and dig into your organization's requirements to drive the strategy
- Design and implement a secure email service approach
- Monitor the age and capacity of security tools and architecture
- Explore growth projections and architecture strategy
- Identify trends, as well as what a security architect should take into consideration

Hands-On Cybersecurity with Blockchain
Rajneesh Gupta

ISBN: 978-1-78899-018-9

- Understand the cyberthreat landscape
- Learn about Ethereum and Hyperledger Blockchain
- Program Blockchain solutions
- Build Blockchain-based apps for 2FA, and DDoS protection
- Develop Blockchain-based PKI solutions and apps for storing DNS entries
- Challenges and the future of cybersecurity and Blockchain

Leave a review - let other readers know what you think

Please share your thoughts on this book with others by leaving a review on the site that you bought it from. If you purchased the book from Amazon, please leave us an honest review on this book's Amazon page. This is vital so that other potential readers can see and use your unbiased opinion to make purchasing decisions, we can understand what our customers think about our products, and our authors can see your feedback on the title that they have worked with Packt to create. It will only take a few minutes of your time, but is valuable to other potential customers, our authors, and Packt. Thank you!

Index

A

Advanced Encryption Standard (AES) 238
advanced persistent threat (APT) attack 35
adware 117
Aircrack-ng 148
Artificial Intelligence
  about 257
  Narrow Artificial Intelligence (Narrow AI) 258
  power Artificial Intelligence technologies 260
  powered cybersecurity 260, 261
  True Artificial Intelligence (True AI) 258, 259
  use cases 262
asset inventory 190
asymmetric encryption
  about 233, 234
  advantages 234
  disadvanatges 234
attack surface reduction 61
attack techniques, online banking
  Channel Breaking Attack 134
  Credential Stealing Attack 134
  Man-in-the-Browser Attack 134

B

BackSwap Trojan 73
Bebloh Trojan 74, 114
BEC attack emails
  credential theft, using malicious software 95
biological virus 110
Blockchain
  auditing 248
  challenges 253
  consensus mechanisms 244
  cryptocurrencies 248
  digital identity 247
  financial applications 248

  future 253
  government purposes 247, 248
  measures 245
  proof of stake 246
  proof of work 245
  recording purposes 246
  technology 244
  technology application 246
Bluelog tool 150
Blueranger tool 150
Bluetooth networks
  Bluebugging 150
  Bluesmack 150
  Bluesnaring 150
Bluetooth
  hacking 150
botnets 11
Bring Your Own Device (BYOD) 162
brute-force attack
  dictionary attack 142
  rule-based search attack 142
  search attack 142
Brutus 144
buffer overflow 125
business
  versus security 162

C

captcha
  about 145
  bypassing 145
Center for Strategic and International Studies (CSIS) 45
characteristics, phishing emails
  attachments 98
  hyperlinks 98
  strange senders 98

urgency 98
characteristics, spam emails
  anonymity 103
  bad grammar 103
  salutation 103
  signature 103
Chief Financial Officer (CFO) 18, 181
Chief Information Officer (CIO) 184
Chief Information Security Officers (CISOs) 18
cloud security 8
Command and Control (C2C) 113
command-and-control (C2C) server 74
Common Weakness Enumeration (CWE) 122
computer virus 110
computer worm
  about 110
  crypto worm 111
  SQL Slammer worm 111
controlled folder access
  enabling 58
cost, of organization security
  about 49
  antivirus systems 50
  Carbanak 49
  encryption 53
  Endpoint Detection and Response solutions
   (EDRs) 51
  firewall systems 52
  intrusion-prevention systems 52
costs, of cyber attack
  about 39, 43
  damaged brand and reputation 46
  data loss 47
  economic losses 45
  fines 47
  litigations 48
  losses, due to recovery techniques 48
  penalties 47
  production loss 44
critical infrastructure security 7
cross-site scripting 128
crypto worm
  about 111
  WannaCry 112
cryptocurrencies challenges

about 252
  exchange risks 253
  theft 252
  unstable value 252
cryptocurrencies wallet
  about 251
  desktop wallet 251
  hardware wallet 252
  mobile wallet 251
  paper wallet 252
  web wallet 251
cryptocurrencies
  about 249, 250
  properties 250
cyber attacks
  categories 29
  costs 39, 40, 41, 42
  cyber criminals 34
  cyber terrorist 33
  hacktivism 30
cyber criminals
  about 34
  Carbanak APT Attack case study 35
  FIN7 case study 34
  OurMine operation case study 36
cyber espionage 11, 13
cyber terrorists
  about 33
  Operation Ababil case study 33
cybercrime 10, 27
Cybersecurity Defence Operations Center (CDOC)
  183
cybersecurity objectives
  banking and financial systems 21
  impacts, to global economy 15
  significance 14
cybersecurity
  about 5
  incidents 154
  objectives 14
  people 6
  processes 6
  scope 7
  technology 7
  terminologies 10

D

Dakota Access Pipeline (DAPL) 31
data breach 11
data in transit
  about 237
  encrypted email servers 238
  encrypted web connection 238
  end-to-end encryption 237
data resting
  about 235
  file encryption 236
  full disk encryption 236
data
  protecting, with cryptography 235
DDoS attack 11, 30, 79
decreased productivity 184
Defense in Depth (DiD) approach
  about 216
  environment, best practices 217
digital economy
  about 24
  critical infrastructure attacks 26
  ransomware threats 25
  smart threats 24
  threats 24
Domain Name System (DNS)
  about 139
  distributed denial of service (DDoS) 140
  packet sniffing 139
dual trust network model 177
dumpster diving 77

E

encryption algorithms
  Advanced Encryption Standard (AES) 238
  Blowfish 239
  examples 238
  RSA 239
  Triple DES 239
encryption challenges
  about 240
  brute force 240
  cryptanalysis 240
  increased computational power 240

encryption
  about 230, 232
  asymmetric encryption 233
  methods 230
  symmetric encryption 232
end user threats
  about 69
  application fraud 70
  card not present fraud 71
  compromised account fraud 72
  credit card fraud 70
  credit card testing 72
  dumpster diving 77
  financial Trojans 73
  mobile fraud 77
  phishing 75
  pretexting 77
Endpoint Detection and Response solutions
  (EDRs) 51
endpoint security
  about 180
  communication interception 182
  decreased productivity 184
  device-based attack 182
  insider threats 183
  malicious code execution 181
  physical access 181
  threats 180, 181
enterprise resource planning (ERP) systems 18
Executive Assistant (EA) 181
exploitation delivery 130
exploitation techniques
  about 124
  buffer overflow 125
  cross-site scripting 128
  format string attacks 127
  integer overflow 126
  memory corruption 126
  one-click attack 128
  race condition 127
  SQL injections 129

F

Fair Credit Reporting Act (FACTA) 219
Federal Deposit Insurance Corporation (FDIC) 75

financial repercussions, of reputational damage 23
financial Trojans
  about 73
  BackSwap Trojan case study 73
  Bebloh case study 74
  Ramnit Trojan case study 74
firewalls
  about 146
  bypassing 146
format string attacks 127
fundamentals
  about 154
  attack surface analysis 155
  data knowledge 154
  monitoring 155
  vendor management 156

G

General Data Protection Regulation (GDPR) 222
Gross Domestic Product (GDP) 45

H

hacking groups
  about 12
  anonymous 13
  Bureau 121 12
  Shadow Brokers 12
hacking tools, wireless networks
  about 147
  Aircrack-ng 148
  Kismet 149
  Wireshark 150
hacktivism
  about 30
  Dakota Access Pipeline case study 31
  Panama Papers case study 32
Health Information Portability and Accountability
  Act (HIPAA) 219
Human Resources (HR) 183

I

ICS-CERT
  URL 30
impacts to global economy, cybersecurity
  about 15

critical dependency of business 18
critical dependency of business processes 19
critical dependency of IT infrastructure 18
economic loss 20
estimation of financial losses 16, 17, 18
finance and cybersecurity 18
incident handling
  about 226
  containment 227
  identification 226
  preparation 226
  recovery and analysis 227
incident response and management
  about 156
  containment phase 158
  detection and analysis phase 157
  eradication 158
  post-incident activity 158
  preparation phase 157
  recovery 158
independent software vendors (ISVs) 121
Indicator of Compromise (IOC) 76, 109, 261
information management 190
insider threats 183
integer overflow 126
Internet of Things (IoT) 10, 180
IT auditing
  about 220
  IT infrastructure, inefficiencies determining 222,
    223
  IT management, inefficiencies determining 222,
    223
  policies, evaluating 221
  processes, evaluating 221
  relevant regulations 222
  risks, determining to company assets 221
  systems, evaluating 221

J

Just Enough Administration (JEA) 67
Just in Time (JIT) 67

K

Kismet 149

L

Local Administrator Password Solution (LAPS) 67

M

malicious programs, BEC attack emails
  Ardamax 95
  LokiBot 96
malware categories
  about 108
  adware 117
  computer virus 110
  computer worm 110
  rootkit 116
  spyware 116
  Trojan 113
malware infection vectors
  about 118
  auto-executed web infection 119
  coded, into existing software 120
  email 119
  injected, by remote attacker 118
  installed, by other malware 119
  network propagation 119
  portable media 120
  user-executed web infection 119
malware, via spam email
  botnets 103
  Storm 101, 102
  Triout 102
malware
  about 10, 107, 108
  trends 117
man-in-the-browser (MitB) 74
Medusa 143
memory corruption 126
Microsoft 365 zero trust network models 179, 180
Microsoft
  about 54
  security features 54
mobile fraud 77
modern endpoint security
  about 184
  breach detection investigation 186
  breach detection response 186

  device protection 185
  identity protection 186
  information protection 186
  threat resistance 185
Multi-Factor Authentication (MFA) 77, 180

N

Narrow Artificial Intelligence (Narrow AI) 258
network intrusions 138
network models
  about 176
  dual trust network model 177
  single trust network model 176
  zero trust network model 178, 179
Network protection
  about 60
  enabling 59
network security 8

O

one-click attack 128
online banking process 133
online banking systems
  attack techniques 134, 135
  attacking 132
  benefits for financial services 133
online behavior 164, 166

P

Panama Papers case study 32, 33
phishing emails
  characteristics 98
phishing
  about 10, 75, 82
  Business email compromise (BEC) 94
  case study 76
  evolution 83, 84
  PayPal phishing email 89
  scams 82
  social engineering emails 85, 86, 88
  spear phishing email 90
  whaling 94
point of sale (POS) 73, 180
power Artificial Intelligence technologies
  about 260

deep learning 260
semi-supervised machine learning 260
supervised machine learning 260
unsupervised machine learning 260
pretexting 77
privileged identities
  about 66
  examples, of compromised privileged identities 66
  protecting 66, 67

Q

quantum technology, impacts
  about 272
  Artificial Intelligence 274
  big data 274
  communication 272
  defense 273
  energy 274
  finance 273
  health 273
  mining 273
quantum technology
  about 267, 268
  atomic bomb, developing 266
  breakthroughs 270, 271
  conventional concepts 266
  encryption systems 266
  environmental influences, protecting 267
  evolution 266
  nuclear magnetic resonance, using 267
  quantum communication 268
  quantum computation 269
  quantum sensing 270
  quantum simulation 269
  quantum software 270
  theoretical paper, publishing 266

R

race condition 127
Ramnit Trojan 74
ransomware 10
reasons, for cybersecurity
  growing cyber attacks 14
  worse cyber attacks 15

Redfang tool 150
Research and Development (R&D) 183
risk assessment 191
risk avoidance 225
risk management
  about 214, 223
  identification 224
  key security principles 215
  risk analysis 224
  risk assessment 225
  risk mitigation 225
  risk monitoring 225
  strategies 224
risk reduction 225
risk retaining 225
risk sharing 225
rootkit 116

S

scope, of cybersecurity
  about 7
  application/system security 9
  cloud security 8
  critical infrastructure security 7
  Internet of Things (IoT) security 10
  user security 9
Secure Development Lifecyle (SDL) 122
Secure Sockets Layer (SSL) 138
security issues
  root cause 196
security management
  cybersecurity initiatives, lacking 163
  failing 163
  organization and planning, lacking 163
  poor leadership 164
Security Operations Center (SOC) 156, 261
security policies
  implement, failure 171, 172
security
  versus business 162
services
  protecting, with cryptography 235
Simple Mail Transfer Protocol (SMTP) 138
single trust network model 176
social engineering 10

spam emails
  characteristics 103
spamming
  about 98
  advertising 100
  email address, obtaining 99
  malware 100
  money making 100
spear phishing 90, 92, 93
spyware 11, 116
SQL injections 129
SQL Slammer worm 111
Stuxnet 7
symmetric encryption
  about 232
  advantages 232
  method 232, 233
system security 9

T

technological transformation
  of financial services 169, 170, 171
threat actors 29
threat landscape evolution 257
threat landscape
  about 69
  threats, against end customers 69
  threats, against financial institutes 78
threats 166, 168
threats, against financial institutes
  about 78
  ATM attacks 78
  blackmailing 79
  denial of service (DoS) attack 79
  POS attacks 78
  ransomware 79
tools, for brute-force attacks
  Brutus 144
  Medusa 143
Torpig 116
Transport Layer Security (TLS) 138
Trojan
  about 113
  Bebloh 114
  Zeus 114

True Artificial Intelligence (True AI) 258, 259
Trustworthy Computing (TwC) 122
two-factor authentication
  about 146
  bypassing 146

U

US National Security Agency (NSA) 12
user security 9

V

vulnerabilities
  defining 193
  detecting 122, 124
  multiplying threats 194
  risk, multiplying 195
  threats, multiplying 194
  to threat 193
vulnerability assessment
  active role 210
  applications and data, pinpointing 211
  assess 209
  business processes, identifying 211
  controls, identifying 212
  hardware structure, determining 211
  hidden data sources, finding 211
  network infrastructure, mapping to hardware 212
  penetration testing, conducting by third parties 213
  scan result, reading 212
  tying, into business impact 210
  vulnerability scans, executing 212
vulnerability management strategy
  about 190
  asset inventory 190
  information management 190
  remediation 192
  reporting 192
  risk acceptance 192
  risk assessment 191
  threat analysis 191
  vulnerability analysis 191
  vulnerability assessment 192
vulnerability management tools
  about 196

BeyonTrust retina network security scanner 205
Burp Suite 202
core impact 204
Enter Acunetix 202
flexera software vulnerability manager 203
McAfee Foundstone's Enterprise 196
Nessus professional 201
Nexpose community 198
Nikto 198
OpenVAS 197
OWASP Zed Attack Proxy 199
vulnerability management
  best practices 207, 208, 209
  implementing 205, 206, 207
Vulnerability Reward Program (VRP) 122
vulnerable network devices 151
vulnerable network protocols
  about 138
  Domain Name System (DNS) 139
  Secure Sockets Layer (SSL) 138
  Simple Mail Transfer Protocol (SMTP) 138

W

WannaCry 112
web protection bypassing
  about 144
  captcha, bypassing 145
  firewalls, bypassing 146
  two-factor authentication, bypassing 146
web servers and web-based systems attack
  about 140
  advanced Google search operators 141
  brute-force attack 142
  buffer overflow 141

SQL injection 140
web protection, bypassing 144
Windows 10 Defender Security Center
  about 55
  app and browser control 56
  device performance and health 55
  family options 56
  firewall and network protection 55
  virus and threat protection 55
Windows 10 defense stack 54
Windows Defender 56
Windows Defender Advanced Threat Protection
    (ATP)
  about 64, 65
  cloud security analytics 64
  endpoint behavioral sensors 64
  threat intelligence 64
Windows Defender Application Guard
  about 62
  URL 62
Windows Defender Credential Guard 61
Windows Defender Exploit Guard 57
Windows Event Forwarding (WEF) 63
wireless networks
  hacking 147
Wireshark 150

Z

Zed Attack Proxy (ZAP) 199
zero trust network model
  about 178, 179
  Microsoft 365 zero trust network models 179,
    180
Zeus Trojan 114

www.ingramcontent.com/pod-product-compliance
Lightning Source LLC
Chambersburg PA
CBHW080626060326
40690CB00021B/4829

* 9 7 8 1 7 8 8 8 3 6 2 9 6 *